The Neural Sublime

The Neural Sublime

Cognitive Theories and Romantic Texts

Alan Richardson

The Johns Hopkins University Press
Baltimore

425960016

© 2010 The Johns Hopkins University Press
All rights reserved. Published 2010
Printed in the United States of America on acid-free paper
9 8 7 6 5 4 3 2 1

The Johns Hopkins University Press
2715 North Charles Street
Baltimore, Maryland 21218-4363
www.press.jhu.edu

Library of Congress Cataloging-in-Publication Data

Richardson, Alan, 1955–
    The neural sublime : cognitive theories and romantic texts / Alan
Richardson.
        p. cm.
    Includes bibliographical references and index.
    ISBN-13: 978-0-8018-9452-7 (hardcover : alk. paper)
    ISBN-10: 0-8018-9452-2 (hardcover : alk. paper)
    ISBN-13: 978-0-8018-9453-4 (pbk. : alk. paper)
    ISBN-10: 0-8018-9453-0 (pbk. : alk. paper)
    1. English literature—18th century—History and criticism. 2. Psycho-
analysis and literature. 3. Philosophy of mind. I. Title.
    PR447.R49 2010
    820.9'3561—dc22   2009026922

A catalog record for this book is available from the British Library.

Special discounts are available for bulk purchases of this book.
For more information, please contact Special Sales at 410-516-6936
or specialsales@press.jhu.edu.

The Johns Hopkins University Press uses environmentally friendly book
materials, including recycled text paper that is composed of at least 30
percent post-consumer waste, whenever possible. All of our book papers
are acid-free, and our jackets and covers are printed on paper with recycled
content.

For Nate and Lida

Contents

Preface

What do literary studies stand to gain from greater engagement with recent work in neuroscience and in the cognitive sciences, in the sciences of brain and mind? This question has already been explored by a series of writers, including myself, who collectively have produced a credible and even pressing set of rationales for what has been called a "new interdisciplinarity," bridging the notorious but increasingly narrow "gap" between the humanities and the sciences.[1] A dedicated and still expanding group of literary scholars have also been voting with their feet—or, rather, their word processors—producing an exponentially growing number of books, articles, and academic dissertations. These works put forth a highly (and healthily) diverse array of means for bringing literary studies and the sciences of mind and brain into dialogue, in areas and subdisciplines ranging from narratology and poetics to performance theory and colonial discourse studies.

A decade ago, when I began working in the field now known as "cognitive literary studies," a handful of pioneering scholars had already produced a small and inspiring body of work, but they had little in the way of professional venues for collaborating with or even getting to know one another, or for disseminating their work and building an audience for cognitive criticism in all its variety. Now an established field with an international audience drawn from virtually every area within the professional study of literature, cognitive literary studies no longer needs to justify its very existence. The question now is not why should students of literature engage with work in the mind and brain sciences but how?

This book does not put forth a single, definitive answer to that question but rather tries out a cluster of potential answers that diverge widely at times in their commitment to one or another possible area or mode of interdisciplinary engagement but are held together by a consistent set of theoretical presuppositions and working hypotheses. Before outlining the chapters to come, however, I want first to provide one modest answer to the "why" question for those readers who may want a little more inducement before following the citations to some of the more elaborate accounts already available in print or online.

Briefly, opening up a dialogue with cognitive science and neuroscience offers those of us in the humanities a new and potentially more robust interdisciplinarity. "Interdisciplinary" research is much talked about by professors of literature—not least in their grant and book proposals—but often, as Linda and Michael Hutcheon have remarked, the research actually produced might better be termed *interdiscursive*: more a matter of reading across disciplinary boundaries and selectively incorporating elements of another discipline's vocabulary, without placing one's home disciplinary perspective into sustained, mutually vulnerable, and potentially transformative dialogue with the rival perspectives of colleagues trained in significantly different areas, with different methods and aims.[2] Whereas interdisciplinary research in the sciences generally involves, at the least, active collaboration among researchers from various disciplines, the reading across disciplines involved in interdiscursive work may involve authors and models long considered dated and of largely historical interest (however venerated as past masters) in their home disciplines. The continuing reliance among literary scholars on Freud and on Freudian accounts of mental functioning is the most obvious example. Up to a few years ago, literature professors had shown surprisingly little interest in the work on mind and language currently being done by leading researchers from the relevant departments in their own universities, despite a widespread emphasis in literary theory on such matters as the self, language and language acquisition, psychosocial development, agency, and the distinctive roles of consciousness and of unconscious functioning in mental life. "Interdisciplinarity" within literature departments has thus sometimes seemed to merely widen the compass of our discipline, making Freud a "literary" author or Saussurean linguistics an adjunct to literary theory, without forcing us to rethink and perhaps revise our disciplinary habits and preconceptions by considering the competing methods, presuppositions, and claims of contemporary theorists and researchers at the leading edge of the disciplines that Freud and Saussure long ago helped to establish.

Stephen Greenblatt opened his influential New Historicist study *Shakespearean Negotiations* with the memorable (and oft-paraphrased) statement, "I began with the desire to speak with the dead." My own paraphrase here might be, "I began with the desire to talk with my colleagues in psychology, linguistics, and neuroscience." That interdisciplinary conversations across the humanities and sciences divide are now underway in many universities in the United States and beyond is, for me, one of the most significant and far-reaching developments for literary studies since the rise of the New Historicism itself. This is by no means to claim that cognitive literary approaches are displacing, much less are in fundamental opposition to, historicist and other contextualist approaches to reading and resituating literary texts that are broadly grouped together as "cultural studies." Rather, as I explain in the introduction, I concur with Ellen Spolsky in viewing cognitive literary criticism as sharing a surprising amount of common ground with poststructuralist and contextualist theories.[3] I also agree with Lisa Zunshine's understanding of cognitive cultural criticism as a logical (if radical) extension of earlier work in cultural criticism, in line with a cognitivist program set out at the beginning of the cultural studies movement by one of its founders, Raymond Williams, though the cognitivist aspect of Williams's thinking has long been ignored.[4]

My response to the "how" question, then, begins by rejecting any simple opposition between cognitive literary studies and the contextualist approaches that have dominated the past several decades of literary criticism and theory. It builds on my earlier attempts, particularly in my book *British Romanticism and the Science of the Mind,* to extend and modify the New Historicism by taking much greater account of newer, more forward-looking models of mind and language, amounting to what I have termed (playfully enough) a *neural historicism.*[5] This book pushes that iconoclastic extension of New Historicism further, however, by making more pronounced and extensive use of models, theories, and findings arising from recent work in neuroscience, cognitive science, and evolutionary biology. I do not regard these fields as intrinsically superior to or more authoritative than the humanities, although I do respect the value of careful empirical study, in the sciences of brain and mind as in literary scholarship. (I also understand how often seemingly "hard" empirical findings are overturned and how weakly supported some allegedly empirical work can turn out to be on a closer look, especially in notoriously problematic fields like evolutionary psychology and sociobiology.) I don't think that the sciences of mind and brain have come anywhere near providing us with a complete set of satisfying answers to our most pressing questions about language, the mind, and human behavior. I do think that some leading researchers and theorists in cognitive science, neuroscience, and evolutionary biology are asking the right questions, however, and asking them in ways that humanists can begin to study with great profit.

Given that, as prominent neuroscientists themselves like to point out, neuroscience at present remains in a "sketchy" stage, with any number of basic questions still hotly under debate, it would seem far too early for humanists to seek (or accept) anything like "consilience" with the mind and brain sciences.[6] More than that, in pursuing an informed intellectual dialogue with their colleagues in the cognitive and neuroscientific fields, humanists may well do best at present to explore a range of the new possibilities opening up rather than to seek too soon for an authoritative grand theory or lay presumptive claim to a fundamental and enduring methodological breakthrough. For this reason, I find the somewhat diz- zying variety of approaches that continue to proliferate within the new field a sign of its early strength rather than of amateurishness or professional disarray. If our colleagues in the cognitive and neuroscientific fields are still (as V. S. Ramachan- dran puts it) "tinkering" in productive and exciting ways in advance of a new sci- entific consensus, we can tinker with them, bringing additional objects of inquiry, different questions, and a certain healthy skepticism (our well-known "hermeneu- tics of suspicion") into the conversation.[7] While some scientists may bridle at the notion of tinkering, literary scholars at least are comfortable with it; we even have a fancy French name for it, *bricolage.*

The chapters that follow capitalize on the current atmosphere of emergent interdisciplinary connections, improvisation, and widening possibilities by adapt- ing several of the new critical strategies developed within recent cognitive literary studies and testing their usefulness in relation to a series of problems, cruxes, and longstanding debates in my home field of British Romantic studies. They include an unexpected variant on the "Romantic sublime" in relation to the neuroscience of illusion; an intervention into the longstanding debate on the Romantic image, drawing on but also qualifying Elaine Scarry's virtual reinvention of imagery stud- ies in *Dreaming by the Book*; a new and more capacious understanding of the figure of apostrophe in Romantic poetry, developed in dialogue with work in cognitive linguistics; a reading of Austen's representation of minds and mental interaction in *Emma* that relies on "theory of mind" theory; a reexamination of the Roman- tic fascination with sibling incest in light of neo-Darwinian accounts of incest avoidance; and an analysis of the representation of an unintelligible yet alluring female speech—what Keats calls "language strange"—in various Romantic poems in light of work in cognitive developmental psychology on infant-directed speech ("parentese") and Ellen Dissanayake's related cognitive-evolutionary account of art and intimacy.

Each chapter seeks to accomplish three tasks: to fundamentally reorient an un- resolved issue within Romantic studies by recourse to cognitive theory, to indi- cate new possibilities for cognitive literary criticism, and to introduce readers to a given area in cognitive, neuroscientific, or evolutionary thought. The chapter on apostrophe, for example, fundamentally recasts literary critical understanding of a trope that became central to poststructuralist readings of Romanticism. It takes cognitive rhetoric (an offshoot of cognitive linguistics) in an unprecedented direction by examining a special kind of trope neglected by cognitive rhetoricians themselves and, in the process, serves to introduce students and scholars of literature to the fields of cognitive linguistics and rhetoric. Thus I see three overlapping audiences for this book: professors and students of British Romanticism, literary critics and theorists already interested in cognitive literary studies, and anyone looking for a detailed, wide-ranging introduction to the interdisciplinary study of literature and cognition that keeps questions of literary history in the forefront.

In putting cognitive and evolutionary literary approaches to work, I am also putting them to the test. Their theoretical claims, their methodological procedures, and their promise for generating new insights are here weighed against the critical practices of an existing literary historical field, one well known for its history of innovation and its rigor. Caught up in the considerable intellectual excitement generated by a new interdisciplinary constellation, we do well to keep in view the *disciplinary* training and practice we bring to the table in our encounter with the mind and brain sciences. Interdisciplinary work thrives on collision as much as collusion; a healthy interdisciplinarity does not involve one group converting to the norms, aims, and ethos of another, but rather participants from all groups joining in a serious and mutually critical conversation in the interests of a new consensus that none could have produced singly. Literary scholars need not feel intimidated in this area, as they bring to the interdisciplinary encounter a long and elaborate history of careful scrutiny of figurative language, representations of mind and behavior, narrative and discursive modes, and other linguistic phenomena currently of great interest to their colleagues in neuroscience and cognitive science. They can bring to the table as well their own sorts of evidence, including a huge, diverse, multilingual and multicultural text base, spanning over two millennia, that most scientific researchers can only begin to access.

A background in British Romantic studies has proved especially helpful to me in this regard. I was trained and have worked for several decades in a field with a long history of interest in topics of great moment for cognitive science and neuroscience, including the imagination, the "unconscious," the origin of language, mind-body relations, human universals, and a developmental approach to the psyche, to give only a partial list. The past twenty-five years of challenging and often exquisitely detailed New Historicist work within that field, corresponding more or less to my own "adult" (postgraduate) life as a scholar of British Romanticism, have made it impossible for me to disregard the crucial historical dimension of the questions raised in this book, my historicist instincts at times acting as a sort of brake on my cognitive speculations. Which is as it should be, since the more it becomes informed by a historical sense, the more legitimately "cognitive" a cognitive literary criticism will prove.

This book grew out of many conversations across disciplines and at the expanding edge of the new discipline of cognitive literary studies, and I wish to acknowledge here at least some of the venues and express my gratitude to some of the participants. One especially important resource has been the monthly seminar on Cognitive Theory and the Arts, hosted by the Humanities Center at Harvard University and co-chaired by Elaine Scarry and Anna Henchman. Seminar guests and participants whose presentations have directly inspired parts of this book include Mahzarin Banaji, Matthew Belmonte, Donald Hoffman, Stephen Kosslyn, Steven Pinker, Rebecca Saxe, and Elaine Scarry. Others whose presentations and questions have proved especially helpful over the years include Elaine Auyoung, Jamshed Bharucha, Alice Flaherty, Allan Hobson, Margaret Livingstone, Vanessa Ryan, Daniel Schacter, and Vernon Shetley. I'm also grateful to Vernon for an invitation to present work related to this book at Wellesley College, with its own lively interdisciplinary group on cognition and culture.

I wish to thank James Heffernan and Michael Gazzaniga for including me in a symposium, supported by Dartmouth University, called "Cognitive Neuroscience and the Arts: Opening a Conversation," held at the Minary Center on Squam Lake at about the time I was beginning this book. I also profited greatly from interdisciplinary conferences on the humanities and the cognitive sciences held at the University of Connecticut in 2006 and at Bucknell University in 2007. I am grateful for the invitation to interact with an international group of researchers from many fields working on empirical approaches to literature at the IGEL conference hosted by David Miall at the University of Alberta in 2004. The chapters that follow were revised, often significantly, based on questions and comments from audiences at UCLA, the University of Michigan, the International Conference on Romanticism held at Marquette University, the International Conference on Narrative held in Burlington, Vermont, the University of Colorado, and Princeton University.

I have been collaborating for some years, formally and informally, with a group of scholars in cognition and literature whose names come up regularly in the pages that follow: Mary Crane, Liz Hart, Patrick Hogan, Ellen Spolsky, Mark Turner, and Lisa Zunshine. My citations of their work only begin to acknowledge how much I owe to them, individually and collectively. Among the many other scholars in cognitive literary and cultural studies whose work and advice have been important to me, I wish to single out a few, including Ellen Dissanayake, Nancy Easterlin,

Francis Steen, and Blakey Vermeule, for special acknowledgment. I am also grateful to Boston College for a sabbatical leave in Spring 2008, during which much of the book was written or revised in its current form. An earlier version of chapter 4 was published in *Style* (as "Apostrophe in Life and Romantic Art: Everyday Discourse, Overhearing and Poetic Address") and an earlier version of chapter 6 was first published in *New Literary History* (as "Rethinking Romantic Incest: Human Universals, Literary Representation, and the Biology of Mind"). I thank the editors of these journals for their suggestions and for permission to reuse the essays here. I also thank Michael Lonegro, of the Johns Hopkins University Press, for his encouragement and advice in the earlier stages of this book's development, Kathleen Keane and Trevor Lipscombe for critical help during later stages, Julia Ridley Smith for skillful copyediting, and Greg Nicholl for seeing the book through to production.

Deborah Blacker has always been ready to answer technical questions about neuroscience and to talk through ideas with me; her help was especially valuable as I began this book. My brother, Brian Richardson, continues to support and inspire me, usually when I need it the most. My greatest inspiration, however, comes from my children, Nate and Lida, who constantly find new ways to surprise, challenge, and delight. It's with great love and admiration that I dedicate this book to them.

The Neural Sublime

CHAPTER ONE

Introduction

Cognitive Historicism

The cognitive revolution can be traced back to the convergence of new paradigms for thinking about language, computer programming, and mental behavior in the 1950s. Since then, it has transformed its home fields of linguistics, artificial intelligence, and psychology and has significantly affected related fields like anthropology and philosophy of mind.[1] Working with one another across traditional disciplinary lines, researchers in these areas have pursued their coalescing interests under the metadisciplinary rubric "*cognitive science*," which in turn has come to overlap so pervasively with new developments in neuroscience and evolutionary biology that many now speak of the "cognitive neurosciences."[2] Perhaps predictably, there has already been talk of a second cognitive revolution or even a third, but these revisionary perspectives, despite important differences in emphasis, seem successive waves of a larger, ever widening movement. Thanks to a series of accessible and often brilliantly written accounts, a good deal of research, speculation, and debate in the cognitive neurosciences has reached a large segment of the intellectual public. Cognitive approaches have been making notable inroads into humanistic fields like film studies, art history, and musicology, which have begun to draw increasingly on the cognitive neuroscience of perception, attention, mental processing, and emotional response.[3]

A decade ago, in the shadow of the "culture wars," the "theory wars," and allied expressions of what William Blake calls "mental fight," it seemed that the academic study of literature might prove the exception. Despite the noteworthy examples of a few pioneering scholars and the obvious interest for literary critics and theorists of powerful new models for understanding language, mind, and human behavior, literary academics as a group seemed bent on resisting any serious attempt to bridge the increasingly irrelevant divide between the humanities and sciences.[4] But the past ten years or so have seen a remarkable increase in work in literature, cognition, and neuroscience, and one can at present even find rival introductions to the new field of cognitive literary studies.[5] What can broadly be called "cognitive" approaches—always keeping in mind that this broad sense *includes* relevant work on the emotions—have already made a significant impact on the study of rhetoric and have become an important presence within the fields of narratology and narrative theory.[6] Given the pressing case for continuing to foster work on poetics (as distinct from literary theory and literary criticism) made by Peter Brooks in the mid-1990s, it should be recognized that cognitive poeticians have done as much as anyone to keep poetics alive and well into the twenty-first century.[7] Newer cognitive perspectives have challenged and enlivened more specialized areas of great theoretical interest, including work on poetic imagery, reader response, and literary universals.[8] Exciting new work has also been done in areas where literary scholarship converges with research in neighboring disciplines, such as discourse theory, pragmatics, and even acoustics.[9]

Most scholarship and research in cognitive literary studies to date has concerned the synchronic aspect of literature, approaching literature and literary language in a systematic manner without any overriding regard to matters of time, place, and social context. Some of the best studies in the new field, in fact, demonstrate a remarkable range of reference across periods and languages, from early Greek epic and Hebrew biblical writings to medieval European romances to late twentieth-century American poetry, embracing Asian, African, and Oceanic traditions as well.[10] Much less attention, however, has been paid to the diachronic aspect of literary studies, to issues in literary history, and to the analysis of specific authors, works, issues, or motifs in terms of their historical, social, and cultural contexts. This relative lack of attention to literary history has proved limiting in several important ways. In practical terms, it has narrowed the potential appeal of the new cognitive approaches, since many literary professionals continue to work within historical fields (traditional or otherwise), numerous conferences are organized along literary-historical lines, and much academic hiring continues to be done in reference to "periods" in literary history. In theoretical terms, this relative absence may have fueled concerns that cognitive approaches to literature are somehow ahistorical in character—unable to account for issues of cultural difference, historical specificity, and change over time. Cognitive literary criticism thus could be (and sometimes has been) seen as resisting, evading, or simply ignoring the historicist and contextualist trends that have played so large and productive a part in literary studies as a whole over the past several decades. Following this line of thinking, early critics of the new field accused its practitioners of being "reactionary," of looking backwards, ironically enough given their iconoclastic and forward-looking adaptation of contemporary developments in cognitive science and neuroscience.[11]

All this is now changing. A number of literary critics—most notably Ellen Spolsky, Mary Crane, Lisa Zunshine, and F. Elizabeth Hart—have been producing work that precisely seeks to bring "cognitive theory," in Crane's parlance, to bear on historicist and related contextualist literary studies. Indeed, in her trenchant essay "Cognitive Literary Historicism," Spolsky calls not for a supplementary relation between cognitive and historicist studies but for their interpenetration. She argues that "cognitive literary study must be embedded within the hard-won recognition of the historical imperative" and, moreover, "that the necessity of that embedding itself argues that cultural/historical criticism must acknowledge the history of the human body and its mind."[12] The "cognitive" in cognitive literary study, in this reading, should not be thought of in transcendent terms, analogous to Kantian categories of thought. Rather, the "cognitive" is historical, naming processes and capacities unfolding (at the species level) in evolutionary time and (at the individual level) in developmental time, always (in both cases) in relation to specific physical and social environments, that are, of course, caught up in a ceaseless process of historical change. "History," by the same token, does not name only the social, cultural, and political but also the biological (including the evolutionary and genetic) and the geophysical. Difficult as it may be (despite myriad disclaimers to the contrary) to avoid thinking in binary terms about mind and body, the biological and the cultural, Spolsky and the authors she draws on seek to do just that, offering concepts such as "coevolution" (6) and "constructivist interactionism" that gesture beyond deeply ingrained dualistic habits of thought.[13]

The attempt, at the methodological level, to think beyond dichotomies of the cultural and biological corresponds, at the epistemological level, to a middle course between objectivist realism on one side and cultural relativism on the other. As Hart has argued, cognitive literary studies seek to move past the sterile "realism/relativism dichotomy of habitual epistemological debate" (331) by assuming a third position analogous to epistemological stances influential for cognitive science, such as Hilary Putnam's "internal realism" or George Lakoff and Mark Johnson's "experientialism" (320).[14] As Hart notes, literary theorists attuned to developments in the philosophy of science have arrived at a closely related "third position" of their own, most influentially in N. Katherine Hayles's notion of "constrained constructivism" (322). Taking for granted the impossibility of a transcendent objectivity or "God's eye" view of the world and acknowledging the profound effect of cultural and other environmental factors in shaping perception and representation, "constrained constructivism" and like theories seek nevertheless to account for the large and undeniable amount of coherence among various accounts of the world, the (never perfect, but frequently good enough) success of communication among members of the same species and even across species, and the affordances and resistances that constantly and materially shape our interactions with and correct our perceptions of the "real," again however partially. "A model of representation," Hayles writes, "that declines the leap into abstraction figures itself as species-specific, culturally determined, and context-dependent," a formulation that draws on cognitive as much as on cultural theory.[15] "Emphasizing instrumental efficacy rather than precision, it assumes local interactions rather than positive correspondences that hold universally." In other words, it assumes an interactionist rather than objectivist epistemology, recognizing the flux and historical contingency of experience, and taking a pragmatic stance in relation to the information constantly streaming in from a given environment. "It engages in a rhetoric of 'good enough'"—a rhetoric that also informs Spolsky's thinking—"indexing its conclusions to the context in which implied judgments about adequacy are made. Yet it also recognizes that within the domains specified by these parameters, enough consistencies obtain in the processing and in the flux to make recognition reliable and relatively stable" (Hayles 32).[16] Conceptual categories, for example, cannot be expected to faithfully reproduce the world "out there," yet neither are they constructed arbitrarily, as poststructuralist theorists sometimes claim. They reflect species-specific capacities (and limitations) and collective historical experience indicating which categories have proved most useful and which have not.

As Hart usefully points out, cognitive literary critics have variously arrived not at a single position between realism and relativism but at a "*set*" of positions on a "continuum" between the two polar (and mutually polarizing) extremes (320).

Hart thus situates specific critics as establishing positions near either extreme or more toward the middle position represented by Hayles. As a group, however, cognitive critics meet the "minimal conditions" defining the "middle-ground" that promises to move cultural theory beyond the "outmoded terms of the realism/relativism debate." Drawing on Hayles, Hart emphasizes that all of the (relevant) cognitive critics "operate from a conviction that there is such a thing as species-specific knowledge and that such knowledge must contribute substantively to our philosophical discussions about knowledge," while also granting that "all knowledge, including species-specific knowledge, is environmentally situated, context-dependent, and culturally indexed," that is, "subject to a lesser or greater degree of constructivity" (326).

Those cognitive literary critics who explicitly address issues of cultural and literary-historical specificity and change have also, by now, developed a set of positions rather than a single, unified methodology, positions that adhere more or less predictably to the epistemological commitments Hart discriminates. Those critics closest to Hart's "realist" extreme, for example, particularly the "evolutionary literary theorists" often grouped together with cognitive critics, are also those most likely to view evolutionary biological history as somehow trumping cultural-historical specificity, elucidating deeply entrenched and presumably all but ineradicable patterns of human behavior that underlie superficial cultural-historical differences. At their crudest, they may suggest, say, that "mating programs" evolutionarily designed into the human genome drive the romantic chess games played out in a given Jane Austen novel, implying that early nineteenth-century debates on gender roles, contested ideologies of feminine "conduct," changes in family structure and the institution of marriage, the rise of a proto-"Victorian" sexual morality, and like issues informing the past several decades of Austen studies account only for superstructural phenomena, matters of mere detail.[17] The "evolutionary" critics may not even meet the minimal conditions for a robust cognitive historical approach, beginning with the acknowledgment, in Spolsky's terms, that given the complexity of the human genetic inheritance, "providing so many possibilities differently actualized in different circumstances and by different people, it will not be possible to answer the new and interesting questions about literature and culture without consulting the historical context of these questions" (*Darwin* 45–46). Historical context is not an "add-on" but an integral part of the cognitive-historical equation.

Toward the other, historicist end of the continuum but closer to a middle position lies the work of Crane, Hart, and Spolsky herself. All, significantly, are professionally identified with the literary historical field of early modern studies, the disciplinary home of the "new" historicism and a hospitable ground for cultural materialist and related historicist approaches. All three critics develop their work in sustained dialogue with their new historicist, feminist, and cultural materialist colleagues, using the same critical language and drawing extensively on work produced from historicist and contextualist perspectives, yet each seeks to address some of the well-known impasses or blind spots encountered in that work by blending in the perspectives of cognitive theory, neuroscience, and (especially in Spolsky) neo-Darwinist theory. Crane, for example, in *Shakespeare's Brain*, notes that historicist and materialist critics, despite their productive interest in both discourse and the body, have not considered the "material site where discourse enters the body," namely, the brain, "where entry into the symbolic occurs, and therefore where the subject is constructed."[18] Assuming (reasonably enough) that Shakespeare's brain would have "functioned as most normal brains do today" (15), Crane can draw on recent work in cognitive linguistics, the cognitive psychology of language acquisition, and the neuroscience of semantic storage and retrieval to elucidate distinctive patterns in Shakespeare's notoriously rich and resonant poetic vocabulary. In every case, however, the specific verbal patterns Crane studies are shown to be significantly enmeshed as well in context-specific processes of ideological change, cultural innovation, and even contemporary developments in theater history.

Shakespeare's Brain can be considered the major example to date of a literary study, focused on a given moment in cultural history, that brings to bear on its subject what Mark Turner has called a "wider notion of human history."[19] In contrast to the usual focus on "cultural and sociological history as it operates over relatively brief temporal spans of decades or centuries," Turner writes, cognitive neuroscience also considers "two other crucial aspects of human history," phylogenetic history and ontogenetic history. Phylogenetic history—Gary Snyder's more poetical term is *deep history*—takes into account "thousands and millions of years" of biological and cultural evolution, including the processes that have resulted in the sorts of genetically guided and neurologically instantiated linguistic structures and mechanisms that interest Crane.[20] Ontogenetic history concerns the "development of the individual mind and brain from conception to advanced age," including the work in developmental cognitive psychology and language acquisition theory on which Crane also relies. These alternate ways of thinking "history" do not displace the literary scholar's traditional focus on sociocultural history but rather complete it. "Cultural, phylogenetic, and ontogenetic history," Turner emphasizes, are "typically viewed in cognitive neuroscience as aspects of human history that do not operate independently" (18).

What gives Crane's distinctive blend of cultural, developmental, and "deep" historical perspectives its special interest for literary scholars, of course, is that she reexamines some of the issues that have proved most vexing for (new) historicist approaches: the author (as opposed to the "author function") and the individual subject, in particular the individual author's brain as the crucial material locus where cultural and biological factors interpenetrate and interact. In addition, Crane can address another well-known lacuna for historicist studies—the question of why the works of one author differ appreciably from those of another working within the same historical circumstances and ideological milieu[21]—by arguing that the "clash of physiological and cultural constraints" (32), the impartial and uneven permeability of a given embodied subject to cultural and ideological penetration, can account for unpredictable differences among contemporaries as well as for the permanent possibility of cultural change.

Spolsky established an early precedent for such arguments in her prescient 1993 study, *Gaps in Nature*. Weaving together a number of claims and models from cognitive science and neuroscience, variously emphasizing the mind-brain's modularity, the "fuzziness" of linguistic and conceptual categories, the "gappy" nature of consciousness, and the friction or noise produced by differences among cognitive and perceptual modules and distinct levels of mental processing, Spolsky argued that the cognitive neurosciences yield a model of human subjectivity every bit as fragmented, discontinuous, and disintegral as a poststructuralist theorist could dream.[22] Yet the very friction or noise endemic to the workings of an embodied mind, for Spolsky, makes for a significant amount of cognitive flexibility and effectively underwrites the possibility of cultural and ideological change. Spolsky sees the gaps and incommensurabilities in human cognitive systems as "necessary and innate aspects of our genetically inherited epistemological equipment" that help account for ideological dissent as well as literary creativity (192). In a striking reversal of the usual tendency to associate "genetically inherited" characteristics with a stable and enduring human "nature" and culturally inherited characteristics with the local and transitory, Spolsky argued that the cultural and ideological conformity and stasis implied by social constructionist accounts of subject formation could be corrected by an appeal to the stubbornness of brain matter. In this way, a "materialist, biologically-based cognitive science" might be enlisted as a valuable "counterweight" to the "materialist historical" trend of contemporary literary and cultural theory (40).

In addition to promoting cognitive flexibility, the complexity of the interactions among cultural and biological inheritances, along with the friction and "inter-modular conflicts" built into the workings of the embodied mind, help account for some of the recurring epistemological crises found in global cultural history (Spolsky, *Darwin* 3). Conflicts among discrete sensory-cognitive modalities can become exaggerated at certain times and in certain places and lead to a culture-wide distrust and devaluation of a given sensory mode, as in the prohibition on certain visual representations, or "iconophobia," found in some but not all Hebrew and Muslim cultures and characteristic as well of the Protestant Reformation in Europe.[23] Or, such distrust may spread more globally and help usher in a period marked by profound epistemological skepticism.[24] That iconophobia and skepticism will recur in human cultures is, for Spolsky, a predictable result of the brain-mind's jagged design, but where, when, and how they will occur depends on the sorts of contingent factors investigated by cultural, social, political, and religious historians.

Along with cognitive flexibility, then, comes a predisposition to certain modes or habits of thought. In other words, given how the mind-brain seems to work, some thoughts are easier to think than others.[25] But this does not make them inevitable in some biologically "hardwired" manner. Crane has argued, in a pro-vocative reading of binary oppositions in Shakespeare's *Macbeth*, that "human subjects rely constantly on binary distinctions" because binary thinking makes for a useful cognitive strategy, especially valuable for real-time problem solving on the fly.[26] Historically, binary oppositions have become (since the seventeenth century) omnipresent as a tool for thinking and for pedagogy in part because they readily lend themselves to logical formalization (111). As we have seen, binary opposi-tions (such as culture/history, nature/biology, or realism/relativism) can become so widely pervasive that they seem difficult if not impossible to think beyond, a pessimistic conclusion sometimes implied by poststructuralist critique. Yet, Crane goes on to argue, cognitive theory reveals that binary thinking is not a "*necessary* constitutive component" of all human cognition and encourages critics to con-sider cognitive models in the interest of overcoming the seemingly "inescapable" pull of the (chronically oversimplified) binary opposition (114, 120).

Cognitive critics have also described some of the more specific ways in which the human mind's particular sort of embodiment and phylogenetic history may make certain modes of thought more readily thinkable than others. In a cogni-tive analysis of the rhetoric and ideology of Anna Barbauld's *Hymns in Prose for Children*, for example, Lisa Zunshine argues for the rhetorical salience and complex ideological effect of key metaphors in Barbauld's seemingly puerile text.[27] By repeatedly insisting, in a manner consonant with the contemporary surge of "catechistic" practices and writings for children, that the child reader is "made" (by God) rather than born, Barbauld strategically conflates two deeply entrenched modes of thought. Citing research and theory in cognitive anthropology, Zunshine identifies two different "domain-specific" modes for processing information, one generally used in relation to artifacts, which are tacitly understood as being defined by their functions, the other more commonly suited for living things, defined instead by their essences (130). (A rabbit missing its signature long ears remains a rabbit; a cup without a handle can readily be seen as a bowl instead.) Displacing human beings into the category of artifacts causes, first, a kind of cognitive frisson (well-known from artificial humanoids like Frankenstein's monster or the Terminator) that seizes the child reader's attention. Second, placing the child into the artifact category may also, for the moment, encourage the child to think of itself in functional terms (one function being to bow down to the Creator in awe and praise). The contemporary ideological import of Barbauld's rhetoric, including its formal relation to the "catechistic" method, can only be accounted for by the kinds of historically specific research associated with cultural criticism and the history and critique of ideology. But, Zunshine writes, a cognitive approach can augment the analysis of "ideologically charged cultural representations" because their effect depends in part on their exploitation of "cognitive contingencies that arise from the constant interplay between the human brain and its environment," an environment saturated with culture. "As an effort to influence human beings," Zunshine continues, "ideology will always be attuned to the intricacies of human cognition," and thus the "exploration of our cognitive makeup becomes increasingly important for scholars invested in cultural studies" (126).

These cognitive critics would have no trouble agreeing that what makes the human mind human is precisely its capacity to create, absorb, and transmit culture—that human beings are "naturally" cultural. That basic commitment does not, however, entail adherence to a "blank slate" conception of a mind passively open to inscription, equally susceptible to any and every sort of enculturation process.[28] The human mind seems just as "naturally" to resist certain kinds of enculturation and, as Spolsky argues, seems even to default towards cultural innovation. Cultural constructionist theories seeking to account for the inevitability of cultural change and ideological contestation (even in the absence of significantly altered economic or other "determinants") have sometimes pointed out that "subject positions" are overdetermined, that human subjects are multiply "inscribed" not only by "social relations of production" (as emphasized in Marxist analysis) but also the "social relations, among others, of sex, race, nationality, and vicinity."[29] This guarantees a certain amount of play in the system, the subject "fixed" to be sure, but "always precariously and provisionally so" (90).

If we tighten the focus here to note that, whatever their vicinity, human subjects are also always embodied and that no enculturation can take place in the absence of a material brain, we have done something more than add yet another item to the standard list of ideological determinants. We have in effect moved beyond the residual behaviorism that has kept poststructuralist cultural analysis from peering into the black box of the human brain, and we have opened up the possibility of a productive dialogue with contemporary work in the mind and brain sciences. That such an opening does not trigger an inexorable slide toward biological determinism or preclude serious attention to historical context and cultural specificity should by now be evident. To the contrary, it may give us more analytically powerful and more detailed ways of addressing the contingencies and resistances that leave historically situated human subjects so "precariously" fixed in a given cultural environment. At the very least, it gives us a wealth of productive new ways to think about language, the imagination, narrative, aesthetic response, rhetoric, poetics, and literary creativity, as well as providing fresh perspectives on authorship, subject formation, individual agency, and consciousness, topics that have proved stubbornly resistant to poststructuralist analysis.

The literary historical field of British Romanticism has proved an especially fertile ground for new historicist and contextualist approaches, and the past quarter century of scholarship in this area has not simply produced new "readings" of familiar texts and authors but significantly expanded the field's focus of attention. A field that, until recently, focused on the work of six poets (all male) and one novel (*Frankenstein*), now embraces a broad range of poetry and fiction by "rediscovered" women writers; the literature of the antislavery movement and the early slave narrative; historical, economic, and polemical works by men and women alike; the Gothic; popular theater; children's writing; and a wide range of novels, including those of Scott and of Austen, the latter long read as though somehow detached from the wider literary culture of the Romantic era. The proliferation of "contexts" for Romantic texts—the French Revolution; the feminist controversy; popular radicalism; colonial slavery and the slave trade; imperial crisis and resurgence, agrarian reform and early industrialism; religious revival and innovation; and profound changes in education and literacy, in book production and periodicals, and in institutions ranging from the poorhouse to the post office—has encouraged the proliferation as well of the sorts of texts, artifacts, and occurrences that might interest a Romanticist.

Romantic-era developments in science and medicine have become increasingly useful as contexts for understanding Romantic-era culture. One important consequence of the recent surge of attention to reading literary works in their scientific and medical contexts has been a new appreciation of just how permeable the lines between literary and scientific culture were in the Romantic era. I have argued that the neuroscience of the era, in addition to being fraught with political and ideological significance, held a special interest for a number of contemporary literary writers. Likewise, some of the most exciting developments in "Romantic brain science" were informed by concepts and preoccupations that had already emerged in the literary and philosophical writings of the time, including those by writers long identified as early "Romantics."[30] An organic and developmental understanding of mind; an unprecedented appreciation for the pervasive role of the "unconscious" in mental life; a protoevolutionary sense of the kinship between human and animal minds; a growing sense (however anxious) of the limitations of conscious introspection and of the split or fragmented nature of individual subjectivity; a renewed emphasis on instinct, intuition, and inherited characteristics; a materialist or "corporealist" approach to mind or at least an acknowledgement of the profound interpenetration of mind and body—all these were common concerns of Romantic-era brain science and Romantic literary writing alike. They are also, of course, central concerns of cognitive neuroscience in the present, a coincidence that has done much to make the pioneering brain science of the late eighteenth and early nineteenth centuries newly interesting to Romanticists today.

Although they play an important background role in the analyses that follow, this book is not centrally concerned with the many resonances between cognitive neuroscience in the present and the pioneering brain science of the Romantic era. It more closely resembles, in aim and spirit, Crane and Spolsky's book-length studies, although I do not attempt to pursue a single large issue from beginning to end. Instead, I have chosen to examine a series of issues from my home field of British Romanticism, each of which inspires a somewhat different engagement with the sciences of mind and brain. As a result, the chapters that follow recruit a number of theories and models from cognitive science, neuroscience, and evolutionary biology, in the interest of reopening or newly addressing a half-dozen problems, cruxes, or special topics in Romantic studies, each of which seems especially ripe for reconsideration along cognitive historicist lines.

Some of these issues have long held major interest for Romanticists, such as the delimitation and description of a distinctively "Romantic" sublime. In chapter 2, I suggest that at least one Romantic version of the sublime can best be understood not in relation to Kantian notions of transcendence but to a materialist, brain-based conception of mind. Chapters 3 and 4, on the relation between mental images and the Romantic imagination and on the rhetorical figure of apostrophe, seek to bring fresh insights to debates that have inspired a great deal of excellent scholarship in the past but have resisted anything like successful resolution. In bringing cognitive linguistics and rhetoric to bear on the seemingly extraordinary figure of apostrophe and (following Elaine Scarry) reconsidering the Romantic imagination in relation to the cognitive neuroscience of mental imaging, I hope at least to productively reframe these thorny topics. As Austen's novels have belatedly come within the purview of Romantic studies, a long-standing interest in "Romantic consciousness" now extends to Austen's innovative narrative techniques for representing consciousness, which I examine (in chapter 5) specifically in relation to what cognitive psychologists and autism researchers term "theory of mind theory." Romantic representations of sibling incest, which have long piqued scholarly interest because of their unusually sympathetic treatment of a topic generally considered disgusting or merely lurid, get a new look (in chapter 6) in relation to work on incest avoidance in evolutionary biology. The final chapter (7) stands out from the rest because it concerns a motif in British Romantic poetry that (to my knowledge) has never been identified as such, although it bears significantly on issues of great interest to Romanticists, including language acquisition, mother-infant relations, and the origins of poetic speech. This chapter also considers the usefulness of evolutionary biology for literary studies, in this case via the "evolutionary aesthetics" of Ellen Dissanayake, as well as work in cognitive developmental psychology and linguistics.

In every case, while looking to work in the cognitive neurosciences as a source for new perspectives, I have tried rigorously to keep the historical specificity of the texts and issues considered here in view. If certain moments, or patterns, or representational methods, or thematic motifs in Romantic-era texts seem to coincide with what we are currently learning about the brain and mind, what in Romantic-era culture makes this convergence possible? If, for example, moments in the poetry of Keats and Shelley evoke the fragility and "gappiness" of a brain-based mind—of a mind that cannot be teased apart from brute matter—it is hardly enough to invoke current scientific orthodoxy on the materiality of mind. Even if (in company, I believe, with all cognitive critics) I hold to a scientific worldview as part of my basic intellectual equipment—what John Searle would call the "background" of my thinking—and I therefore accept unhesitatingly that "the mind is what the brain does," I am not at liberty to project that belief back onto the writers of the Romantic era.[31] True, there is every reason to believe (again in keeping with a basic scientific worldview) that minds were no less dependent on brains in the Romantic era than they are now. But there is no reason to think, in advance of historical research, that Romantic-era subjects held this to be the case. To the contrary, it has been well-established that in many times and places, most if not all people would find the notion of a material mind, or a mind identified with the brain, counterintuitive or even shocking. Even today, many Americans, probably a majority of them, believe in some kind of disembodied mind- or soul- or spirit-stuff that persists independently of the brain and can outlive the body's dissolution. In the Romantic era, such a view was certainly the dominant one, and it was held by scientists as well as by laypersons. What seems obvious now may have been anything but obvious in the past.

However, in this case, the material embodiment of mind was certainly *thinkable* in the Romantic era. In fact, materialist or "corporealist" conceptions of mind formed one aspect of radical intellectual culture and appealed as well to a growing number of scientists and medical doctors, many of whom had links to contemporary political radicalism. Materialist notions of mind were by no means dominant, but, at least in intellectual circles, they were notorious. It has been demonstrated that Keats and Shelley (not to mention Coleridge, Wordsworth, and many other Romantic-era writers) were directly exposed to such notions and that Shelley, Coleridge, and (arguably) Keats personally held such notions at times. Scholars have begun to delineate, as well, a pronounced physiological cast to the psychology of the sublime experience as theorized by Burke, who cannot be called a "materialist" but whose conception of mind shares some crucial elements with the materialist psychologies that emerged by the end of the eighteenth century. Why then, hasn't Romantic criticism considered the possibility of a "neural sublime" before now? Probably because, viewing the sublime almost exclusively through its later, Kantian, version, no one has thought to look for a nontranscendent or even anti-transcendent sublime. Recent work on the neuroscience of perception, however, and especially the neuroscience of perceptual illusions, has made possible a very different perspective on the Romantic sublime, one that has long been available in the archival record but has remained nevertheless effectively out of view.

All this is not to imply that the (scientific) fact of the mind's embodiment is trivial. Avoiding the relativistic extreme (which might hold that, for cultures that do not locate the mind in the brain, a serious head injury would not affect mental functioning), we can reliably assume that human minds have always and everywhere been instantiated in brains and required reasonably intact brains in order to function reasonably well. As a result, we could expect that brain-based conceptions of mind have arisen throughout history in many times and places, whether as widely accepted notions or as minority views arising from empirical observation. We could expect to (and do) find such conceptions present throughout the historical archive well above what would be predicted from mere chance, far outnumbering alternative theories that might locate the mind in the liver, in the dominant hand, in a sacred talisman, or in the stars. The most refined idealist philosophy could, in theory, always be challenged by a good blow to the head. But, retreating as well from the realist extreme, we recall that empirical observation is no simple thing. What we see is conditioned by what we already think, the "background" that forms our largely unquestioned assumptions and beliefs, the discursive systems that give form to our thoughts and expressions, and, not least, the species-specific cognitive equipment that may favor some thoughts and modes of thought over others. Hayles writes, in relation to sociological studies of science, that constrained constructivism "invites—indeed cries out for—cultural readings of science, since the representations presented for disconfirmation have everything to do with prevailing cultural and disciplinary assumptions." On the other hand, she continues, "not all representations will be viable. It is possible to distinguish between them on the basis of what is really there" (34). Extending this argument to the history of science, we can expect certain representations to have proven more frequent in occurrence and more robust in their effects over time, though we should not expect to find anything like an unbroken history of scientific progress. Human beings have never had unmediated access to the real, nor can one easily imagine how such access might ever come about. Yet the real has always had ways of making itself felt.

These ways do not include writerly intuition, much less prophecy. One of the great lessons of the cognitive revolution has been just how much of mental life remains closed to introspection—much more, it is sometimes claimed, than Freud himself supposed.[32] I see no reason to exempt even writers of great literary achievement from this rule, which has to do not with the presence or absence of "genius" but with the inherent limitations of our species-specific cognitive equipment. Certainly, some artists have demonstrated unusually acute powers of observation and thus achieved uncommon insight into the workings of their own minds and external senses and into the mental behaviors of others. But historicist critique has rightly taught us to be wary of projecting current representations back onto past texts and artifacts simply because these representations capture phenomena that must always have been there, supposedly perceptible by any artist with sufficient intuitive or observational powers, independent of that artist's epistemological frame and culturally contingent biases and presuppositions. If Austen, for example, represents something very like "theory of mind theory" in her later novels, it is not enough (at least for me) to argue that, as an indisputably great observer of human nature, she saw and recorded behaviors that scientific psychology would take another 170 years or so to discover. Noting a coincidence between current representations of mind and mental behaviors and the literary representations of the past represents the beginning, not the end, of a process of literary interrogation. What, if anything, in the social, philosophical, and scientific discourses of the time made it possible for Austen to observe these behaviors as such and to think them worth representing in her fiction? Can one find analogous representations in the early psychological thought of the period, whether or not one can establish conclusively that Austen had read such accounts? Was there anything in Austen's experience as a woman, as femininity was then constructed, that would have encouraged her observation of the mental behaviors in question? Can one relate Austen's alleged depiction of "theory of mind" behaviors to contemporary developments in the practice of fictional representation, such as the recent invention (sometimes attributed to Austen herself) of free indirect discourse?

Questions such as these plunge us back into the contingent, local, historically specific character of the given text, event, or artifact subject to analysis and help us guard against naively imposing present understandings on the past or, worse, using past texts to allegorize later models and theories in the manner of much psychoanalytical literary criticism. A given cognitive historicist reading will gain credibility not from the neatness of the fit between past and present representations, or from the cleverness with which such a fit is finessed, but from careful scholarship, serious consideration of alternative explanations, critical judgment, and the persuasiveness of specific examples. Even when a given text or series of texts seem closely to "anticipate" (whatever that means) a current model or theory, careful consideration of competing hypotheses may suggest instead that this is a matter of coincidence or of convergent cultural evolution—two distinct discursive cultures arriving at a closely comparable model by different means and for different reasons (see chapter 6). Convergence does not necessarily amount to identity, nor repetition to anticipation.

Taking a vital interest in what cognitive science and neuroscience are learning about stable, species-specific features of the human mind and its workings will not provide literary studies with ready-made answers to its own questions but rather will help generate new, alternative hypotheses for literary analysis. Even aspects of mind and mental activity that seem to occur with minimal variance over time and across cultures have histories; they are interpreted, represented, and valued in relation to specific historical and cultural milieus. As Hayles points out, the empirical investigations of the sciences reflect "prevailing cultural and disciplinary assumptions" and cannot be adapted carelessly or wholesale for use in literary and cultural analysis. Nor should good empirical work carried out according to high methodological standards be cavalierly dismissed, even (or especially) when its findings seem to challenge cherished assumptions in the humanities. Models and theories from the sciences of mind and brain (themselves still of a largely provisional character) can help humanists locate blind spots, false dichotomies, and disciplinary limitations in their own thinking and can open up new methods or even whole areas of critical investigation. The chapters that follow consider just a few ways that such an interdisciplinary venture might develop. They will succeed to the extent that they help inspire others to begin similar investigations of their own.

CHAPTER TWO

The Neural Sublime

Keeping up with the literature in the sciences of mind and brain can involve more than just reading. Books written for a general intellectual audience in particular—cognitive neuroscientific "crossover" books—frequently enlist the reader as coexperimenter. They ask the reader to perform a series of self-experiments, often involving visual illusions or like forms of cognitive bewilderment, experiments intended to replicate well-known findings that give us a palpable sense of the differences between our conscious experience of mind and perception and the obscure and curious workings of our brains.

Here are a few classic examples, which I in turn will ask you, the reader of this book, to try out on yourself. Fix your eyes on a stationary object across the room—a lamp, a picture, a doorknob—and rotate your head a little to the right and then to the left. Although your eyes are moving, you notice that the object does not move with them, thanks to supplementary information routed to your brain from your vestibular system. But now close one eye and fix the other on the same object and then, as gently as possible, push your eyeball a little toward the bridge of your nose. This time, the object does move, although you "know" perfectly well that it remains stationary. But this knowledge is powerless to override the illusion. The brain, it turns out, does not always work seamlessly, and the conscious reason, despite its sense of being in charge of such matters, can be tricked in the wink of an eye.[1]

One of the brain's most impressive tricks on the conscious mind, which happens whenever there's light enough to see by, involves the blind spot that everyone has in each visual field thanks to the small area in the retina where the entry point of the optic nerves causes a gap in the retinal array of photoreceptors. Hold your finger, the tip at eye level, ten to twelve inches from the center of your gaze. If you keep looking straight ahead, while moving your finger slowly to one side—about fifteen degrees—your fingertip will disappear: that's the blind spot. You can see the same effect, perhaps more easily, with an exercise involving two black disks on either side of a plus sign.[2]

Revealing the blind spot. Courtesy of Daniel Dennett.

Close one eye, hold the diagram eight to ten inches away with your gaze fixed on the central cross, and one dot will disappear. You can make the dot on the other side disappear by closing the other eye. If you practice this a little, you can make the disks blink on and off like inverse Christmas lights, dark instead of bright.

This one proves a little more intriguing, and maybe a little more disturbing. Not only is it easy to trick the conscious mind but apparently the brain is doing this *all the time*, filling in the blind spot (of which, until the first time you try these experiments, you remain happily unaware) with information culled from the surrounding visual field. The brain is at least partly creating the world that the mind perceives; this idea will not seem so strange to readers of Wordsworth.

The brain has other ways of "filling in"—of taking the initiative in creating the perceived world—and neuroscientists never seem to tire of demonstrating these to the rest of us. Another classic diagram (with its many variations), the Kanizsa triangle, shows how the neural mechanisms of perception trick us into seeing fairly vivid contour lines where there is only blank space.

The Kanizsa triangle. Modified from Gaetano Kanizsa, *Organization in Vision* (New York: Praeger, 1979).

In the example above, not only do contour lines appear but the white triangle they outline looks brighter than the surrounding white space it stands out from. (A photometer would detect no such difference.)[3] Such illusions, as the cognitive scientist Donald Hoffman puts it, suggest that "to experience is to construct," in vision as well as "in each [sensory] modality and without exception" (48).

Many of the universal cognitive rules guiding such constructions seem to have arisen over the course of evolution in order to give us the pragmatically useful (if philosophically suspect) sense of a relatively stable object world. If, for example, a figure is broken up by what look like solid bars, we will construct an occluded, equally solid-looking geometrical figure behind them; if the figure is altered so that we no longer assume such occlusion, we see just an odd collection of smaller two-dimensional figures.[4]

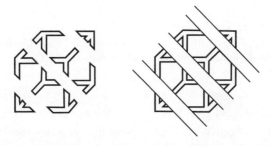

Imaginary occlusion. Modified from Gaetano Kanizsa, *Organization in Vision* (New York: Praeger, 1979).

Other figures, however, can evoke *instability* by playing on the same basic rules of perception. The famously ambiguous duck-rabbit figure, for example, which presents two equally plausible gestalts, flips back and forth almost at random as one gazes at it.[5]

The duck-rabbit. From Joseph Jastrow, "The Mind's Eye," *Popular Science Monthly* 54 (1899).

The still more famous Necker cube, perhaps because each competing construction gives us an equally abstract geometrical design and not a mimetic representation, seems to flip entirely at random, although you can train yourself to reverse it more or less at will.[6]

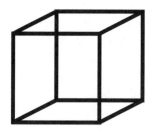

The Necker cube. Adapted from Louis Albert Necker, "Observations on Some Remarkable Phenomena Seen in Switzerland: And an Optical Phenomenon Which Occurs on Viewing a Figure of a Crystal or Geometrical Solid," *London and Edinburgh Philosophical Magazine and Journal of Science* 3 (1832).

But why would you want to? Why would anyone spend so much time staring at illusory and ambiguous figures that a certain amount of expertise in manipulating them begins to develop? Why should figures that, as Keats says, "tease us out of thought" yield fascination rather than annoyance, pleasure rather than anxiety?

When, some years back, I began reading textbooks in cognitive science and popularizations of neuroscience, I soon wondered at the avidity with which I performed every such self-experiment asked of me—at times, repeatedly. Their function in advancing the argument of the book, whether a work of neuroscience, of philosophy of mind, or of cognitive psychology, seemed clear enough. Guiding the reader through self-experiments in perceptual and cognitive illusion serves to disarm skepticism provoked by the more startling cognitive and neuroscientific claims. They dishabituate our habitual relation to perception and our own thinking process, defamiliarizing ordinary cognition (to borrow the terminology of Russian formalism) and breaking down our resistance to a brain-based notion of mind. By discrediting conscious introspection, revealing its literal as well as figurative blind spots, such illusions leave us open to the counterclaims of cognitive and neuroscientific theory. These claims are made on behalf of the considerable amount of *un*conscious processing characteristic of perception and cognition and, ultimately, on behalf of the immensely complex and (from the viewpoint of consciousness) disturbingly alien brain that makes possible this constant work of unconscious processing.

One can readily see, then, why such illusions would prove rhetorically useful to the author, but what makes them so appealing to the reader? I'm happy to add that this almost compulsive pleasure in cognitive illusions does not seem to be simply one more eccentricity of my own. As I began attending and sometimes hosting seminars featuring demonstrations by colleagues in the mind and brain sciences, I learned that these researchers frequently begin their presentations with demonstrations of visual and other cognitive illusions, in part because these are guaranteed to engage the audience. The more spectacular the illusion, the more rapt the audience (myself included) seemed to become. Illustrating what is called "change blindness," for example, one presenter (Donald Hoffman) gave us alternating brief looks at two seemingly identical slides, always with a blank slide in between, asking us when we could see the differences between the two photographs. After many repetitions, first one, then another, and finally all of us test subjects saw that fairly significant objects (including, I recall, a whole wing of a farm building) had been edited out of one photo.[7] Why did it take so long to notice the difference, to actually see rather than skeptically looking to confirm that the two scenes were nonidentical? Because while the brain constructs the object world that we perceive, it does so more economically than we might suppose, simply leaving out details low in salience. It is as though one's digital camera were to capture the friends and family in a crowded party scene but silently edit out the plants and pets.

To begin a presentation on cognition and "racial" discrimination, the cognitive social psychologist Mahzarin Banaji took the group through a demonstration of the related but even more spectacular phenomenon of "motion blindness." Watching a filmstrip of a simple ball game and instructed to follow the motion of a ball tossed from one player to another, we were asked if we noticed anything else, anything unexpected. No one had. Slowing the film down, Banaji then revealed (to our collective amazement) that we had entirely missed a female figure, dressed in white, walking directly through the group of players across the center of the picture plane.[8] Following the motion of the ball had blinded us to the seemingly irrelevant figure, reducing her to an eerily invisible specter.

One could imagine several possible responses to such presentations, which collectively demonstrate how the conscious mind is fed a mere simulacrum, and a sketchy one at that, filled in here, edited there, of an only apparently stable and clearly outlined object world. The perceptual illusions so tellingly engineered by researchers like Hoffman and Banaji might provoke resistance, irritation, incredulity, or a deep, existential anxiety. Perhaps at times they do provoke all of these reactions. But what I've witnessed, again and again, is a reaction closer to awed astonishment, breaths sharply taken in and issuing out again in sighs, in murmurs of "Oh," or "Ah," or "Oh Wow" or (if there are younger scholars present) "Omigod!" And such demonstrations, in print and in real time, seem deliberately designed to provoke such reactions. Francis Crick, for example, calls his book, replete with such illusions, *The Astonishing Hypothesis* and Hoffman underscores the "shock" accompanying the sudden conviction that the brain constructs what the conscious subject sees (23). In this way, the rhetoric of illusion so pervasive within popular cognitive science and neuroscience overlaps with the rhetoric of the sublime. Does the connection run deeper? Is the experience of undergoing a perceptual illusion somehow related to the psychological experience that writers since Longinus have called the "sublime"?

One could begin by noting a certain structural problem in the relation of the conscious subject to each kind of experience. In *Art and Illusion*, a book that anticipates by some decades the current surge of interest in neuroscience and the arts, E. H. Gombrich states that, "though we may be intellectually aware of the fact that any given experience *must* be an illusion, we cannot, strictly speaking, watch ourselves having an illusion."[9] With an imaginary contour figure, for example, we can cover certain parts and see that the bright areas are just so much blank space on the page, but we can't then, taking our hands away, simultaneously see the contours *and* see that they are not there. Otherwise, it would not really count as an illusion. Guy Sircello, bringing a measure of philosophical rigor to the sublime in his notable essay "How Is a Theory of the Sublime Possible," similarly holds that the "sublime, as an object of experience, is epistemologically inaccessible," since (for Sircello) the sublime experience by definition exceeds ordinary "human powers of knowledge or description."[10] Yet, I would suggest, there are cognitive technologies that enable us, at least, to catch ourselves in the act of having such experiences. In regard to illusion, for example, Buddhist traditions offer meditation techniques that constitute, in the words of neurologist and Zen practitioner James Austin, a "long-range program of systematic training" precisely in recognizing and breaking through the illusory or virtual character of human cognitive experience so trenchantly described by neuroscientists like Hoffman, Banaji, and Crick.[11] Without committing ourselves to years of mindfulness training, however, we can still develop at least a feel for the virtual character of our habitual relation to the perceived world by savoring those disjunctive moments when our brains switch us from one reading of the Necker cube to the other, or when the black disc disappears into the blind spot, or when we first catch conscious sight of the missing objects in a change blindness demonstration. Indeed, this verging on a theoretically impossible experience, watching ourselves having an illusion, may account for part of the pleasure, part of the compulsive appeal, of such illusions.

In regard to the sublime, Sircello has already suggested several possible responses to the paradox of a psychological experience that by definition eludes human knowledge and description. Perhaps the sublime moment constitutes "a genuine experience of what is, or seems to be, inaccessible to *ordinary and familiar* modes of epistemological access" (547). To compare (very) large things to (very) small ones, this would make the sublime experience analogous to perceiving the blind spot in our visual field. Perhaps, Sircello suggests in his conclusion, "epistemological transcendence . . . may not concern 'the real' at all, but only the limitations of any attempts to grasp it, whatever it is taken to be" (549), rendering the sublime analogous to change blindness and motion blindness demonstrations, which comparably reveal our "radically limited access" to what Sircello calls, for want of a better term, "reality." In that case, sublime discourse could be seen as a cognitive technology for triggering the "*intuition of nothingness*" that he finds in examples of the sublime from Wordsworth to Bodhidarma (the "First Patriarch" in the Zen tradition) to Bataille, each of which suggests the emptiness of our habitual apprehension of what we take to be a graspable and permanent object world (547).

All of this is to assume, of course, that sublime discourse does recount an actual cognitive experience, something I do assume, in agreement with Sircello and most theorists of the sublime before the twentieth century, and in disagreement with more recent accounts that would limit the sublime to a purely linguistic, rhetorical, or textual phenomenon. Even Longinus, sometimes said to think of the sublime largely in rhetorical terms, conceives of a sublime experience prior to and independent of its linguistic expression, as in his discussion of the "elevation of thought" requisite to produce sublime discourse and his example of the silence of

Ajax, "a naked thought without words [that] challenges admiration, and strikes by its grandeur."[12] From the beginning, then, there has been a cognitive element to the sublime that helps to connect earlier speculation on the topic going back to Longinus, to the influential accounts of Edmund Burke and Immanuel Kant in the eighteenth and early nineteenth centuries, and to more recent philosophical discussions like Sircello's. One might expect that critics working with cognitive approaches to culture would sooner or later arrive at a "cognitive sublime," to add to the ever-growing list of sublimes—Gothic and Romantic, Egotistical and Sympathetic, American and Indian, Racial and Androgynous, and still more—that have been posited over the years.[13] Sure enough, the philosopher and film theorist Cynthia Freeland has already proposed a cognitivist account of the sublime, which retains key elements of Kant's philosophical reading of the sublime without remaining limited by what she terms Kant's "primitive theory of mental faculties."[14] Freeland's thinking on this subject is by no means predictable, but perhaps the very existence of *some* cognitive reworking of Kant's famously psychologized version of the sublime could have been predicted by now.

The "neural sublime," however, might seem to pose a different story, implying as it does an account of the sublime that features the brain as much as it does the mind. Kant's influential theory of the sublime, especially as it has been taken up and rehearsed by later writers, notably leaves the body and its brain behind to posit an idealized Reason that, in the course of the sublime moment, succeeds in touching on the noumenal itself, however obliquely, however indescribably. Kant dismissed Burke's theory of the sublime, after all, as a "physiological" or "merely empirical" exposition of the subject, unqualified to speak to the universality of aesthetic taste revealed by the sublime experience and so required to give place to a transcendental treatment of the subject such as Kant's own.[15] Although Kant's aesthetic theory may be more closely bound to the human body than critics often suppose (disembodied spirits, Kant insists, cannot experience beauty, and "pure intelligences," lacking any means for aesthetic presentation, would equally fail to experience the sublime [52, 131]), the Kantian sublime definitely trends toward valuing the mentalistic over the physiological, the abstract over the empirical. Kant's sublime might itself be described as a cognitive sublime, but a neural sublime would seem to remain, by contrast, tied to the phenomenal, tethered to the body and its limitations—and what kind of a sublime would that be?

One advantage, then, of a "neural sublime" concerns the way it disrupts teleological readings of the sublime tradition, such as Samuel Holt Monk's, that trace the growing internalization or psychologizing of the sublime to its culmination in

Kant's *Critique of Judgment*.[16] In relation to Romantic poetry, it asks us to reconsider the competing accounts of Burke and other writers in the British tradition,
not as so many stepping stones leading to Kant but as intriguing constructions
in their own right that, after all, would have been much more familiar to British
Romantic-era writers than would have been Kant, then known only to a few. It
would also challenge what seems to be a growing critical consensus that the sublime moment in canonical Romantic poetry inevitably, as in Kant's model, "erases
the body."[17] If anything, the sublime experiences that most interest me in poets like
Keats and Shelley could best be described, not as transcendental moments or asser-
tions of linguistic mastery over the body, nature, or the feminine but as instances
of a corporeal sublime. Perhaps the neural sublime even verges on constituting
an antisublime—something equally true of certain constructions of the feminine
sublime and of the ecological sublime.[18]

If the prestige of Kant's transcendental approach to the sublime has served to
occlude the neural sublime of the British Romantics, a comparison with the sublime rhetoric of illusion in recent neuroscience may help to bring it back into focus.
I contend that the neural sublime does not, as in Kant, trigger in the beholder the
apprehension of a higher Reason but rather, as in the neuroscientific demonstrations recounted above, yields up a disturbing but compulsive glimpse into the
ordinarily secret workings of the brain. I do not wish to claim that all instances
of the sublime encountered in Romantic writing can or should be understood in
terms of this "neural" sublime—many, perhaps most of them cannot—but that
an important and highly revealing subset of them can best be understood in this
manner. Discriminating a neural sublime from among the various instances of the
sublime in Romantic poetry will also help to tie that body of writing back to the
most considerable account of the sublime widely current at the time, the sublime
of Burke.

Burke's sublime, although overtly (and now notoriously) gendered masculine,
is no less firmly tied to the body for that. Burke's sublime appears distinctly earthly
and physical not only in relation to the Kantian idealist sublime to come but in
comparison to a good deal of earlier sublime writing as well. From the early English translations of Longinus on, the sublime experience often evokes metaphors
of transport or rapture—finding oneself carried out of one's body and above the
earth the way prey might be carried off by an eagle or other raptor. "For the sublime not only persuades," according to Longinus (in a 1743 translation), "but even
throws an audience into transport" ("On the Sublime" 22). Theorists of the sublime
in this period regularly feature the terms "ravished" (*Sublime* 43, 80), "transported"

(49), and "ecstasy," etymologically, the state of being taken beyond or above one's ordinary state, although qualified by Shaftesbury as a "reasonable ecstasy" (77). According to James Burgh, in 1761, the sublime "transports," "ravishes," and "ought to hurry us out of ourselves" (117). John Dennis epitomizes this tradition when he says that sublime writing produces "an invincible force, which commits a pleasing rape upon the very soul of the reader" (37).

Burke's thinking, in contrast, makes part of a revisionary countertradition, arising somewhat later in the eighteenth century, that understands the sublime less as divine rapture than as physical rupture. Imagining the mind as an organ or a muscle, writers like Joseph Priestley, William Duff, and Thomas Reid emphasize the effortful character of thinking the sublime, a labor of conception that invokes metaphors of enlarging, stretching, dilating, and swelling, no longer suggesting a conceptual rape (pleasing or not) so much as the mental pregnancy that might result from it. The mind, Priestley writes in his 1777 lecture on the sublime, "must, as it were, enlarge itself, to conceive a great object" (*Sublime* 119). For Duff, in the *Essay on Original Genius* (1767), the sublime poet "labours to express in his compositions the ideas which dilate and swell his Imagination" (*Sublime* 175), adding that the poet will often fail to find adequate words and "sinks under the immensity of his own conceptions," attesting to the cognitive aspect of the sublime and inverting the upward trajectory of the dominant "transport" metaphor. For Reid, writing in 1785, "it requires a stretch of imagination" to grasp the "true sublime," the apprehension of which entails "a kind of violence" in the mind of the beholder (178). In Burke's theory of the sublime, this violent distention of the mind becomes paramount, and the terms *rapture* and *transport* drop away altogether. Locating the sublime in the body rather than in an out of the body phenomenon, Burke makes the sublime a corporeal experience that, in the last analysis, depends on changes in the central nervous system, a stretching and subsequent relaxation of the nerves.

Vanessa Ryan has argued, a good deal more charitably than Kant, for a "physiological" reading of Burke's sublime, stressing its irrationality and its close links to the body, the nerves, and the passions. In this way, Ryan argues, Burke represents an extension of eighteenth-century British thought on the subject, "which emphasizes the overpowering of reason by the passions," while Kant's sublime in contrast "presents a break with British thought rather than its culmination" (268). For Burke, as Ryan shows, the sublime forestalls and outruns the reason rather than attesting to its preeminence, as in Kant. "Hence," Burke writes, "arises the great power of the sublime, that far from being produced by them, it anticipates our reasonings, and hurries us on by an irresistible force."[19] The Burkean sublime, which at bottom arises from events Burke locates within the nervous system, is in Ryan's phrase a "physiological sublime," while "Kant's sublime is an entirely spiritual consciousness" (278).

Burke's understanding of the human mind developed throughout the *Philosophical Enquiry* looks forward in a number of ways to the brain-based, "corporeal" psychologies I have described elsewhere (in *British Romanticism and the Science of the Mind*) as an important and previously neglected dimension of Romantic-era thinking about the mind. Burke sets out to trace mental events to ultimate "physical causes" (55) and assumes that human beings share a species-typical perceptual apparatus because they share the same sensory and neural "organs" (65). He accepts (against mainstream empiricist thought) the existence of innate notions and responses, such as a "natural" liking for sweets (66) and a universal ability to accurately perceive the "passions" of other people through "natural and uniform principles" (73) of basic human emotions and their expression. (This makes Burke an important early precursor of what are now called "Theory of Mind" theories.)[20] "Our minds and our bodies are so intimately connected," Burke emphasizes, that "one is incapable of pain or pleasure without the other" (163).

The painful pleasure, or pleasing pain, of the sublime ultimately rests on psychophysiological events that Burke compares (like Duff) to a "sort of swelling" that proves, however violent, nonetheless "extremely grateful to the human mind" (96). But why should swelling and distention, and seemingly aversive emotional states like fear and terror, produce pleasure when they issue in the sublime? Burke resolves this seeming contradiction with an appeal to the pioneering neuroscience of his time. The sublime, the "strongest emotion which the mind is capable of feeling" (86), involves at bottom a "tension, contraction, or violent emotion of the nerves" (162), a process of stretching and contraction analogous to muscular motion as the nerves labor to transmit the powerful emotions associated with vast or terrifying objects and with grand or suggestively obscure ideas. This neurological process is pleasing because, so long as it stops short of damaging the neural apparatus, it provides "exercise" for the "finer parts" of the sensory and nervous "system" (165). This may sound like a proto-Darwinian argument—human beings evolved to crave sublime emotions because they proved adaptive for neural fitness and thus survival and reproduction—but adaptationist arguments serve creationists just as well as they do evolutionists, and Burke himself gives full credit to "Providence." Whether evolved or divinely implanted, the thrill of the sublime functions like the rush of an aerobic workout, toning the nerves and buffing up the sensory organs.

The Romantic sublime, or at least the version of it that concerns me here, shares Burke's physiologism but not his interest in mental calisthenics. Rather, the neural sublime mode presents a mind stretched to and even past the breaking point, without necessarily leading to that snapping back that would complete the analogy with a flexed and then relaxed muscle. Its emphasis on cognitive breakdown can also be viewed as an extension of eighteenth-century sublime theory, at least in the work of those theorists who emphasize the effortful character of the sublime as an experience just too big and intense for the ordinary mind to handle. Joseph Addison, for example, in the *Spectator* series on the pleasures of the imagination, writes in relation to the sublime that the imagination "loves to be filled with an object, or to grasp at anything that is too big for its capacity" (*Sublime* 62). Shaftesbury, in a rhapsodic address to the Deity of nature, declares that "in thy immensity all thought is lost; fancy gives over its flight, and wearied imagination spends itself in vain . . . Thus having often essayed, thus sallied forth into the wide expanse, when I return again within myself, struck with the sense of this so narrow being, and of the fulness of that immense one; I dare no more behold the amazing depths, nor sound the abyss of *Deity*" (73). (Note again the directional shift from the sublime as something toward which we are carried up and away, to the sublime as an abyss or void opening within or beneath us.) Emphasizing, as does Burke, the mental "exertion" called forth by the sublime, Priestley quotes Mark Akenside on man's penchant for "thoughts beyond the limits of his frame," at once a brief for the "true sublime in sentiment" and a poetic instance of it (120). For Sir Joshua Reynolds, the "awe of the sublime" constitutes a "sentiment of *power* out of *our power* to produce or control"; in its capacity to overwhelm our cognitive abilities, the sublime thus verges on "horror, deformity, madness! an eminence from which the mind, that dares to look farther, is lost!" (126). Mary Wollstonecraft will go one step further to imagine a "sublime" of outright insanity in *The Wrongs of Woman*, as her heroine, Maria, imprisoned in a madhouse, expatiates on the examples of mental breakdown all around her. Contrasting the spectacle of insanity with the ruins of "monumental" art, a stock example of the sublime since Burke, Maria finds the former still more productive of a disturbing, negative sublime: "The view of what has been done by man, produces a melancholy, yet aggrandizing, sense of what remains to be achieved by human intellect; but a mental convulsion, which, like the devastation of an earthquake, throws all the elements of thought and imagination into confusion, makes contemplation giddy, and we fearfully ask on what ground we ourselves stand."[21]

At the same time, this sense of "mental convulsion" or cognitive collapse brings the Romantic neural sublime closer to Kant's sublime in terms of its dynamic structure and its emphasis on temporary mental failure, while as an experience taking place in the brain it represents an extension of Burke's physiologism and neural speculations. Although the Burkean and Kantian versions of the sublime have sometimes been seen as incommensurable, they might instead be seen as coalescing in the neural sublime of the British Romantics.[22] Kant's sublime centrally involves a dynamic cognitive sequence, parsed into three distinct moments in Thomas Weiskel's influential and admittedly heuristic analysis.[23] The Kantian sublime (1) begins with an attempt on the part of the mind to grasp at the infinite or infinitely vast, entailing (2) failure and a moment of mental collapse, which is then (3) followed and compensated for by a "feeling" that the "*mind has a power surpassing any standard of sense*" (Kant 106). This third moment, at which the finite mind comes into transient, inarticulate, yet transformative contact with the transcendent, marks the ultimate victory of the Reason making up for the defeat of the imagination (106). It's the intervening moment of breakdown—and with it "a momentary inhibition of the vital forces" (98)—that most resembles the Romantic neural sublime. Yet, in the Romantic version, the subject is left not marveling at the power of Reason but rather stunned by the capacity and complexity of the human brain.

I have elsewhere described the neural sublime at work in certain poems by Keats, a poet who was directly exposed (through his medical studies) to the new, neuroscientific psychology of the era and to many of the latest findings concerning the brain, widely regarded (at least in medical circles) for the first time as the massively complex organ of cognition we continue to see it as today.[24] The brain, within the neural sublime mode, reveals its power and its extent in moments when consciousness fails just at the point of some hoped-for revelation. Not in spite of but because of its network of interconnections with the rest of the body, "brain" for Keats often conveys a richer and more capacious sense of mental life than "mind," including not only conscious rational thought but emotive, unconscious, intuitive, and involuntary cognition as well. Lamia's "sciental brain"—with its ability to "unperplex bliss from her neighbor pain," an analytical feat highly reminiscent of Burke's sublime theory—evinces how the term *brain* can come to exceed *mind* rather than illustrate its debility, as the term *brain* (and compounds like *brain sick*) generally do in neoclassical satire. When, in contrast, the Romantic brain does fail, it fails not comically but in an awesome and sublime manner, underscoring the extent and labyrinthine complexity of the embodied mind in touching its limits. ("Nothing unearthly," Keats writes in the sonnet "On Receiving a Laurel Crown from Leigh Hunt," "has enticed my brain/Into a delphic labyrinth.") Even at moments when thought attempts a conceptual flight evoking the long tradition of sublime transport or rapture, the brain remains embodied and grounded, revealing its "delphic" or abysmal depths as the alternate and final source of sublimity. As early as in *Endymion*, a priest in the tradition of Shaftesbury's rhapsode expatiates on "thinkings" that "dodge/Conception to the very bourne of heaven,/Then leave the naked brain" (1: 294–95). The brain's nakedness, I would argue, ought to be taken in a double sense in this passage. On the one hand, as conscious thought reaches its limit and flickers out, the brain is left conceptually bare, momentarily impoverished and bereft of ideas. And yet this very experience of conscious quietude and conceptual emptiness provides a glimpse into the underlying presence and workings of the brain in all its nakedness. The brain's voidness in such moments paradoxically comes to signify the mind's power as well as its ultimate limits, what Keats elsewhere calls the "dim-conceived glories of the brain" ("On Seeing the Elgin Marbles").

It is not Keats, however, but P. B. Shelley who uses the term *brain* in its modern sense more extensively than any other Romantic poet and in ways that reflect his long-term interest in materialist or quasi-materialist thinkers like Priestley, Erasmus Darwin, Pierre-Jean-Georges Cabanis, and William Lawrence.[25] Shelley's own materialist phase—including a conviction that human thought is "no more than a relation between certain parts" of matter, "that infinitely varied mass of which the rest of the universe is composed," is evident from his "Essay on a Future State," composed by early 1812.[26] Although Shelley had disavowed materialism, including his materialist understanding of mind, by the end of that year, his use of the term *brain* continued to convey a sense of brain as mind comparable to that found throughout the materialist psychologies of Cabanis (a youthful enthusiasm of Shelley's) and Lawrence (his physician and friend later in life). Despite its separation of "body and soul," for example, *Queen Mab* describes mental events in a markedly materialist register: "the weak touch/That moves the finest nerve,/And in one human brain/Causes the faintest thought" (2: 104–7).[27] This is only one of many places where Shelley uses *brain* in place of the generally preferred term *mind*. In the verse *Letter to Maria Gisborne*, for example, Shelley writes that his "visionary rhyme" (probably referring here to *Prometheus Unbound*) was "Struck from the inmost fountains of my brain" (169), and in *Julian and Maddalo* he speaks of how the "swift thought" of animated conversation "flew from brain to brain" (30). The brain is also, as Shelley makes clear in *The Revolt of Islam*, the site where human experiences of the sublime take place:[28]

> those who saw
> Their tranquil victim pass, felt wonder glide
> Into their brain, and became calm with awe.
>
> (4478–80)

The brain provides the locus for our experience of the sublime; however, for Shelley as for Keats, the brain can itself become a source of the sublime.

Shelley's most spectacular and memorable descriptions of brain events come at moments when, through sensory or emotional or conceptual overload, or some combination of all three, the mind blanks out and seems to undergo a physical collapse or meltdown. The initial and studiously paradoxical description of the title charmer in the *Witch of Atlas* seems to bring Burke's opposed categories of the beautiful and the sublime into vertiginous fusion, defying the capacity of the brain to withstand the resulting conceptual overload:

> A lovely lady garmented in light
>   From her own beauty—deep her eyes, as are
> Two openings of unfathomable night
>   Seen through a Temple's cloven roof—her hair
> Dark—the dim brain whirls dizzy with delight
>   Picturing her form.   (81–86)

Struggling, in *Hellas*, to take in the sublime speech of Ahasuerus, in which the vastest conceptual scale imaginable ("this Whole / Of suns, and worlds, and men") is exposed as a mere shadow of "thought's eternal flight," Mahmud is thrown into the state I am terming the *neural sublime*:

> "Thy words stream like a tempest
> Of dazzling mist within my brain—they shake
> The earth on which I stand, and hang like night
> Of Heaven above me."   (786–89)

Most memorably, perhaps, Shelley describes the experience of cognitive dissolution as one overpowering vision gives way to the next in the *Triumph of Life*: "And suddenly my brain became as sand" (405).[29] This is Shelley's own signature version of Keats's "naked brain," with the entire cognitive apparatus momentarily wiped blank, as a wave washing over the beach erases all existing tracks from the sand. Notice how the classical sublimity of the ocean is here transferred to an image that evokes instead a brain temporarily void of thought.

These moments in Shelley coexist uneasily with the idealist tenor of his mature verse, perhaps nowhere more strikingly than when an encounter with a spiritual presence provokes a distinctly material and darkly sublime version of mental collapse. The crucial passage in *Alastor* that describes the poet's visionary encounter with his "veilèd maid" relentlessly stretches, in the manner of the British sublime countertradition, the hero's sensory and emotional capacities.[30] Gradually, it comes to overtax as well the reader's ability to parse the deliberately thorny syntax and to continue to visualize "imagery" that challenges any attempt to sustain a coherent mental image.

> Sudden she rose
> As if her heart impatiently endured
> Its bursting burthen: at the sound he turned
> And saw by the warm light of their own life
> Her glowing limbs beneath the sinuous veil
> Of woven wind, her outspread arms now bare,
> Her dark locks floating in the breath of night,
> Her beamy bending eyes, her parted lips
> Outstretched, and pale, and quivering eagerly.
> His strong heart sunk and sickened with excess
> Of love. He reared his shuddering limbs and quelled
> His gasping breath, and spread his arms to meet
> Her panting bosom; . . . she drew back a while,
> Then, yielding to the irresistible joy,
> With frantic gestures and short breathless cry
> Folded his frame in her dissolving arms.
> Now blackness veiled his dizzy eyes, and night
> Involved and swallowed up the vision; sleep,
> Like a dark flood suspended in its course,
> Rolled back its impulse on his vacant brain.
>
> (lines 172–91)

This is a negative sublime with a vengeance. The *Alastor* poet is left with a brain literally emptied out of content. In place of the idealist notion of thought without a brain, here is a brain bereft of thought—the mind's instantiation in brain revealed by its momentary extinction. The corresponding effect on the reader is well described by Shelley in his essay "On Life." "We are on that verge where words abandon us, and what wonder if we grow dizzy to look down the dark abyss of how little we know" (*Prose* 174), the reader's own negative sublime. There is no compensation aside from that awful vacancy and accompanying dizziness. No Kantian transcendent Reason appears to rescue our sense of human dignity; we are left blinking in the sublime darkness of an overtaxed brain.

The profound vacancy of this negative sublime raises the question: Does the neural sublime involve pleasure, at least for the reader, if not for the swooning subject? And, if it does, why would vicariously experiencing the loss of self and a glimpse, however faint, of the naked brain seem at all pleasant? Here I would like to return to the analogy of perceptual illusions with which I began. As I've suggested, perceptual illusions (as well as certain chronically ambiguous figures) yield an unexpected yet undeniable dividend of pleasure in the very process of suggesting that conscious perception is unreliable and that the vivid and apparently stable object world it presents to us is illusory and marked by a kind of emptiness, as in the blind spot demonstration. Significantly, the analogy I am posing between perceptual illusions and sublime experiences for Burke seems not to be an analogy at all but rather a matter of identity. Burke, that is, includes certain visual and motoric illusions in his *Enquiry* as instances of the sublime, not as mental experiences he likens to the sublime. Commenting on the philosophical precision of Milton's sublime phrase "dark with excessive light," for example, Burke explains that "extreme light, by overcoming the organs of sight, obliterates all objects, so as in its effect exactly to resemble darkness." Burke suggests a kind of self-experiment designed to demonstrate this fact, one that I would urge readers *not* to attempt: "After looking at some time at the sun, two black spots, the impression which it leaves, seem to dance before our eyes. Thus are two ideas as opposite as can be imagined reconciled in the extremes of both; and both in spite of their opposite nature brought to concur in *producing the sublime*" (121; my emphasis). I'm not certain that many readers will agree with Burke that such inverse afterimages (which we now sometimes experience as a result of a camera's flash) are sublime, but it remains telling that Burke himself would think so. A bit earlier in the *Enquiry*, in relation to the sublime tendencies of our notions of infinity, Burke cites motoric and auditory as well as visual illusions as productive of sublime effects: "Whenever we repeat any idea frequently, the mind by a sort of mechanism repeats it long after the first cause has ceased to operate. After whirling about; when we sit down, the objects about us still seem to whirl. After a long succession of noises, as the fall of waters, or the beating of forge hammers, the hammers beat and the water roars in the imagination long after the first sounds have ceased to affect it . . . If you hold up a straight pole, with your eye to one end, it will seem extended to a length almost incredible" (115).

Burke's first example, in which objects still seem to whirl when we first stop after spinning around, may sound vaguely familiar to students of Romantic poetry. Wordsworth describes a closely related illusion, illustrating the same principle, in the famous ice-skating episode of *The Prelude*, as the poet recalls how he would glide at top speed along the lake:

> And all the shadowy banks on either side
> Came sweeping through the darkness, spinning still
> The rapid line of motion, then at once
> Have I, reclining back upon my heels
> Stopped short—yet still the solitary cliffs
> Wheeled by me, even as if the earth had rolled
> With visible motion her diurnal round.[31]

I'm less interested in claiming this passage as an instance of the influence of Burke's *Enquiry* on Romantic poetry (although I believe it is such an instance), than in offering it as one more example of the Romantic neural sublime. Wordsworth produces a sublime sense of seeing the earth itself move on its axis by means of what is clearly a cognitive illusion, its mechanism well described (if not explained) by Burke: "The senses strongly affected in some one manner, cannot quickly change their tenor, or adapt themselves to other things; but they continue in their old channel until the strength of the first mover decays" (115).[32] The ice-skating passage is widely considered a high point of *The Prelude*, sometimes associated with the "spots of time" passages, but what exactly does it illustrate? That even as a boy, Wordsworth liked to produce situations, analogous to self-experiments, through which the brain could play its tricks on the mind, causing the senses to swim and the object world to become temporarily unhinged through a perceptual illusion.

The sublimity of this and other instances of the neural sublime does not depend on an intuition of a transcendent realm somehow above the ordinary mind but rather on a palpable if vertiginous sense of the active brain that subtends the ordinary workings of mind. Where the Kantian sublime, in other words, claims to produce an intuition of the supersensible, the Romantic neural sublime instead, in the manner of perceptual illusions, offers an intuition of what is ordinarily subsensible. It is, to bend Keats's phrase a little out of context, a "material sublime," not a transcendent one, earthly rather than lofty and physiological rather than spiritual. In its acceptance of rather than wishful freedom from human material embodiment, it overlaps with what Christopher Hitt has called the "ecological sublime," with its definitive instance in Thoreau's late Romantic revelation during his descent of Mount Katahdin in Maine[33]: "I stand in awe of my body, this matter to which I am bound has become so strange to me. I fear not spirits, ghosts, of which I am one,— *that* my body might,—but I fear bodies, I tremble to meet them. What is this Titan that has possession of me? Talk of mysteries!—Think of our life in nature,—daily to be shown matter, to come in contact with it—rocks, trees, wind on our cheeks! the *solid* earth! the *actual* world! the *common sense*! *Contact*! *Contact*! *Who* are we? *where* are we?" With the neural sublime, something closely analogous happens with that part of the body termed the *brain*, which grows strange, awesome, and of titanic proportions in relation to the conscious subject, overwhelming it and yet leaving it with a sense of what Wordsworth calls "possible sublimity."

For Hitt, Thoreau's sublime moment of "Contact!" with nature involves not a rejection of transcendence but a novel (and I would stress, almost perverse) manner of conceiving of it. "For this *is* a kind of transcendence—but not transcendence of the physical world. Rather, by crossing the threshold of discursive conceptualization, the speaker transcends *logos*." The raw experience of contact with material nature, not least including the intimate materiality of one's own body, shorts out the conceptual grid through which one ordinarily perceives (and attempts to master) the material world. Hitt goes on, turning the Kantian sublime on its head. "For whereas in Kant the discovery of reason abrogates the natural world, in Thoreau the discovery of nature abrogates reason" (616). "To be more precise," Hitt continues, "a sublime encounter with nature seems to have the power to jolt us momentarily out of a perspective constructed by reason and language"—a formula that applies equally well to the experiences of perceptual illusion that jolt us momentarily out of the cognitive categorizations by which we parse the perceived world in order to intuit the neural mechanisms working beneath them.

The pleasure of such a sublime—a pleasure accompanied by a disturbing sense of loss and disorientation for the conscious subject—would have to consist in the feeling of "contact" itself, of material (rather than spiritual) fusion with the environmental surround. The neuroscientist V. S. Ramachandran posits a similar source of pleasure, arguing that one's perceived sense of an integrated, consciously controlled body, one's body image, is itself a kind of proprioceptive illusion generated by neuronal mechanisms, a "phantom in the brain."[34] Why do we find pleasure, Ramachandran asks (and he assumes that we do), in learning from advances in neuroscience that there is no permanent and unified self, no "soul separate from our minds and bodies" that might survive death? He begins his answer by deflating one traditional notion of the sublime, the lofty flight of the soul: "Far from being terrifying, this idea is very liberating. If you think you're something special in this world, engaging in a lofty inspection of the cosmos from a unique vantage point, your annihilation becomes unacceptable." In place of this, Ramachandran (leading into a concluding sublime quotation from the Upanishads) offers a sense of material fusion with the cosmos: "But if you're really part of the great cosmic dance of Shiva, other than a mere spectator, then your inevitable death should be seen as a joyous reunion with nature rather than as a tragedy" (157).

Maybe. I want to conclude instead, however, by noting one last sublime trope of popular neuroscience, by which not the soul, nor the Reason, but the brain itself expands to cosmic proportions and figuratively swallows the universe. This rhetorical move recalls Kant's "mathematical sublime" in asking us to imagine a number so large that imagination is bound to fail, but in this case in order to convince us of the awesome scope and potential residing in the three pounds of neuronal matter within our skulls. "But here is an astonishing fact," writes Gerald Edelman in *Bright Air, Brilliant Fire*. "There are about one million billion connections in the cortical sheet. If you were to count them, one connection (or synapse) per second, you would finish counting some thirty-two million years after you began." But that's just counting connections. "If we consider how connections might be variously combined, the number would be hyperastronomical—on the order of ten followed by millions of zeros." And *hyperastronomical* here is apparently meant literally, suggesting that the vast extent of potential brain space is somehow larger than the universe that contains it, for there are comparatively only "about ten followed by eighty zeros' worth of positively charged particles in the whole known universe!"[35] Paul Churchland arrives at the same sublime point, a bit more soberly, in his own philosophical introduction to brain science. "If we assume, conservatively, that each synaptic connection might have any one of ten different strengths, then the total number of distinct possible configurations of synaptic weights that the brain might assume is, very roughly, ten raised to the trillionth power . . . Compare this with the measure of only 10^{87} cubic meters standardly estimated for the volume of the entire astronomical universe."[36] Emily Dickinson had it right: the brain *is* wider than the sky.[37]

This mathematically sublime notion of the brain would not have been available to writers of the Romantic era, although there was a good deal of excitement at the time regarding the newly discovered complexity of the brain. As early as 1793, in the *Visions of the Daughters of Albion*, Blake already speaks of the brain (rather than the mind) as "infinite."[38] The Romantic neural sublime clearly depends on this emergent sense of the brain's awesome complexity and capacity, but I think it owes still more to the desire for at least a negative encounter—the dark afterimage of a brightness glimpsed through the void—with what might be called a "brain's eye view" of the world, a view stripped (as in Hitt's reading of Thoreau) of the usual overlay of conceptual and linguistic categories, an unfiltered and unedited encounter with the real. Austin, at the beginning of his book of *Zen-Brain Reflections*, states that Zen Buddhism invites us "to ask the naïve and seemingly incredible question: what is this world *really* like without our intrusive self-referent self in the picture?" Or, rephrasing the question in terms of what Keats calls the "naked brain," "let's suppose a brain drops off all its subjective veils of *self*-consciousness. What, then, does the rest of its awareness—its pure, objective consciousness, perceive?" (xxv). According to Sircello, this seemingly impossible experience would make for a paradigmatic instance of the sublime. This is the antitranscendental revelation toward which the Romantic neural sublime gestures but stops short—leaving us dizzy, faint, or emptied out, and deeply unsatisfied. Which, for the Romantic poet, can be a good thing in itself.

CHAPTER THREE

The Romantic Image, the Mind's Eye, and the History of the Senses

Does the expression "the mind's eye" tell us anything meaningful and useful about how we think, read, and daydream, or is it an arbitrary and misleading metaphor? Do we in some manner "see" the mental pictures we create in acts of the imagination, or do we just imagine that we do? These might appear to be questions of interest primarily for students of the artistic imagination, and they have provoked debate among theorists of literature and aesthetics from the eighteenth century to the present. The same questions, however, have inspired a good deal of (sometimes heated) argument in the cognitive sciences as well. What has been termed the *imagery debate* broaches such fundamental questions as the nature of mental representations, the encoding mechanism that makes remembering as well as imagining possible, and the consequences of human embodiment for mental life.

The empiricist philosophers whose works the Romantics grew up reading had made pictorial-like mental images central to their accounts of human psychology. From Thomas Hobbes, they inherited the notion that the "imagination," that is, the faculty of storing and producing images in the mind, begins with the "image made in seeing" or with other images (less properly so called) gleaned from other sensory modalities. Thus, Hobbes famously remarks, "imagination is therefore

nothing but *decaying sense*," and without the sensory images captured from perception and stored in the memory, the mind would have very little to work with.[1]
John Locke traces most (though not all) of our ideas to sensory experience as
well, holding that "our *simple Ideas* are *clear*, when they are such as the Objects
themselves, from whence they were taken, did or might, in a well-ordered Sensation or Perception, present them."[2] In other words, the more faithfully (simple)
ideas resemble the acts of sensation and perception from which they were initially
taken, the more clear and reliable they will prove. The mind's eye, for Locke, functions best when it best reproduces the images gleaned by the bodily eye. Words are
notoriously unreliable for Locke precisely because they tend to drift away from
perceived (or mentally represented) objects, losing the clarity and distinctness of
sensation.

The guiding postulate of a fairly tight resemblance between the mental image
and the perceptual act that initially produced it, either in whole or in parts later
rearranged by the imagination, proved immensely influential not only for eighteenth-century philosophy and psychology. It also informed much educational
thinking of the time, inspiring, for example, the "object lesson" central to rational-
ist and Romantic educational theories alike.[3] By learning through manipulating
objects themselves rather than through mere words about objects, children would
form clear ideas based on direct experience that could help minimize the linguistic drift decried by Locke and other thinkers in the empiricist and sensationalist
traditions. "Never," Jean-Jacques Rousseau cautions in *Emile*, "substitute the word
for the thing." This emphasis on direct contact with the object world, however,
could come at the expense of any high valuation of literary experience, as Rousseau
famously attests: "Reading is the plague of childhood."[4]

Yet literary critics themselves often insisted that the images provoked in reading
should approach Lockean ideals of clarity and distinctness, and therefore should
readily lend themselves to visualization. By 1757, in the *Enquiry* on the sublime,
Edmund Burke describes this position as the dominant one: "The common notion
of the power of poetry and eloquence, as well as that of words in ordinary conversation, is that they affect the mind by raising in it ideas of those things for which
custom has appointed them to stand."[5] A bit later, Burke restates "idea" as the
"*picture*, or representation of the thing signified by the sound" (190). At a time
when visualizing during reading has become something of a lost art, or at least one
that is rarely encouraged or taught, eighteenth-century demands for visual clarity
in judging poetic imagery may strike us as naively literalistic, not only picky but
wrong-headed, as when Samuel Johnson complains, of the "Metaphysical" poets,

that "in forming descriptions, they looked not for images, but for conceits."[6] Milton himself does not escape Johnson's strictures: "His images and descriptions of the scenes or operations of Nature do not seem to be always copied from original form, nor to have the freshness, raciness, and energy of immediate observation" (1: 123). Quoting John Dryden, Johnson adds that Milton viewed nature "through the spectacles of books"; coming from Johnson, this is no compliment.

For Burke, of course, the obscurity of Milton's imagery is no fault but makes part of Milton's claim to sublimity; a clear idea, after all, is "another name for a little idea" (106). Burke argues, against mainstream opinion, that forming mental images, far from being necessary or automatic to verbal processing, requires a special "act of the will" and that, in "ordinary conversation or reading," it is the exceptional case when "any image at all is excited in the mind" (193). Words evoke not so much "ideas" (images) drawn from prior sensory experience as a whole web of associations with the word in question as it has been used in various contexts; Burke's approach to language is thus associationist or (one might say today) connectionist.[7] How else to account for the celebrated excellence of the descriptions in the nature poetry of "Mr. Blacklock, a poet blind from his birth" (192)? Poetry affects us more than do the other arts because, not in spite, of its distance from concrete imagery and its evocation of complex networks of verbal and conceptual associations. The "images raised by poetry," Burke argues, in striking contrast to Johnson, are "always" of an "obscure kind" (106). He illustrates his point with an "amazingly sublime" passage from the book of Job, its sublimity "principally due to the terrible uncertainty of the thing described" (106). Not the "power of raising sensible images" but the "union of affecting words" in (potentially) infinitely extensible associational networks gives poetry its "energy" as well as its sublimity (193).

Burke's iconoclastic preference for the shadowy web of verbal associations over the alleged clarity and "raciness" of the mental image became normative, according to recent critical consensus, for Romantic poetic theory. W. J. T. Mitchell, in his influential essay "Visible Language," acknowledges that both basic approaches to understanding the effect of poetic imagery—that poetry "makes us see" with the mind's eye or, alternatively, that (in Shelley's words) "the deep truth is imageless"— were "alive and well" during the late eighteenth and early nineteenth centuries in Britain.[8] But, Mitchell goes on, the "antipictorialist position" was now "dominant," at least among the "major, canonical Romantic poets." For these writers, the key term *Imagination* is typically "contrasted to, not equated with, mental imaging," conveying instead a "power of consciousness that transcends mere visualization"

(49). Mitchell supports this claim with a now quite familiar list of citations: Wordsworth's characterization of the eye as the "most despotic of our senses," Coleridge's dismissal of allegory as an inferior "picture language," Keats's casual remark (in a letter) that "descriptions are bad at all times" (49). For a later critic like William Galperin, the Romantic poets' "imaginative iconoclasm" and their corollary turn to the power of consciousness—the "way that the 'I' demonstrably supplants the *eye* as the prime agent of perception in Romantic aesthetics"—has become so well established that it practically begs to be deconstructed.[9]

Deconstruction has a way of enshrining the very oppositions it seeks to undo, and there are other options, including the resort to good old-fashioned scholarly qualification. Certainly, one could point out that the attitudes of the "major, canonical Romantic poets"—in this case (given the inclusion of Blake) a canon only established in the 1950s—would not ordinarily prove representative of the wider literary culture of the Romantic era. It would be impossible, for example, to understand the contemporary appeal of Walter Scott's poetry—the most popular early nineteenth century poet (until eclipsed by Byron) as well as one of the most highly valued by his peers—without acknowledging that antipictorialism was hardly "dominant" at the time or that by "Romantic aesthetics" Galperin means something other than the attitudes and assumptions most commonly informing Romantic-era reviews. Scott's poetry appealed, to critics and to a broad popular audience alike, precisely because its descriptive passages could evoke vivid mental pictures, gaining Scott the appellation the "Wizard of the North." More needs to be said about Scott in this regard, and will be later in this chapter. For now, I quote a contemporary of Scott's, whose passing strictures on the age of Alexander Pope reveal that at least some Romantic-era readers, contrary to Burkean theory, did in practice look to poetry as a source of clear and vivid mental images. "It is remarkable," he writes, "that, excepting the nocturnal Reverie of Lady Winchelsea, and a passage or two in the Windsor Forest of Pope, the poetry of the period intervening between the publication of Paradise Lost and the Seasons does not contain a single new image of external nature; and scarcely presents a familiar one from which it can be inferred that the eye of the Poet had been steadily fixed upon his object." This startlingly capacious claim is supported by allusions to disappointing descriptions of night in the poetry of Dryden and Pope, followed by a remark that more or less turns Burke's analysis on its head. "A blind man, in the habit of attending accurately to descriptions casually dropped from the lips of those around him, might easily depict these appearances with more truth." For Burke, the poetical descriptions of the poet blind from birth reveal the marginality of pictorial images and the centrality of verbal associations to both poetical composition and reading. Here, instead, the blind man, impoverished in his relation to the natural world, serves to convey the inferiority of a poetry bereft of vivid imagery based on first-hand visual experience: even a blind writer could do better than *that*.

As many readers will have recognized, the author of this particular critique is not some forgotten reviewer of Scott or George Crabbe, but the poet William Wordsworth, writing in the 1815 essay supplementary to the Preface to *Lyrical Ballads*.[10] The same Wordsworth who elsewhere complains of the "tyranny" of the eye (*The Prelude* 1805.XI.179) can criticize earlier poets for relying too little on that same eye, having claimed (in the Preface itself) that, in contrast: "I have at all times endeavoured to look steadily at my subject" (285). Wordsworth, the canonical Romantic poet par excellence, seems to advance both a pictorialist and an antipictorialist position at once, a contradiction well worth exploring. Happily, F. A. Pottle advanced an authoritative discussion of this very problem more than half a century ago in "The Eye and the Object in the Poetry of Wordsworth," an essay that used to be standard reading in the field and still holds vital interest today.[11]

Pottle's careful analysis of the status of the eye and the mental image in Wordsworth's poetics shares some common ground with the "antipictorialist" view. "It is a great mistake," Pottle cautions, "to consider Wordsworth a descriptive poet" (280), and the scenes and subjects in a good number of Wordsworth's more successful poems, steeped in the poet's memory and transformed by imaginative revision, correspond to "nothing Wordsworth ever saw with the bodily eye" (274). What Pottle insists upon, however, is that Wordsworth's natural imagery nonetheless reflects a "lifelong habit of close, detailed, and accurate observation of the objects composing the external universe" (279–80). In contrast to Johnson's Milton, who allegedly viewed natural scenes through reading glasses, Wordsworth relies on the naked eye and over a lifetime of vivid sensation builds up a rich mnemonic repertoire of precise natural images. In a "literal, physiological sense," Pottle stresses, Wordsworth did indeed "look steadily at the natural objects" that inform his poetry. Yet, Pottle goes on, this looking is only where Wordsworth typically begins the imaginative process that results in a fully developed work of the imagination, and the "eye," mentioned in the Preface, that "looks steadily is not the physical eye." Wordsworth's "subject" (oddly, the terms *subject* and *object* are used more or less interchangeably in Pottle's essay) is "a mental image, and the eye is that inward eye which is the bliss of solitude." There is, after all, no contradiction between Wordsworth's cultivation of the bodily eye and his ultimate appeal to the "inward eye" of imaginative revision, for these describe two distinct phases at the beginning and toward the end of a single creative process. Wordsworth "starts with a mental image of a concrete natural object," a mental image that retains the vividness and naturalistic detail of actual sensation, and then "looks steadily" at it, using not the bodily but the "mind's" eye, until he "sees what it means." What it means includes emotional as well as cognitive significance, or rather, for Wordsworth poetic "meaning" prioritizes the emotional impact and import of a natural object or occurrence. According to Pottle, Wordsworth arrives at the final vision, embodied in the achieved poem, through a process of simplification; as he looks steadily at the object, he "simplifies it" and continues to "simplify and interpret until the object becomes the correlative of a single emotion" (280).

Much as I agree with Pottle's analysis of the basic trajectory in Wordsworth from an initial state of "vivid sensation" (Wordsworth's phrase) to an internalized image transformed by the mutations of the memory and the workings of imagination, I find the last part of his formula problematic. A "single emotion" does not, for me, capture the complex play of dissonant emotions one finds in poems like "Surprised by Joy" or "Anecdote for Fathers" (what *is* the emotion being conveyed?) or any number of poems that provoke an emotional impact easier to register and to feel than to articulate or describe. "I Wandered Lonely as a Cloud," Pottle's exemplary text in this essay, may indeed end on an especially unified emotional note: "And then my heart with pleasure fills, / And dances with the daffodils." Even so, I still take exception to the notion of simplification. It encourages Pottle, I believe, to move too quickly from the bodily eye to the "inward" eye, failing to register just how complex the physiology and psychology of seeing become in that same poem and how greatly the poem's representation of those acts add credibility to its conclusion. Here I would turn instead to a more recent critical work, Elaine Scarry's powerful analysis of literary imagery in *Dreaming by the Book,* which, not surprisingly given Scarry's special interest in flowers, includes a reading of Wordsworth's daffodil poem.[12]

For Scarry, Wordsworth serves as a prominent example of the "great sensory writers," literary artists widely celebrated for the "vividness" of their imagery and descriptive passages (21, 15). Vividness or "vivacity" (perhaps another word for what Johnson calls "raciness") does not, as Scarry argues, come easily or without special procedures. The mental images we ordinarily form, for example when daydreaming, are notoriously pale and difficult to sustain. Under special circumstances, however, as when under the spell of a great sensory writer like Wordsworth, Gustave Flaubert, Emily Brontë, or Thomas Hardy, we can entertain mental images that charm and engage us by their unusual vivacity. Comparable to being led through certain tasks under hypnosis—or guided as test subjects through a cognitive psychology experiment—as readers we follow highly specific sets of instructions that enable us to recreate such vivid images with and within our own brains. This process is what Scarry means by imagining "under the instruction of great writers," in other words, dreaming by the book (6).

The unexpected parallel between readers and experimental subjects is by no means an incidental one. The writers who interest Scarry in this book, forming a long tradition that runs from Homer to Seamus Heaney and John Ashbery in the present, share a number of subtle and subtly effective insights into the perceptual process, insights gained from studying their own acts of perception and from close reading of the sensory writers of the past. Pioneering cognitive psychologists of a sort, such writers "give us a transcript of how the brain works because they look at the images turning up in their own minds" with extraordinary "concentration and dedication" (244). By then "reproducing the deep structure of perception" in their descriptive passages, they manage to "enlist our imaginations," as we read them, in "mental actions that in their vivacity more closely resemble sensing than daydreaming" (9, 16).

Scarry's reading of "I Wandered Lonely as a Cloud" is developed with such impressive economy that it would be impossible to distill it further by way of summary. It needs to be read in full, and it more than repays the effort. Taking her own reader, couplet by couplet, through the first dozen lines of the poem, Scarry demonstrates in utterly convincing detail how programatically Wordsworth makes his initial perception of the daffodils—an act of sensation so intense that it merits epic style ("Ten thousand saw I at a glance")—equally vivid for an attentive reader. Wordsworth employs a dazzling succession of the literary methods Scarry describes earlier in her book for giving imagined scenes the vibrancy and shine of actual sensation. These include "radiant ignition" (we can readily imagine, with uncommon vivacity, spots of light, like the stars in Wordsworth's simile for the flowers, or the sun-drenched daffodils themselves), "stretching" (a more complicated but equally effective method for getting readers to "see" images in motion), and the eliciting of felt eye-movement as Wordsworth encourages the reader to follow the darting, dancelike movements of his own shifting gaze ("Beside the lake, beneath the trees"). The first half of the poem guides its readers through an activity less like comprehension than "composition," provoking a quick succession of "pictures moving on the mental retina," images shining and dancing, like the daffodils themselves, in the mind's eye.

This series of guided mental exercises, Scarry goes on, brilliantly anticipates the poet's own internalization and recreation of the imagined scene (as much a dramatic scene as a pictorial one, given all the motion Wordsworth has managed to evoke in the first two stanzas). In the second half of the poem, Wordsworth "gradually lets the moving picture vanish from view, then stages its return" in a manner that again encourages the reader to mentally rehearse each phase in the poet's transition from vivid sensation to images scanned with the "mental retina" alone. But Wordsworth, as Scarry points out, has skillfully (and strategically) placed the reader and the poetic speaker in distinct positions in relation to the work of image making. For the speaker, the first two stanzas "concern an act of perception" and the second two "concern his act of mental composition." For the reader, in contrast, both halves of the poem "require the same act of imagining." First, we "must mentally construct the flowers" (over the course of the first twelve lines); then, "having folded into our minds a sequence of carefully positioned instructions," we quickly run through this sequence again in recomposing the "moving picture" of bright flowers dancing in a breeze. When the flowers "flash upon that inward eye / Which is the bliss of solitude," that "flash" will again provoke "radiant ignition" in the reader's own mind, while "folded into that flash are all the practices rehearsed in lines 1–12."

The double trajectory that Scarry locates in this single poem both parallels and helps to fill in the trajectory that Pottle identified at work in a given act of poetic composition. Each describes a process of internalization, from an experience of charged sensation to the vivid rehearsal of the experience, in perceptual tone and emotional valence, though not in every detail. Pottle shows most interest in how this internalization occurs in the mind of the poet, while Scarry is more concerned with the poetic speaker (not, in her reading, wholly distinct from the biographical poet) and with the reader, who experiences a kindred series of mental images by following the speaker's implicit recipe for composing them, even as the poet recounts his own movement from external sensation to internal imagining and rehearses this movement for us. Scarry fills in crucial blanks missing in Pottle's account by demonstrating that the moment of sensation itself is a highly complex event involving more psychological procedures than we might otherwise suppose, that describing this complexity entails a second level of procedural detail that allows the reader to recompose elements of the poet's remembered or imagined perceptual experience, and that the reader's composition (under implicit authorial instruction) of a series of moving mental images gives the poem's concluding stanzas their credibility and power, at least when the poem works. (It fizzles for some readers, notoriously including Coleridge.) The internalized vision at the end of the poem can now be seen not as a preferred alternative to the visual experiences recounted and celebrated in its two first stanzas but as a reenactment of them, one that that reader can mentally stage in turn.

Scarry's analysis, in this exemplary reading and throughout her book as a whole, restores the continuity between the visual image and creative imagination that "antipictorialist" accounts of literary imagery deny or discount. Scarry's inspiration comes not only from the "great sensory writers" themselves but also from recent cognitive science and neuroscience, particularly from Stephen Kosslyn's research on visual imagery. Kosslyn has long been the most important single advocate of the "imagist" side of the imagery debate.[13] In contrast to the position that all thinking is at bottom propositional, so that (for example) the mental images we think we see are, like the icons on our computer desktops, expressions of computational code, Kosslyn and his allies contend that mental images have physical properties akin to perceived visual images. Kosslyn and other researchers have demonstrated that when we perform certain mental operations with visual material, such as rotating a two-dimensional figure to see if it matches a second figure, or calculating the route from one point to another on a memorized map, the time it takes us to arrive at an answer corresponds to the spatial distance between the two (pre- and post-rotated) positions or the two points on the map. That is, we behave precisely as would be predicted if mental images do in fact share basic features with perceptual images. These mental imagery "effects" can (like any other mental phenomena) be explained propositionally, but mental rotation and other visualization experiments remain persuasive to many. For the layperson, the imagist position holds a great deal of intuitive appeal: when asked, for example, which has a darker green color, a pine tree or a grass lawn, most everyone will resort to a mental image in trying to decide. Whether mental images ultimately prove propositional or visuo-spatial "all the way down," digital or analog, such "imagery effects" retain a force of their own and may be all we need to understand the power of an analysis like Scarry's.

Kosslyn's position has become still more persuasive with the advent of new brain scanning techniques such as fMRI (functional magnetic resonance imaging), which can specify which brain areas become active during the performance of carefully designed mental imaging tasks. Again as predicted by the "imagists," in "almost every study, mental imagery activates modality-specific visual cortex areas." When we imagine color, for example, the brain's visual areas associated with color perception become active. At least some types of mental images seem to be "spatially mapped" in the brain, again suggesting the "spatial nature of image representation," in contrast to the propositional view.[14] Cognitive neuroscientific researchers (including Kosslyn) now speak of two overlapping systems in the brain, one for perceiving images—a kind of bottom-up processing—and one for generating them, a top-down activity that produces images at several distinct levels of resolution. The process that involves the highest level of resolution, producing what Kosslyn calls "depictive imagery," corresponds to what we usually mean by "seeing with the mind's eye." Many of the same neural processes, he concludes, "underlie [both] perception and depictive imagery": just as Scarry's analysis of poets like Homer, Wordsworth, and Heaney would lead one to believe.[15]

In reasserting the continuity between the visual image and the creative imagination, work like Kosslyn's (and Scarry's) on mental imagery can help remind us that, for the Romantics, visual perception itself is already "creative." Departing from what they see as the passivity of empiricist accounts of perception, Romantic-era writers as diverse as Blake, Wordsworth, Coleridge, and Shelley all assert the creative nature of everyday perception, although we may gradually become dulled to the extraordinary character of ordinary perception through what they term "habit" or "custom" or the "film of familiarity." Wordsworth famously writes that the eye and ear both perceive and "half create" the object world as we experience it, a process of "*active*" grasping, construing, and representation of the world that Wordsworth traces to infancy in the "blest babe" passage of *The Prelude*.[16] Coleridge terms this process the "primary imagination," meaning (to begin with) that in constructing and reconstructing an intelligible object world, moment by moment, the agent of human perception participates in the creative activity of the deity itself, "the repetition in the finite mind of the eternal act of creation in the infinite I AM."[17] Such attitudes will sound mystical to some, but they may sound neuroscientific to others. Donald Hoffman is only one among many current neuroscientists who stress the active and creative nature of what only appear to be simple acts of perception, and Hoffman (as we have seen) shows no qualms about sharing his own sense of wonder at this process, even as he seeks to better understand and explain it.[18]

Many Romantic-era statements one might take as evidence of "antipictorialism" prove, in context, more concerned with distinguishing this active, creative account of perception from the comparatively mechanistic models of certain influential eighteenth-century thinkers. Many, but not all. Although I have been arguing, along lines set out by Pottle and independently developed, much more recently, by Scarry, for the continuity between visual perception and the creative imagination associated with (if not definitive of) canonical Romanticism, I cannot stop there. There is much more to this particular story. Wordsworth's comment on the "despotic" tendency of the eye, for example, still does not seem to square entirely with his contrary insistence on looking steadily at his poetic objects, nor does the force of *despotic* disappear with the acknowledgement that, for Wordsworth, a poet should begin but not *end* with the bodily eye. That quotidian vision, however marvelous and creative in itself, still needs to be transmuted into something more, well, visionary. At times Wordsworth, with some of his best-known contemporaries, seems instead to want to short-circuit habitual vision, to turn away from the visual system altogether, perhaps in favor of a different sensory modality. It is, for example, when we figuratively turn from seeing to hearing—with "an eye made quiet by the power / Of harmony"—that we "see into the life of things" ("Lines ... Tintern Abbey," 47–49). Such turns from seeing to using a different sensory modality, in the pursuit of a different sort of "vision" altogether, have long and rightly been understood as characteristic of canonical British Romanticism.[19] Even after the significant continuity between the visual sense and the visionary imagination has been acknowledged, rendering any simple alignment of canonical Romanticism with antipictorialism highly problematic, a distinct residue of ambivalence toward the bodily eye and quotidian vision remains and demands critical attention.

The human senses have a cultural history in addition to a "natural history," and the eye in particular, as in the work of Foucault with his emphasis on the panopticon, can be said to have a political and ideological history.[20] Taking these broadly social historical perspectives into account may help justify the residue of ambivalence toward the visual system, the "despotic" sense, frequently encountered in Romantic-era texts. One should keep in mind, however, that natural and cultural histories represent distinct disciplinary perspectives but cannot finally be kept firmly apart in any broad account of the human species and its past. It has been argued, for example, from a cultural historicist perspective, that the "common human predilection for all things sweet" stems not from some "biological disposition" but originates "in colonialism and the mass import of raw sugar to Europe which first made it possible."[21] There is some truth to this claim, but it is only a half-truth. There is a reason, that is, that modern-era colonialism fed and inflamed a craving for sweets and not for, say, bitters, despite the minor fad for quinine that also made part of the European colonial experience. Human beings were already predisposed to crave sugars and fats for sound adaptive reasons, which, as evolutionary psychologists like to point out, only became potentially maladaptive when sweets became (initially through colonialism) more readily available than ever before. The cultural and evolutionary perspectives on our human sweet tooth supplement rather than contradict one another, each contributing to a larger "biosocial" view.[22]

Much the same could be said of the increasing preeminence of the eye and the visual sense in the modern era. Foucault helped inaugurate an entire subfield of social analysis of the "disciplining of the gaze," and cultural historians have identified a range of "scopic regimes" emerging by the mid-nineteenth century (Jütte 186–87). Romantic-era Great Britain, the birthplace of Jeremy Bentham's panopticon, played no small part in the increasing dominance of the visual sense, through the production of mass-produced visual materials, the transformation of urban streets into a series of visual spectacles (lamented by a vertiginous Wordsworth in the London books of *The Prelude*), and the development of new visual experiences like the panorama and the diorama (Galperin 34–71). But if the eye strengthened its "despotic" rule over the sensorium during the early nineteenth century, its dominance was already an old story. The preeminence of vision in the hierarchy of the senses goes back at least to Aristotle, and even ideologically inspired histories of the senses concede that the "privileged position of the *sense of sight* is in no way a by-product" of modernity but dates back at least to antiquity (Jütte 61–64). This, too, could only to be expected, given the natural history of the senses. Vision and visual processing take up an inordinate share of the resources devoted to the sensory and cognitive systems. Diane Ackerman claims that as much as "seventy per cent of the body's sense receptors" are devoted to vision (230), and according to Hoffman, "nearly half of the brain's cortex" has been given over to visual intelligence (xi). The "despotism" of the eye begins with its dominance over a large fraction of the brain.

It is not so surprising, then, that a series of literary movements—beginning with Romanticism—that seek to defamiliarize the frozen world of "habit," frequently challenge the eye's dominance as one aspect of a poetic program for disturbing and dishabituating stock perceptual processes. Such defamiliarization finds theoretical justification in a series of influential twentieth-century approaches to literary analysis, most notably in the works of the Russian Formalists, who make defamiliarization or "estrangement" a definitive feature of literary art. Boris Eichenbaum, in fact, locates the first major theoretical breakthrough of the Russian Formalist school in Victor Shklovsky, Leo Jakubinsky, and Osip Brik's rejection of the poetic "image" central to the dominant theories of the time. They collectively challenged the implicit ascendance of the visual sense in Symbolist theories with a contrasting emphasis on the role of pure sound in poetry, leading to the Formalist interest in nonsense verse and repeated sounds.[23] Roman Jakobson, an early member of the Russian Formalist movement, retains this polemical opposition between image and sound throughout his career, discussing the legitimacy of a poetry "devoid of images" in his famous essay "Linguistics and Poetics" and developing the "poetry of grammar" as one alternative to an imagistic poetry.[24] The pioneering cognitive poetician Reuven Tsur further develops this Formalist and Structuralist emphasis on the "musicality" of verse and the role of poetic sound, citing, for example, the French Symbolists' inclusion of imageless and even nonsemantic material in such works as Arthur Rimbaud's "Voyelles."[25] In Paul Verlaine's memorable phrase: "De la musique avante toute chose." Scarry herself acknowledges the way that the sounds of poetry involve an immediate sensuous appeal that contrasts with the slower work of mental image-making—poetry, she writes, keeps its "metrical feet in the material world" (9). Ellen Esrock, in her own study of readers and mental imagery, *The Reader's Eye*, provides a revealing survey of twentieth-century literary critics and theorists who agree in demoting visual imagery in favor of a Burkean emphasis on language and verbal associations, part and parcel of the "linguistic turn" characteristic of the literary culture of that era (39–78). Even a work like Frank Kermode's *Romantic Image*, which might seem to provide an exception, ignores visual imagery in favor of the Romantic (and post-Romantic) "symbol," a term that for Kermode evokes a complex pattern of verbal and cultural associations rather than an image recreated with the mind's eye.[26]

Despite Wordsworth's insistence on the poet's eye and the vivid clarity of the poetic image (statements that find agreement in Coleridge's writings), Romanticism has long been associated with a deliberate confounding of the senses in order to challenge the habitual dominance of the visual.[27] In her valuable study of the five senses in literary history, Louise Vinge writes that in the "age of Romanticism," rigid distinctions among the senses began to collapse as various writers sought ways to combine or confuse the senses through devices like synesthesia. According to Vinge, "mixed sensations, associations, synaesthesias" appealed more to the "Romantic imagination" than did the "rational five-sense pattern, which had now been almost totally eclipsed."[28] The textbook example would be Coleridge's line, "a light in sound, a sound-like power in light" from "The Aeolian Harp," and many other examples readily come to mind.[29] More recently, and explicitly working from neuroscientific theories of sense perception, Gabrielle Starr has written on the significance of "multi-sensory imagery" in literature and especially in poetry, a topic with obvious relevance to a Romantic writer like Keats, whose poetry features throughout her essay. Again, readers of Romantic poetry will quickly think of canonical examples—the "jellies soother than the creamy curd," and the "lucent syrops, tinct with cinnamon" from "The Eve of St. Agnes"—and Starr does not disappoint.[30]

In addition to defamiliarizing habitual perception by combining or confounding the senses, many Romantic poems often employ the opposite strategy: a deliberate exposure of the gaps between the senses, even an exaggeration and exploitation of these gaps. Anyone familiar with the wildly and often desperately suggestive language of wine description ("the dominant flavors of berry, oak, and barnyard give way to a silky finish, with notes of chocolate and leather") will need little convincing that the modalities of taste and olfaction resist any ready translation into propositional language, each accessing a distinct realm of experience that the other senses simply cannot provide. The gap between the visual and auditory modalities, exposed for example in the spectacular failure of nineteenth-century "program music" is no less pronounced. (What melodies and harmonies "sound like" a sub-Alpine forest seen through a light fog?) Although we can be quite good at putting information from discrete sensory channels into recognizable assemblages (as a birdwatcher might put a flash of color, a half-heard series of chirps, and a characteristic flight and perching pattern into the accurate perception of a kingfisher glimpsed well upriver), the various sensory modalities do not neatly line up and cohere but instead tend to give us remarkably different *kinds* of information, usually compatible but by no means fully commensurable. Neuroscience has shown great interest in such gaps among the senses and between the various senses and our efforts to translate them into propositional language. Some have hypothesized dual or multiple cognitive coding systems, suggesting that the discrete sorts of perceptual information resist mutual translation, or translation into a common master code, all the way down to the smallest and most fungible units of cognitive currency.[31]

The gaps and disparities characteristic of our perceptual-cognitive systems have proved of special interest to cognitive literary theorists. Ellen Spolsky, beginning with her important book *Gaps in Nature* (1993), has argued for the evolutionary advantages of the gaps among the sensory and linguistic modalities as well as the consequences of these ineluctable gaps for literary and cultural history. A "gappy" and discontinuous sensorium may actually be preferable to a smooth, integral one because the resulting tension or noise in the system could help make crucial information more salient. One's ears and eyes might be signaling that all is still, calm, and well, but the nose, picking up a faint but distinct and persistent smell of acrid smoke, could disrupt this sense of well-being; the very disparity between the messages coming in from distinct sensory channels could itself prove highly salient and provoke investigation and ultimately life-saving action. Because the sensory modalities fail to entirely cohere, each remains free to "disagree" with the others, and the resulting disturbance within the cognitive system becomes a way to keep the system alert, open to contradictory signals, self-correcting. In this way, Spolsky views human cognition as revisionary by nature, enabling the human organism to identify and deal with dissonant or contradictory messages about the external environment as well as assuring that cultural change is inevitable, thanks to the gaps, friction, and slippage in a largely effective but chronically disintegral brain-mind.[32]

Spolsky takes particular interest in how such gaps provoke literary creativity, in how, for example, poets may invent startling but effective metaphors in attempts to bridge the gaps in the cognitive system (26, 115–29). But literary artists may also choose to explore these gaps, even exacerbate them, using one sensory modality to revise or correct a different one. Wordsworth's subtle transition from sight to sound ("an *eye* made *quiet* by the power of *harmony*") in "Tintern Abbey" makes one of only many instances found throughout his poetry. "The Solitary Reaper," a poem centrally concerned, like "I Wandered Lonely," with the internalization of a remembered scene, begins with a decidedly visual image—"Behold her standing in the field / Yon solitary Highland lass!"—but shifts from mind's eye to mind's ear by the poem's end: "That music in my heart I bore / Long after it was heard no more." The speaker of Keats's "Ode to a Nightingale," a poem set in virtual darkness, turns from a tritely fanciful visual scene ("and haply the Queen Moon is on her throne / Cluster'd around by all her starry fays") to a keenly etched imagery of olfaction:

> I can not see what flowers are at my feet,
>   Nor what soft incense hangs upon the boughs,
> But, in embalmed darkness, guess each sweet
>   Wherewith the seasonable month endows
> The grass, the thicket, and the fruit-tree wild;
>   White hawthorn, and the pastoral eglantine;
>   Fast fading violets covered up in leaves . . .

In Shelley, as we have seen in relation to the sublime mode, visualization can be pushed to the breaking point—"And saw by the warm light of their own life / Her glowing limbs beneath the sinuous veil / Of woven wind" and then the sense of touch and/or the internal sense of interoception might take its place: "His strong heart sunk and sickened with excess / Of love."[33] In each of these instances, the visual sense is not supplemented but rather displaced, sometimes violently. The senses of hearing, or smell, or interoception function less to provide an additional aspect of what the visual sense has already glimpsed than to reveal something altogether different, something the visual sense chronically misses and could never supply.

In this way too the history of the senses suggests that Romantic literary art makes part of a wider culture, one including developments in the sciences. For, in contrast to the what a more purely literary history like Vinge's might imply, the medical and physiological discourses of the early nineteenth century are marked not by a confluence of the senses but by a greater discrimination among them. As Robert Jütte writes in his *History of the Senses: From Antiquity to Cyberspace*, developments in nineteenth-century science "fostered the separation of the senses" as technological and methodological advances ("new methods and instruments") made finer measurements of and sharper differentiation among the senses possible (236). This greater discrimination can already be seen in the work of leading brain scientists of the Romantic era. The pioneering neurologist Charles Bell, in his seminal treatise *Idea of a New Anatomy of the Brain* (1811), argued for the existence of distinct neural pathways linking the various sensory organs and receptors to dedicated "organs of the brain," maintaining that "each organ of the sense . . . is utterly incapable of receiving the impressions destined for another organ of sensation."[34] He even provided a self-experiment for those desiring confirmation of this claim, suggesting that the reader touch a "sharp steel point" to various papillae on the tongue and note how while "one papilla produces a [tactile] sense of sharpness," another will convey a "metallic taste" but no sense of touch whatever.[35] Franz Josef Gall, the "organologist," advanced (not surprisingly) his own modular theory of the senses, in keeping with his view of the brain as an "assemblage of particular organs."[36] Romantic-era brain scientists even challenged orthodox thought to posit more than five senses, as when Pierre-Jean-George Cabanis notes the importance of sense impressions "received in the internal organs" and recognizes the need to posit such internal senses as those later termed interoception and proprioception.[37]

The relation of poetic imagery in the Romantic era to the visual sense, to the external—and internal—senses generally, and to the creative imagination turns out to be much more complex than most commentators have wished to acknowledge. To begin with, one finds widespread recognition of the dominance of the visual sense, but this recognition can lead to seemingly contradictory responses even for a single given Romantic author. The powerful vivacity of the visual sense can be accepted and exploited, with a correspondingly tight relation implied between the physical eye and the poetic imagination, as Scarry has shown so brilliantly to be the case in Wordsworth's "I Wandered Lonely as a Cloud." At the same time, Wordsworth is equally exemplary in maintaining a certain disparity between visual and visionary imagining, as Pottle argued long ago, and the Romantic poet may at times even lament the "despotic" sway of the eye and summon the visionary imagination by recourse to a different sense, or to an imageless "spirit and a feeling" (quoting, once more, "Tintern Abbey"). Romantic writers may choose to defamiliarize sense experience, again in the interests of challenging the eye's habitual dominance, by conflating the senses through various synesthesias or by combining them in their use of multisensory imagery. Yet all the while the distinctions among the various senses persist and may even be exaggerated in passages that underscore and exploit the "gaps" between the senses, disparities that become increasingly marked as well in the neurology and brain science of the era. In every case, the dominance of the visual sense is acknowledged, whether to be prized for its sharpness and vivacity; to be tempered, qualified, or enriched by one or more alternative sensory modalities; or, finally, to be temporarily dethroned in the interests of defamiliarization. Different as they are, our appreciation of each of these poetic strategies, all of which may meaningfully be considered "Romantic," can be enriched by what is being discovered about the history, both the natural history and the social history, of the senses.

Before ending this discussion, I want to consider at least briefly how the history of the senses, natural and social, can interact with the history of reading. Toward the very end of her book, in a paragraph tucked into the acknowledgments section, Scarry responds to concerns (which she does not share) that as the "dazzling new technologies in the visual arts" continue to proliferate, readers living in the image-saturated cultures of the future may "lose the ability to dream by the book, to let their own minds become the surface on which pictures get made" (249). It could be argued that, to a certain degree, this has happened already. Anyone who regularly teaches introductory or even advanced courses on poetry at the college level will know that students today do not ordinarily visualize as they read poetry but need to be explicitly, and sometimes repeatedly, instructed to do so. (I found this to be the case even when teaching a literature course expressly designed for architecture students, a group one might expect to be uncommonly visually oriented.) Scarry's own book, in fact, can be regarded as a pedagogical as much as a critical tour-de-force: it teaches readers to adopt (or to further develop and refine) the imaging practices it describes. Eighteenth-century critics apparently could take it for granted that readers visualize when reading poetry; twenty-first century English teachers cannot.

Esrock takes a pessimistic view of this situation in *The Reader's Eye*. Noting that the "forming of visual images" in reading was "well accepted" through the early twentieth century, she laments that current critical approaches "do not identify visualization as a scholarly or even an educated response to texts" (180). Translated into classroom practice, this "marginalization" of imagery and visualization (78) means that virtually "everything in the student's training discourages imagining" (180). Even in the college literature classroom, imaging "is rarely advocated" (I'm happy to find myself in the minority here) and may be "explicitly discouraged" (180). Commenting on Italo Calvino's *Invisible Cities*, Esrock questions whether contemporary readers have collectively suffered a "failure of vision," an "inability to visually imagine in a culture saturated with television and other technologies of mass-marketed imagery" (176)—to which we can now add computer technologies and the Internet.

Esrock's concerns, supported by her survey of antipictorialist tendencies in twentieth-century literary theory (a tradition that, we have seen, goes back to Burke), cannot easily be dismissed, although the success of Scarry's *Dreaming by the Book* suggests that many readers are willing to go back to a style of reading that gives a greater role to the "mind's eye." "Go back" can be understood in a genetic as well as historical sense, as many children seem still today to visualize as they read. How else to understand the many complaints regularly overheard when a popular book becomes a movie and certain characters are judged not to "look right"? (The first Harry Potter film, which came out at the height of the Harry Potter book craze, provoked many such comments among children, at least among those in my vicinity.) Perhaps image making while reading constitutes a sort of default tendency, especially among readers with a visually oriented "cognitive style" (Esrock 123–24).

Whether or not readers "naturally" default toward imaging while engaged with printed texts, it seems clear that a significant shift has indeed occurred over the past century or so, from a reading culture that accepted and even expected a certain amount of visualization to one that actively discourages such activity, at least for readers beyond the early school years. Eighteenth-century and Romantic-era theorists, critics, and book reviewers have left a great deal of evidence suggesting that imaging while reading was at least widely perceived as a common practice and that clear, vivid images readily susceptible to recreation with the mind's eye long remained an important desideratum in poetry, even (at times) for poet-theorists who, like Wordsworth and Coleridge, have been generally associated with antipictorialism. Poets who once enjoyed vast popularity and now are read almost solely by literary historians and scholars—James Thomson, author of *The Seasons*, would be a prime example—may have lost their readerships largely because of a shift in reading practices away from visualization. The same claim could be made in relation to Sir Walter Scott, still valued (and popularly read) as a novelist, but virtually forgotten, outside of specialist scholarship, as a poet.

Early on in *Waverley*, in relation to its hero's tendency to lose himself in books or in his own daydreams, Scott speaks of that "internal sorcery, by which past or imaginary events are presented in action, as it were, to the eye of the muser."[38] Scott's poetic appeal had everything to do with his own quasi-magical ability (again, the "Wizard of the North") to craft imagined scenes and actions that readers could readily recreate with the mind's eye. William Hazlitt, in his *Lectures on the English Poets*, presents Scott as the "most popular of all the poets of the present age, and deservedly so."[39] (It is all the more striking that this was written in 1818, when Scott's poetic reputation was already being eclipsed by Byron's.) "He describes," Hazlitt goes on, "that which is most easily and generally understood with more vivacity and effect than anybody else." *Vivacity* here means for Hazlitt what it does for Scarry: "Mr. Scott has great intuitive power of fancy, great vividness of pencil in placing external objects and events before the eye." His poetic power is "picturesque rather than *moral*," and (like Scarry's great sensory writers) he not only can make imagined scenes vivid but can put them into motion as well: "Few descriptions have a more complete reality, a more striking appearance of life and motion, than that of the warriors in the Lady of the Lake" (155). Although Hazlitt himself would later revise his opinion, losing interest in Scott the poet in favor of Scott the novelist, generations of readers would continue to value Scott's descriptive poetry—until the middle of the twentieth century when, as Esrock has shown, visualizing while reading fell out of critical fashion and virtually ceased to be taught.

Other reasons could be cited for the decline in Scott's popularity: contemporaries saw him as a careless versifier, and (as even Hazlitt conceded) his poetry was seen to lack "depth" at a time when rivals like Wordsworth and Coleridge were promoting a poetry of internalization, "deep" psychology, and layers of symbolic resonance. Yet it seems more than coincidental that visually oriented, highly descriptive poets like Thomson and Scott lost wide readerships just as appeals to the mind's eye were losing much of their purchase. It could be argued that, even should criticism such as Esrock's and Scarry's help spark a renewed vogue for readerly imaging, and an emphasis on visualization return to the classroom, a poetry like Scott's that relies too exclusively on visual appeal still would not find many new fans. In a postmodern marketplace of images already overcrowded with offerings streaming in from film, television, and portable computers, "sorcery" like Scott's may seem tediously labor intensive and decidedly low tech. It says something highly significant about the human mind-brain that, before there was anything like film, poets like Scott were providing "moving pictures" for screening by the mind's eye. It could be argued that film did not create a new craving for vivid, moving images but arose to fill that hunger with a speed, readiness, and lack of effortfulness never before possible, a visual analogue to the way colonial sugar production supercharged a natural taste for sweets. But with film and video technicians now providing ready-made, audience-friendly scenes and action sequences, why expect the majority of readers to invest much effort in the "mental Olympics" that, for Scarry, make us fit consumers of literary imagining (195)?

Such questions about the future of reading are easier to raise than to resolve. What remains certain is that, in relation to the future of critical reading, new work in neuroscience and the cognitive sciences will continue to help inspire literary scholars as they develop their own fields in important new directions. But no one today can say what precisely those directions will be. Scarry's revealing and provocative work on conscious dreaming under "authorial direction" (31), instigated by the research of Kosslyn and others into mental imaging, and developed in ways that cognitive psychologists can appreciate but could never have anticipated, provides a telling example of the unpredictable ways that new work can arise out of unexpected interdisciplinary connections. Adding the perspectives of literary and social history, not to mention the "deep" or "natural history" of the senses, can help situate and more sharply define work like Scarry's, while doing nothing to diminish its excitement. Learning from key developments in cognitive neuroscience can help us to put the image back into accounts of the literary imagination. The natural and cultural history of the senses, perspectives that ideally should complement rather than rival one another, remind us in turn that the human imagination does not somehow transcend history but itself remains a richly historical phenomenon.

CHAPTER FOUR

Romantic Apostrophe

Everyday Discourse, Overhearing, and Poetic Address

The new field of convergence between literary studies and the cognitive sciences, still emerging and still widening in focus, has from the beginning found crucial inspiration in a fundamentally new understanding of figurative language. Soon after the cognitive revolution began in earnest, the study of rhetorical figures, especially metaphor, became a key research area for cognitive linguists, computer scientists, and cognitive psychologists.[1] Their interest was inspired in no small part by the notable failures of early artificial intelligence programs to handle figurative utterances that human speakers readily took in stride. One early text-processing program (called FRUMP), fed a news article beginning "The death of the Pope shook the world," issued the following summary: "There was an earthquake in Italy. One person died."[2] Why did it seem so unlikely, if not unimaginable, that a native speaker would make such an error? What did the effortless and automatic interpretation of rhetorical figures say about the architecture of human cognition and the widespread, perhaps universal properties of natural languages? Once consigned largely to rhetoric, itself increasingly seen as a minor subdiscipline of literary scholarship, the study of figurative language suddenly became a topic of great moment for cognitive science.

Two cognitive theorists in particular, the linguist George Lakoff and the philosopher Mark Johnson, made metaphor crucial to their novel conception of what would eventually be called the *figurative mind*. As the title of their first book, *Metaphors We Live By* (1980), suggests, for Lakoff and Johnson metaphor is pervasive in everyday language and metaphorical mappings characterize even pre-linguistic thought processes.[3] Where an earlier philosophical tradition had long viewed figurative language as ornamental and deviant, Lakoff and Johnson insisted on the constitutive character of figurative thought and on the naturalness of figurative language. As they summarized it in retrospect, *Metaphors We Live By* presented "evidence that conceptual metaphors are mappings across conceptual domains that structure our reasoning, our experience, and our everyday language."[4] Mark Turner, one of the first literary scholars to notice the growing importance of figurative language for cognitive research, declared that rhetoricians now had a key role to play in the "science of the mind."[5] If, as Lakoff and Johnson argued, our effortless (and largely unconscious) production and comprehension of rhetorical figures reveal the figurative structure of thought and speech, then for Turner the "literary mind is the fundamental mind" and the traditional concerns of literary analysis can be refashioned within the larger orbit of cognitive science.[6] A number of cognitive psychologists, including Ellen Winner, Richard Gerrig, and Raymond Gibbs, agreed, and controlled studies of how human subjects use figures like metaphor, metonymy, and irony soon made a central part of their research agendas. Gibbs became an important proponent of the key claims staked out earlier by Lakoff and Johnson; his 1994 book, *The Poetics of Mind*, summarizes years of empirical research designed to show that "human cognition is fundamentally shaped by various poetic or figurative processes."[7]

In retrospect, it seems unfortunate but unsurprising that so few scholars in literature departments shared Turner's early enthusiasm for the cognitive study of figurative language. For the rise of what Turner called "cognitive rhetoric" in the 1980s was largely eclipsed by an equally challenging, and at the time much more compelling, recasting of metaphor and related figures of speech in the service of deconstruction. Paul de Man's essay "The Epistemology of Metaphor," first published in 1978, set the tone for much of the work that followed in emphasizing the "proliferating and disruptive power of figural language," what Jacques Derrida had earlier called the "abyss of metaphor" (253).[8] Derrida and de Man were no less persistent or ingenious than Lakoff and Johnson in uncovering the latent metaphoricity of discourses of many kinds, including philosophical and scientific discourses claiming objectivity and linguistic transparency. But where cognitive rhetoric celebrated the generative power and conceptual coherence of figurative thought—in a word, its felicity—deconstruction instead stressed the "catastrophic" effect of figures that render the texts that harbor them "suspended and unresolved."[9] "Rhetoric," in de Man's formulation, "radically suspends logic and opens up vertiginous possibilities of referential aberration"—a "figural potentiality" that de Man would identify with "literature itself" ("Semiology" 10). For de Man, no less than for Turner, rhetoric was regaining its lost prestige in discriminating the relentlessly figurative element of virtually all linguistic production: "It does not take a good semiotician long to recognize that he is in fact a rhetorician in disguise" ("Epistemology" 27). For the deconstructive rhetorician, however, figural language remains deviant, and rhetorical readings aim to elicit the disruptive, vertiginous, aberrant workings of metaphors and other tropes.

The trope of apostrophe has come to epitomize the excessive, disruptive, and insistently literary character of rhetorical figures as perhaps no other. Jonathan Culler notoriously argued that apostrophe, classically defined as a diversion or "turning away" of a speaker's utterance from a primary addressee to a second auditor (who might be absent, dead, or imaginary), functions to "complicate or disrupt the circuit of communication" ("Apostrophe" 135). In Culler's influential reading, apostrophe exemplifies "all that is most radical, embarrassing, pretentious, and mystificatory" in lyric poetry, and may be identified "with lyric itself" (137). Although Culler's interest in this figure goes back to his 1975 book *Structuralist Poetics*, where the germ for his "Apostrophe" essay can be found, his formulation here is attuned with the thinking of de Man, who makes the "figure of address" primary to the definition of the lyric ode and "paradigmatic for poetry in general" ("Lyrical Voice" 61).[10] Other critics influenced by de Man, including Mary Jacobus and Cynthia Chase, also produced work in the 1980s arguing for the disruptive and even "dangerous" character of apostrophe (Jacobus 171) and granting it "paradigmatic" status for the "lyric mode" (Chase 211).[11] This "radical" view of apostrophe has by now taken on the bland authority of the student handbook. In her *Course Guide* for the *Norton Anthology of Poetry*, for example, Debra Fried (citing Culler) warns beginning poetry students about the "problematic" nature of apostrophe, remarking that the "breathless 'Thou's and 'Oh's of the Romantic ode can seem to make apostrophizing hard work" (65).

Apostrophe would seem, then, to pose a special challenge for the cognitivist approach to figurative language. Lakoff, Johnson, Turner, Gibbs, and their adherents all assume a fundamental continuity between literary and everyday language, underscoring the pervasiveness of rhetorical figures but viewing them as facilitating rather than undermining textual coherence and successful communication. As the figure for linguistic disruption and literary deviance par excellence, repressed by the critical tradition and "problematic" for readers and audiences—"above all," as Culler stresses, "embarrassing" (135)—apostrophe might appear inherently unassimilable to a cognitive rhetoric or a poetics of mind. Nevertheless, in what follows I propose to develop a cognitive account of apostrophe, one that can cover a wider range of instances and functions than those considered by deconstructive rhetoric and one that remains sensitive to distinctions, including historical distinctions, that other accounts tend to elide.

A cognitive reappraisal of apostrophe might begin by noting that, pace Culler, apostrophes are not invariably embarrassing or at the very least do not always embarrass to the same degree. Consider these two examples from the same poet, both of them addresses to daughters.[12] First: "Stern Daughter of the Voice of God! / O Duty!" And now this one:

Surprised by joy—impatient as the Wind
I turned to share the transport—Oh! with whom
But thee, deep buried in the silent tomb.

The address to the personified abstraction, Duty, indeed sounds highly "poetic" and rather awkward. But Wordsworth's apostrophe to his child, who has died so recently that the poet has not yet lost his habit of looking to her, does not (at least for me) provoke any embarrassment whatsoever. Or consider two examples from a single poem (Coleridge's "This Lime Tree Bower My Prison"). First, this sequence of apostrophes:

Ah! slowly sink
Behind the western ridge, thou glorious Sun!
Shine in the slant beams of the sinking orb,
Ye purple heath-flowers! richlier burn, ye clouds!

And now this apostrophe from the same stanza, a few lines above:

they wander on
In gladness all, but thou, methinks, most glad,
My gentle-hearted Charles!

Or try to set an embarrassment value for each of two alternative readings of the same line by Anne Yearsley, the apostrophe that opens her *Poem on the Inhumanity of the Slave-Trade*. Is "BRISTOL, thine heart hath throbb'd to glory" equally embarrassing when one takes it to be addressed to the city and slaving port, as it is when one takes it to be addressed to Yearsley's patron and the poem's dedicatee, "the Right Hon. and Right Rev. FREDERICK, Earl of Bristol" (Yearsley, ii, 1)?[13]

Why does it sound more natural and felicitous, less awkward, to address an apostrophe to a patron instead of a city, to an absent friend rather than to a present sunset, to a recently dead daughter and not an abstract entity? A view of apostrophe committed to maximizing its linguistic deviance, its communicative failure, and its literariness or poeticality cannot answer this question. The more one attends to the entire range of figures of address, from the bombastic—"richlier burn, ye clouds!"—to the conversational—"but thou, methinks, most glad"—the more it appears that the "problematic" theory of apostrophe accounts for only one end of a larger continuum. To account for the more familiar and less "poetical" uses, one can turn instead to cognitive theories of language and communication as they bear on works of verbal art.

Richard Gerrig's cognitive psychological study of reading, *Experiencing Narrative Worlds*, provides a good place to start. In a chapter on language use in narrative worlds, Gerrig proposes to extend speech-act theory to better account for hearers of communicative utterances who are *not* the designated addressees of those utterances. A cognitive psychologist who has collaborated with Gibbs, Gerrig similarly understands verbal acts in literary works as continuous with "ordinary processes of language use" and as recruiting the same "cognitive processes."[14] Although he does not use the term, Gerrig evidently has apostrophe in mind when he mentions poetic phrases "nominally directed toward nonsensical addresses" like the sun or stars. Criticizing theories that are forced to posit "special mental acts dedicated to the experience of poetry," Gerrig claims instead that readers bring "vast experience" with comparable utterances in everyday discourse to aid in their comprehension of seemingly "nonsensical" poetic addresses (111, 126). Gerrig's first example is taken from a magazine article describing how the AIDS activist Larry Kramer dealt with having Ed Koch, then the mayor of New York, as a neighbor. Kramer detested Koch's AIDS policies and would loudly berate him in the lobby of their apartment building until the building management threatened Kramer with eviction. After that, whenever he would find himself with Koch in the lobby, Kramer would instead address his dog, Molly, with comments such as, "There's the man who murdered all of Daddy's friends" uttered loudly enough for the mayor to overhear them (105).

The example of Kramer, Molly, and Koch works especially well because the dog, Molly, is no less "nonsensical" an addressee than would be a nightingale or a personified abstraction. It is easier than one might at first think to come up with quotidian examples of remarks nominally intended for uncomprehending addressees that are clearly meant to be overhead by a second auditor. My experience as a parent suggests that one commonly addresses infants with remarks made for the benefit of the other parent: "Don't worry, honey, I'll get up and change your diaper again because Mommy is *just too busy* reading the *New Yorker.*" Culler inadvertently provides an example of his own, when he imagines a man cursing a late bus in the rain: "'Come on, damn you! It's been ten minutes!'" Culler suggests that if the man "continues apostrophically when other travelers join him on the corner, he makes a spectacle of himself" ("Apostrophe" 141–42). In fact, the man looks much odder if he apostrophizes the bus when no one is present—if he's seen talking out loud to himself. If he curses the bus in the presence of others waiting at the stop, he's intending the remark to be overhead by them and may even get a chorus of approving chuckles or empathetic groans in response. It is by no means uncommon to apostrophize the dead at a funeral—"*X*, we will miss you"—and the effect is anything but embarrassing. Everyday apostrophes may be still more common among certain religious communities. A colleague who grew up in a predominately Catholic neighborhood, for example, recalls her friend Maureen's mother, Mrs. Flanagan, frequently making remarks along the lines of, "Jesus! Don't let these girls drive off a bridge on their way home from that party," a plea or warning to the girls issued in the form of an apostrophic prayer. The nuns at their high school, Marian Catholic, would often reprove them with phrases like, "Jesus, Mary, and Joseph, what am I going to do with these kids!" Many of us, I expect, have childhood memories of similar remarks, regardless of religious affiliation.

As Gerrig explains, however, the everyday analog to apostrophe does not require a mute, inanimate, dead, or divine addressee. Whenever a conversation takes place before a third party, for example, the speakers ordinarily tailor their remarks to take the presence of an overhearer into account (104). Some remarks may be primarily intended for the overhearer (whom Gerrig terms the "side-participant" to distinguish this communicative position from an unintended or deliberately excluded "overhearer" [106]).[15] John Keats neatly describes this triangular communicative relation in a letter written to his brother George but intended to be read as well by George's wife, Georgiana: "I must take an opportunity here to observe that though I am writing *to* you I am all the while writing *at* your Wife—This explanation will account for my sometimes speaking *hoity-toityishly*"[16] (2: 204). And in "ordinary conversations with three or more participants," Gerrig points out, any given utterance might be explicitly addressed toward only one of the hearers, but each participant is expected to listen to and keep track of the flow of talk, deftly and unconsciously shifting between "addressee" and "side-participant" roles throughout the conversation (104). (When teachers answer a given student's question in the classroom, they expect or at least hope that the other students are taking an active side-participant role and craft their remarks accordingly.) In stark contrast to the exotic and aberrant role given to apostrophe by Culler and other deconstructive rhetoricians, Gerrig sees the three-way communicative relation assumed by apostrophe as a natural extension of normative and habitual conversational practice.

In focusing on the social and pragmatic functions of linguistic behavior, and arguing for the persistence of those functions in works of verbal art, Gerrig could find precedents in the "sociological poetics" put forth by the Bakhtin group in the 1920s. In his resonant essay "Discourse in Life and Discourse in Art," V. N. Volosinov builds from his basic definition of verbal discourse as "social event" to describe a triadic communicative relation similar to Gerrig's constellation of speaker, addressee, and "side-participant."[17] Looking out the window on a dreary day and uttering the semantically empty term *well* in a reproachful tone, Volosinov's imagined speaker has made use of intonation not to address a comment on the weather to his listener but to allow his listener to overhear a comment directed to an underdetermined *"third participant"*—perhaps nature, the snow, or fate.[18] Volosinov explicitly relates this model quotidian utterance to the figure of apostrophe: "Intonation has established an active attitude toward the referent, toward the object of the utterance, an attitude of a kind verging on *apostrophe* to that object as the incarnate, living culprit, while the listener—the second participant— is, as it were, called in *as witness and ally*" (103). Volosinov uses the terms *speaker*, *hero*, and *listener* in place of Gerrig's *speaker*, *addressee*, and *side-participant*, but the triadic relation remains constant and in each case constitutes an everyday analog to poetic address.

The same triadic communicative relation informs classical accounts of apostrophe. As L. M. Findlay notes in an early dissent from Culler, according to Quintilian's *Institutio Oratoria*, "what is heard apostrophically by one or more select addressees is also overheard by the remainder of the exordium's original audience."[19] Quintilian, who classes apostrophe among the "figures of thought," describes it as the "diversion of our words to address some person other than the judge" in a situation of rhetorical pleading.[20] Quintilian's definition of apostrophe underscores both its pragmatic function and the judge's role as overhearer (or side-participant), both of which are elided in Culler's dyadic, "I-thou" (or rather, I-"*you*") model (142).[21]

Culler quotes Northrop Frye (who in turn is glossing John Stuart Mill's dictum that the lyric is "not heard but overheard") to claim that the poet "turns his back on his listeners" in pretending to address a muse or friend, a natural object or personified abstraction (137). But to turn *aside* from one listener to another does not mean to turn one's back on the former and in fact (as Gerrig and Volosinov describe in their different ways) makes part of normal conversational practice. It is through such practice that readers learn to "habitually take a side-participant stance" in relation to literary works, according to Gerrig (124). Considered in this way, there is nothing inherently deviant, abnormal, or "embarrassing" in the use of apostrophe. To counter Culler's self-referential opening example—a lecturer on apostrophe, presumably Jonathan Culler, intoning "O mysterious apostrophe, teach us to understand your workings!" (135)—one need only imagine Culler's colleague in the audience turning to a friend and whispering, "Oh, Jonathan! That's such a loaded example!" In this case, the apostrophe might become embarrassing only if uttered loudly enough for the lecturer, its nominal addressee, to hear.

Quintilian's discussion also makes clear that an apostrophe need not be addressed (as some handbooks have it) to an "absent person" or "abstract or inanimate entity."[22] "Some person other than the judge" could as readily be present as absent. Confining his examples to apostrophes that "turn away from empirical listeners by addressing natural objects, artifacts, or abstractions" allows Culler to strengthen his case at the expense of considerably narrowing the definition of his leading term (138). De Man similarly limits discussion to the "fiction of an apostrophe to an absent, deceased, or voiceless entity," anticipating his conclusion that "language, as trope, is always privative."[23] This narrowing of the trope's field appears all the more remarkable in light of Culler's and de Man's shared focus on Romantic texts. For in poetry of the Romantic era, as Michael Macovski has asserted, addressees tend to "appear before their respective speakers as direct, face-to-face respondents."[24] Macovski accordingly reads apostrophe as a figure not for communicative breakdown or the "privative" nature of language but for "dialogue" and for language as "social process" (11, 38). Angela Esterhammer has demonstrated the importance of a similarly "dialogic" element in the linguistic theory of the era, with a pronounced interest in the social, pragmatic, and "performative" aspects of language.[25]

Esterhammer gives special attention to Thomas Reid, the leading philosopher of the Scottish "common sense school," who advanced an early version of speech-act theory in works first published in the 1780s. Predictably, Reid's brief discussion of apostrophe places it in close proximity to ordinary linguistic practice and, significantly, it occurs at the end of a discussion of the "social operations of mind."[26]

"In all languages," Reid claims, "the second person of verbs, the pronoun of the second person, and the vocative case in nouns, are appropriated to the expression of social operations of mind, and could never have had place in language but for this purpose: nor is it a good argument against this observation, that, by a rhetorical figure, we sometimes address persons that are absent, or even inanimated [*sic*] beings, in the second person. For it ought to be remembered, that all figurative ways of using words or phrases, supposes a natural and literal meaning of them" (74). Rhetorical figures for Reid are not linguistically aberrant but constitute special uses of "natural" utterances. Apostrophe exemplifies rather than derails the social and communicative function of linguistic acts.

Acknowledging the overlap between figurative language and everyday speech, and the communicative gesture latent within the figure of apostrophe in particular, does not mean, of course, that all uses of this figure will sound natural or evoke the social character of language. When Byron in *Childe Harold* exclaims, "Roll on, thou deep and dark blue Ocean—roll!" (IV.179), it does sound excessive and, yes, embarrassing. An adequate theory of apostrophe would need to cover not just the familiar and communicative instances characteristic of Romantic "conversation" poems and excluded by de Man and Culler, but the problematic cases so ingeniously analyzed by them as well. It would also need to account for the rise in awkwardness when poets invoke nonhuman rather than human auditors. Hugh Blair, whose *Lectures on Rhetoric and Belles Lettres* (1783) remained the most popular guide to rhetoric throughout the Romantic era, actually reserves the term *apostrophe* to cover *only* addresses to human beings. All other apostrophes are regrouped instead within a special "degree" of the related figure prosopopoeia (or "personification").[27] Here is how Blair defines apostrophe:

> It is an address to a real person; but one who is either absent or dead, as if he were present, and listening to us. It is so much allied to an address to inanimate objects personified, that both these figures are sometimes called apostrophes. However, the proper Apostrophe is in boldness one degree lower than the address to personified objects; for it certainly requires a less effort of imagination to suppose persons present who are dead or absent, than to animate insensible beings, and direct our discourse to them. (1: 338)

Blair's definition of apostrophe shares Culler's exclusion of what the latter calls "empirical listeners" (138), but it also excludes the artifacts, objects, and abstractions that play such a crucial role in Culler's argument. Blair, too, acknowledges the greater departure from ordinary discourse in addressing "insensible beings" but significantly describes this as an increase in "boldness" rather than awkwardness or embarrassment.

However historically intriguing, Blair's redefinition of apostrophe proves theoretically unsatisfying. It leaves far too much out of consideration, excluding the present human auditors evoked so frequently in Romantic-era poetry and relegating nonhuman addressees to the "third degree" of prosopopoeia. The line Blair draws between human and nonhuman addresses is suggestive but too sharp: apostrophes to the dead, who are at once human and inanimate, would seem to fall in between. One might do better to place poetic instances of apostrophe along a rough continuum largely according to addressee, from present and intimate (though silent) human companions to inanimate objects, with distant or huge and lifeless objects (like stars or oceans) at the far end. The overlapping distinctions between animate and inanimate, human and nonhuman auditors call for special discussion but *not* for distinct and exclusive categories. Borderline cases, in which the addressee hovers between categories, can prove especially instructive, suggesting that Romantic-era poets keep sight of distinctions like the one posed by Blair but choose to confound them. In the rest of this chapter, I sketch out a continuum approach to apostrophes, keeping in view their connections with everyday discourse and their more pronouncedly odelike or "poetical" effects.[28] I end by suggesting, however, that the degree of what Blair calls "boldness" may vary not just from one instance of apostrophe to the next but from one historical era to another.

The addresses to silent auditors that punctuate Romantic "conversation poems" closely resemble the everyday speech situations Gerrig describes—so closely that their apostrophic character can easily be missed. Macovski, in a rare discussion of these familiar apostrophes, notes that the apostrophic incorporation of the addressee makes a signature aspect of Romantic style (21). Often the addressee is not just familiar but familial. Wordsworth turns to address his sister in the final section of his "Tintern Abbey" poem—

> Oh! yet a little while
> May I behold in thee what I was once,
> My dear, dear Sister!—

as Coleridge turns to address his infant son in the concluding stanzas of "Frost at Midnight": "Dear Babe, that sleepest cradled by my side . . . " It is remarkable, though rarely remarked upon, that Coleridge's address to the infant Hartley does not strike readers as unnatural or strained, although the child is in a prelinguistic stage and an unconscious state. No doubt Coleridge's address seems natural because parents habitually address infants in this way, generally to convey attitudes or information to side-participants: "Aha, you messed up your diaper *again*"; "Oh, so you're finally asleep, you little insomniac!" The function of such addresses varies and shows various degrees of complexity. Readers have noticed that the apostrophe to Dorothy in "Tintern Abbey" collapses difference into sameness, as the address to a feminine other turns her into a virtual mirror image of the poet's younger self ("May I behold in thee what I was once").[29] The apostrophe to infant Hartley, on the other hand, seeks to maximize otherness:

> My babe so beautiful! it thrills my heart
> With tender gladness, thus to look at thee,
> And think that thou shalt learn far other lore,
> And in far other scenes!

Yet in asking Hartley vicariously to live out the Wordsworthian childhood that Coleridge envies, the poem threatens again to collapse difference into self-identity, as earlier when the "*stranger's* face" becomes that of the poet's sister: "My play-mate when we both were clothed alike!" By implicitly evoking the social character of linguistic exchange, apostrophes in these poems underscore the strong gravitational pull of self-regard even in seeking to break its hold.

Apostrophes to intimate friends, whether present or absent, share the familiar conversational feel of those to close relatives. They often provide a sense of ratification, as do the addresses to "gentle-hearted Charles" in Coleridge's "This Lime Tree Bower," or Wordsworth's apostrophes to Coleridge throughout *The Prelude*: "Ah! need I say, dear Friend! that to the brim / My heart was full" (4: 333–34). Such apostrophes reflect a collaborative writing culture in which poems were typically circulated in manuscript or inscribed into familiar letters, often intended (like Keats's letters to George and Georgiana) for multiple recipients. Yet they also reflect anxieties raised by the professionalization of poetry, increasingly written for an anonymous, paying readership rather than a circle of patrons and friends, by providing an insulating layer between the poet and the book-buying public. The double apostrophe to William and Dorothy Wordsworth, for example, provides Coleridge with an internal audience guaranteed to assent to his revisionary views in "The Nightingale" (the same poem that, with its subtitle, introduces the very term *conversation poem*): "My Friend, and thou, our Sister! we have learnt / A different lore." Byron exposes this device by inverting it in *Don Juan*, shifting the reader's position from side-participant to poetic addressee, while announcing his poetry's dependence on the literary marketplace: "But for the present, gentle reader! and / Still gentler purchaser!" (1: 221). Addresses to the reader carry a certain defamiliarizing charge not just because they expose a text's artificiality but because they jostle readers out of their accustomed "side-participant" position to become, momentarily, what Volosinov calls the "heroes" of apostrophic invocations.

Familiar apostrophes do not always provide a ratifying, insulating effect but can perform instead what Macovski terms an "agonistic" function (24–26). Coleridge's addresses to "pensive Sara" play this role in "The Eolian Harp," her silent but active presence in the poem inspiring him to abandon its intimations of pantheism: "But thy more serious eye a mild reproof / Darts, O beloved Woman!" Note, however, that in shifting from the familiar "Sara" to the abstract "Woman," Coleridge's final address to his wife moves several degrees toward the "bold" or "embarrassing" pole of the apostrophic spectrum. Similar shifts in function and boldness value can be seen in the series of changes in poetic addressee that help give such a different feel to the various drafts of the poem now known as Coleridge's "Dejection" ode.[30] In its early manuscript version as *A Letter to ———*, Coleridge addresses a different Sara, not his wife but his obsessive love interest, Sara Hutchinson: "O Sara! we receive but what we give / And in *our* Life alone does Nature live" (33). In this version the tone is familiar, seeking for assent, yet also monitory, almost pedagogical. When, in a partial transcription of the poem in a letter to William Sotheby, the addressee becomes Wordsworth, the apostrophe takes on an agonistic function, at least to readers aware of the two poets' history of disagreement on this very point: "O Wordsworth! we receive but what we give, / And in our Life alone does Nature live" (40). In its final form, with the addressee now an unnamed "Lady," the apostrophe again sounds rather didactic but also less conversational, more awkward: "O Lady! we receive but what we give" (55). Although the poet represents the Lady as an intimate—"friend devoutest of my choice"—the shift from proper name to abstract noun saps the address of the familiar tone that characterizes the earlier versions.

In between the addresses to intimates found in conversation poems, so familiar from everyday discourse that they often fail to register as apostrophes at all, and the disruptive addresses to artifacts and abstractions that epitomize the apostrophe for readers like de Man and Culler, lies a large middle ground of addresses that neither command nor evade readerly attention. Addresses to human beings become more noticeable as they become more abstract and as their objects become more removed from the poet or poetic speaker in intimacy, place, and time. Compare the speaker's apostrophe to his presumed daughter in Wordsworth's "It Is a Beauteous Evening"—"Dear Child! dear Girl! that walkest with me here"—with that to an idealized infant in the "Immortality" ode: "Thou little Child, yet glorious in the might / Of heaven-born freedom on thy being's height." Apostrophes to whole classes of persons, even if a relationship is being claimed, also sound more "rhetorical" than addresses to intimates: "We have offended, Oh! my countrymen!" (This last is from Coleridge's highly apostrophic poem, "Fears in Solitude," to which I will return.) Apostrophes to other poets may appear more strained as the poet is removed in time: compare Coleridge's "O Wordsworth" to Keats's "Oh Chatterton!" and then to Wordsworth's "Milton!" And yet, apostrophes to earlier poets are so thoroughly conventionalized that they generally sound less awkward than addresses to others of the mighty dead, no matter how far removed in time. It's hard to imagine using the apostrophe "Oh Plato! Plato!" for any purpose other than comic effect, as Byron does in *Don Juan* (1: 116). But an apostrophe to Sappho would not sound so ludicrous.

My discussion has moved from addresses to the living to invocations of the dead without comment up to now. Why does there seem to be a continuum in moving from the living Wordsworth, to the recently dead Chatterton, to the long dead Milton, rather than an absolute divide between breathing addressees and those in the ground? An absent apostrophic "hero," such as Charles in "This Lime Tree Bower," can after all still read the lines addressed to him. But Chatterton could never read the apostrophes that Coleridge, Keats, and other writers of the era kept addressing to that icon of the beautiful, young, dead poet. In many cultures, of course, the dead remain with the living and receive offerings and oblations, prayers and supplications accordingly. Romantic-era Britain was not entirely such a culture, but the dead may well have seemed nearer than they do in the twenty-first century. Christabel's apostrophe to her mother (in a poem set, admittedly, in an earlier, pre-Protestant England)—"Oh mother dear! that thou wert here!"—summons a real presence, at least according to Geraldine's response: "Off, woman, off! this hour is mine!" (Coleridge, "Christabel," 202, 211). But think again of contemporary verbal behavior at a funeral or memorial service. Even someone long dead can be apostrophized without departing from normative speech codes, though it may sound a bit stagy and strained: "Oh Frank, if you could have known before you died that your son would one day curse me in my own house!" It may be easy to address dead people simply because it is people that one habitually addresses, as Blair suggests in defining the "proper Apostrophe."

Certainly, apostrophes to living animals sound less natural, more stilted, than apostrophes to human beings, present or absent, living or dead. A remarkable tonal shift occurs in "The Nightingale" as the speaker turns once more to address his friends after apostrophizing the bird of the title: "Farewell, O Warbler! till tomorrow eve, / And you, my friends, farewell, a short farewell." It sounds as though the poet were using two different figures altogether, as Blair would have it. Poets can use the principles of abstraction and of multiplication to further heighten the unnaturalness of the animal apostrophe, as in the "Immortality" ode: "Ye blessed Creatures, I have heard the call, / Ye to each other make." Although addressed to animate beings, such apostrophes diverge much more noticeably from ordinary linguistic usage than do addresses to the inanimate dead, who cannot talk or even bleat back.[31]

The silence of the dead in apostrophic relations has been interestingly read by de Man as impelling a rather Gothic scenario, in which the poet's wish to make the dead speak bears the "latent threat" that the "living are struck dumb, frozen in their own death" ("Autobiography" 78). For de Man, who, like Culler, reads apostrophe in terms of a dyadic relationship, the "symmetrical" structure of the figure implies its reversibility.[32] If, however, one understands apostrophe in terms of a triadic relation, as Quintilian, Volosinov, and Gerrig all do, then the muteness of the dead might be less notable than the inability of the dead to overhear. That is, the dead can still function as "hero" of an apostrophe but no longer as Volosinov's "witness" or Gerrig's "side-participant." Wordsworth's sonnet "Surprised by Joy" gains much of its poignancy—and it is hard to think of a more poignant poem—by playing out this transformation in the relations among speaker, addressee, and witness. Let me quote the sonnet's opening lines once more:

> Surprised by joy—impatient as the Wind
> I turned to share the transport—Oh! with whom
> But thee, deep buried in the silent tomb,
> That spot which no vicissitude can find?

The speaker turns to his daughter, not to address her but to share an attitude, much as the speaker in Volosinov's example calls in the listener "*as witness and ally*": "I turned to share the transport." But the poet's daughter has died, and his habitual gesture, his turning toward her, becomes the "turning away" that etymologically defines apostrophe: "Oh! with whom / But thee." If one reads the passage slowly and sequentially, the exclamation "Oh!" functions to encapsulate this movement in a single, overdetermined phoneme. In the second line, "Oh!" implies a semantically empty yet meaningful term like Volosinov's "Well!," readily interpretable by a present listener in full possession of the "extraverbal pragmatic situation" (98). As in, "Oh! how beautiful," or, given the extraverbal context, simply "Oh!" When the death of the addressee becomes manifest in line three—manifest not just to the reader but to the momentarily forgetful poet as well—the "Oh!" is reinterpreted as a bereaved father's cry of pain, eloquent in its inarticulateness. But, as well, the "Oh" of grief harbors the "O" of apostrophe, marking, with the pronounced caesura that precedes it, the apostrophic turn itself. The pain arrives with the knowledge that the daughter is left with *only* the position of "hero" or addressee in any apostrophic relation. Wordsworth's apostrophe becomes a moving comment on the communicative structure of apostrophe.

If the dead *could* speak back, then the latent threat that de Man describes—that the "living are struck dumb"—might, in a triadic reading of apostrophe, apply to a living witness rather than to the apostrophic speaker. Just such a fate seems to befall the unnamed listener in "A Spirit's Return," which Felicia Hemans sometimes described as her most fully realized poem. Addresses to the listener, a "gentle friend" and apparently a disappointed suitor, occur frequently enough to give the poem a dialogic quality, although only the female speaker's voice is ever heard. That voice also utters a series of more daring apostrophes—"O thou rich world unseen! / Thou curtain'd realm of spirits"—that lead up to the revelation that through "fiery" and "magic" words she has indeed managed the impossible: "Communion with the dead!" In telling contrast to Byron's Manfred, evoked via the poem's epigraph, Hemans's speaker manages to call her beloved back from the grave and actually have a two-way conversation with him:

I drank in *soul!*—I questioned of the dead—
Of the hush'd, starry shores their footsteps tread,
And I was answered.

The speaker gains not death but life—"I drank in *soul!*"—when the beloved's spirit speaks back. The "gentle friend," however, seems to disappear from the poem at its conclusion, frozen out of the scene as the speaker turns definitively toward her disembodied lover, the addressee of her final series of speech acts: "shall not *I*, too, be, / My spirit-love! upborne to dwell with thee?" In a poem replete with and thematically concerned with performative utterances, Hemans asserts a dyadic relation between a living and dead speaker by taking skillful advantage of the triadic structure of apostrophe.

In their ambiguous status as inanimate bodies and as disembodied souls, the dead readily become subjects of apostrophic address. Apostrophes to inanimate objects or to abstractions, however, might seem to belong where Blair puts them—in another category altogether. To deconstructive readers, apostrophes that border on prosopopoeia (in its sense of "personification") appear outright "mystificatory" (Culler 137), even "hallucinatory" (de Man, "Lyrical Voice" 67). Cognitive rhetoricians take a quite different view. Lakoff and Johnson include personification among the common "metaphors" we live by, citing such quotidian uses as "This fact argues against the standard theories" and "Inflation is eating up our profits" (33–34). For Lakoff, causation is "one of the most fundamental of human concepts" and always assumes, in its "prototypical form," some kind of agent (*Women* 55). No surprise, then, that utterances will posit agency even when no overt agent can be discriminated, as in "it's raining." Turner argues that, even in a world disenchanted of "river gods and wind deities and tree spirits," we regularly "project features of animacy and agency" onto nonhuman objects and abstract entities in order to think about them in human terms, the terms most familiar to us from habitual reflection on our own actions (*Literary Mind* 20–21). This habitual projection explains why apostrophes to inanimate objects are so readily understood, even when they sound comically strained: "Come on, old car, start this time, you can do it!" Blair himself recognized the pervasiveness of personification long ago, stating that "there is a wonderful proneness in human nature to animate all objects" and that "very frequent approaches" to personification occur in "common conversation." Although "at first view" personification seems to "border on the extravagant and ridiculous," its use is "extensive" and its "foundation laid deep in human nature" (1: 324–25). Blair remains instructively ambivalent regarding personification, holding that, when properly used, it strikes readers as "natural and agreeable," yet it still retains the emphasis on "boldness" that for him distinguishes personification from apostrophe (1: 324).

A cognitive rhetorician might diagnose this ambivalence by pointing to the conflicting operations of two distinct and equally common human tendencies. In a useful introduction to metaphor and conceptual blending theory (an offshoot of cognitive linguistics), Joseph Grady and his coauthors note that the perceived degree of metaphoricity in a given utterance may vary with the perceived degree of distance between the categories being brought together. "A sentence starting with 'If I were a cloud' strikes us as more figurative than one starting with 'If I were you,'" even though the latter poses an equally impossible metaphorical blending.[33] Certain cognitive anthropologists and psychologists see category distinctions between human and nonhuman, and between animate and inanimate, as especially salient, fundamental, and widespread across geographically and genetically distinct cultures.[34] One common human tendency, then, the attribution of agency to many kinds of entities, might run up against a second, the deeply entrenched category distinction between the human agent and the inanimate object. Without the latter distinction, indeed, one could hardly develop a reliable theory of other minds.[35]

Apostrophes to inanimate objects, then, should prove readily comprehensible yet also carry a note of strain or artificiality, heightening their perceived degree of poeticality: "And O, ye Fountains, Meadows, Hills, and Groves, / Forbode not any severing of our loves!" Notice how Wordsworth heightens the sense of "boldness" not only by multiplication, offering a whole list of inanimate addressees, but by nonstandard, "poetical" sounding forms like "ye" and the apostrophic "O" itself. Apostrophes of this sort want to be noticed. They do the kinds of work described so well by Culler, de Man, Jacobus, and other critics writing in the 1980s: willing objects to function as subjects; imposing a relation between subjects onto a subject-object relation; constituting by the very act of asserting a powerful, poetic voice; and underscoring the special temporality of writing. Their preferred linguistic register is not the colloquial but the vatic, as throughout the poetry of Blake: "O Earth, O Earth, return!" Macovski underscores the difference between dialogic addresses to silent auditors and apostrophes to inanimate objects, noting that the latter, as throughout the poetry of Shelley and Keats, ironically posit a listening subject in order to wishfully collapse the subject-object distinction (9–10). "Be thou, Spirit fierce, / My spirit! Be thou me, impetuous one!" Their evocation of a high poetic, if not prophetic, stance leaves such apostrophes temptingly open to travesty. A parodist need only ratchet the vatic tone up a notch, as in this send-up of Erasmus Darwin: "Great Babylon is fallen! Shout, shout, ye Meads! / And, oh! ye Corn-fields, wave your happy heads!"[36] Apostrophes to hills, cornfields, the Earth, and other inanimate objects often do strike readers with the "brazenness" deconstructive rhetoric attributes to them (Culler 152). They form, however, the extreme end of a series moving from conversational addresses to present and absent intimates, through apostrophes to the distant and departed, to the apostrophes to animals, plants, artifacts, and inanimate nature so readily parodied.

Addresses to personified abstractions might seem still more brazen, but to my sensibilities they lie somewhere between "O, Sara!" and "O, ye Fountains." The very profusion of mythological references and motifs in premodern poetry may leave readers prepared to give abstract entities something akin to human form. The opening address of Wordsworth's "Ode to Duty"—"Stern Daughter of the Voice of God! / O Duty!"—seems less, not more, bold than the same poet's apostrophe to a living creature: "O Cuckoo! Shall I call the Bird, / Or but a wandering voice?" ("To the Cuckoo"). In Hemans's poem "The Image in Lava," the apostrophe "Love! human love! what art thou?" does not jar so much, perhaps because readers of poetry are used to thinking of Love as a goddess and seeing visual representations of goddesses in human form. Abstract entities less familiar from mythology, especially when encountered in a series, lose this quality of relative familiarity: "O world! O life! O time!" (Shelley, "A Lament").

Even at their most bold or brazen, however, apostrophes remain readily comprehensible; they may disturb the reading process but they do not short-circuit it. Or as Blair puts it, when skillfully handled they remain "agreeable," however removed from ordinary usage. In his essay "Process and Product in Making Sense of Tropes," Gibbs argues for a distinction between the comprehension and the full understanding of rhetorical figures.[37] If metaphor, metonymy, irony, and (we can now add) apostrophe are not only present in everyday language but constitutive of ordinary thought processes, these figures should prove readily interpretable. Psycholinguistic research undertaken by Gibbs and others strongly suggests that the comprehension of such figures does not indeed require special cognitive procedures. As products of understanding, however, a given instance of figurative language may elicit extended interpretive activity, provoking judgments of relative "poeticality" such as those made throughout this essay. The figurative mapping "If I were you" neither stalls interpretation nor slows it down; "If I were a dead leaf thou mightest bear" (from Shelley's "Ode to the West Wind") does not stall immediate *comprehension,* although it may well cause readers to slow down and prolong their efforts to *appreciate* such an unusual conceptual blend. Cognitive rhetoric posits the comprehensibility and felicity of figurative tropes just as resolutely as deconstructive rhetoric insists on their disruptive and "vertiginous" qualities (de Man, "Semiology," 10). Gibbs's distinction between comprehension and appreciation can account both for the coherence of figural language and for the dishabituating, slowing-down effect that any number of poeticians have made a hallmark of "literariness."[38]

In concluding, I want to emphasize that the perceived degree of naturalness or boldness in a given use of figurative language may well vary along with historical changes in cultural and linguistic practice. Although Gerrig does not discuss historical shifts in readers' experience of rhetorical figures and other literary devices, he does acknowledge that the "common ground" or "body of shared assumptions" that readers bring to their engagement with texts can change over time and vary among discrete "interpretive communities" (118). One remarkable distinction between academic readers in the present and Romantic-era readers of poetry concerns the prevalence of religious discourse and changing statistical patterns in regularly attending religious services. The vast majority of readers and writers in the late eighteenth and early nineteenth centuries would have been present at some form of public or family worship weekly if not more often. Even professed freethinkers and atheists would most likely have attended religious services as children, and those services would ordinarily have included public prayers and other devotional practices manifesting the same triadic structure as apostrophe. Whether prayers to God—who, as Wordsworth's Goody Blake puts it, is "never out of hearing"— can be considered "proper" apostrophes may be a question for theological debate as much as for literary theory to decide. But public prayers to God, however sincere, always aim to be overheard by the congregation, and (as with prayers for the health of the royal family) may be framed with an ideological agenda no less than with spiritual concerns in mind. At a time when, as Esterhammer writes, the "role of public utterance" had been heightened and expanded by the French Revolution and its aftermath in Britain—an era of loyalty oaths, patriotic anthems, royal and church investitures, and overtly politicized sermons—addresses to an unseen being meant for the edification of an overhearing public may have proliferated as rarely before or since (51). So, at least, Coleridge complains in "Fears in Solitude," decrying the plethora of wartime mandates "Stuffed out with big preamble, holy names, / And adjuration of the God in Heaven" (101–2).

In such a cultural and linguistic climate, apostrophes like those that throng "Fears in Solitude" may have sounded more familiar, however abstract or nonsensical their addressees, than they could be expected to sound to modern ears.[39] How different in tone are Coleridge's apostrophes from those that might be heard at a Dissenting service? "Therefore, evil days / Are coming on us, O my countrymen!" (123–24); "But O dear Britain! O my Mother isle!" (182); "Spare us yet a while, / Father and God!" (129–30). Or consider the addresses studding Anna Barbauld's trenchant antiwar poem, "Eighteen Hundred and Eleven": "Yet, O my Country, name beloved, revered" (67); "And think'st thou, Britain, still to sit at ease, / An island queen amidst thy subject seas" (39–40). Apostrophes like these have nothing like the familiar conversational feel of those to present or absent intimates, but they may have sounded familiar enough to contemporary audiences. Apostrophes in general—even those to inanimate beings or personified abstractions—may have sounded "bold" to varying degrees without ever eliciting the modern critic's "embarrassment," except when deliberately exaggerated in the interests of parody. Jane Austen and other Romantic-era novelists regularly include apostrophes when representing familiar discourse, as in this sample from *Mansfield Park*: "'Poor William! He has met with great kindness from the Chaplain of the Antwerp,' was a tender apostrophe of Fanny's, very much to the purpose of her own feelings, if not of the conversation."[40] Or, toward the end of the same novel, as Fanny reacts (in soliloquy) to a letter from Edmund: "Edmund, you do not know *me* . . . Oh! write, write. Finish it at once!" (414). "Bolder" apostrophes can be used to characterize a more affected character, like the poetical enthusiast Marianne from Austen's *Sense and Sensibility*: "Oh! happy house, could you know what I suffer in now viewing you from this spot, from whence perhaps I may view you no more!"[41] Apostrophes may have been a defining feature of the high Romantic ode, but they were by no means excluded from the nineteenth-century domestic novel.

Let me end by underscoring some of the advantages of a conversation among literary scholars and cognitive scientists as they converge on the traditional concerns of rhetoric. Cognitive theory provides a cogent and productive new way to think about figurative language—as pervasive rather than exceptional, as normative rather than aberrant, as constitutive rather than ornamental. It revives an older sense of tropes as not merely linguistic phenomena but as "figures of thought," going beyond rhetoricians from Quintilian to Blair, however, in hypothesizing that various figurative operations characterize large tracts of cognitive activity at a fundamental level of processing. In relation to the figure of apostrophe, a cognitive approach can elicit a richer, more extensive, more complex understanding of that trope, revealing its rootedness in ordinary linguistic behavior and delineating an entire spectrum of usages from the transparently familiar to the obtrusively strange. A cognitive reading can help restore promising but neglected paradigms from within literary theory, such as Volosinov's triadic scenario for modeling apostrophic exchange, while reasserting in the process the pragmatic and social functions of rhetoric that deconstructive theorists ruled out of consideration.

But cognitive science can stand to learn from literary and cultural studies as well, first by being reminded that the analysis of figures like metaphor and apostrophe *does* have a long and rich history. Literary scholars resist, by habit and by training, reliance on the simplified examples that play such a large role in controlled studies, refusing to consider any theory of figurative language remotely satisfying until it can deal with what F. Elizabeth Hart calls the "acrobatic" effects characteristic of complex literary texts.[42] Literary analysts can extend the compass of cognitive rhetoric by seeking to account for the salience and difficulty—even the violence—of novel, ambiguous, and self-consciously literary usages, supplementing cognitive work on "comprehending" rhetorical tropes by providing methods and examples of more fully "understanding" them, to return to Gibbs's important distinction. Finally, literary scholars can vastly enrich notions of "extraverbal context" and "common ground" by specifying the cultural and historical differences that may affect the production and reception of rhetorical figures over time. As more literary theorists, critics, and historians begin speaking to notions of cognitive rhetoric and figurative thought, cognitive scientists would do well to reply—or at least to overhear.

CHAPTER FIVE

Reading Minds—and Bodies— in *Emma*

Narrative theory and narrative poetics have proved especially rich areas for the new approaches emerging at the interface of literary studies and the sciences of mind and brain. In this case (as with cognitive approaches to figurative language) cognitive science can be seen to have taken the initiative. The titles of certain now classic books and articles in the field suggest how, by making narrative central to studies of how the mind works, leading cognitive researchers presented an opening to their colleagues in narrative studies; these include Roger Schank and Robert Abelson's *Scripts, Plans, Goals, and Understanding: An Enquiry into Human Knowledge Structures* (1977), Schank's *Tell Me a Story: Narrative and Intelligence* (1990), and Daniel Dennet's "The Self as Center of Narrative Gravity" (1988), originally entitled, "Why Everyone Is a Novelist."[1]

A growing number of literary researchers have responded to this implicit invitation, and cognitive approaches to narrative now represent a significant tendency within narrative studies and theories of the novel.[2] Significantly, novelists themselves, including some of the most notable living practitioners of the dominant literary narrative form, had already found their way to cognitive science in advance of the recent surge of interest among literary academics. If "everyone is a novelist," as Dennett claims, then why shouldn't professional novelists take special interest in and exhibit special insight into the investigations of mind and consciousness being undertaken by cognitive theorists, neuroscientists, and psychologists? This question has now been worked out in several different ways, giving new life to what was once called the "novel of ideas" and attesting to the tensions as well as the significant overlaps between cognitive and novelistic modes of exploring the human mind. Several novels, in fact, stage intellectual confrontations between fictional representatives of cognitive science and literary art, each laying claim to insights that the other badly needs and just as badly lacks. Most systematically (and closest to a traditional novel of ideas), David Lodge, in *Thinks* (2001), stages a series of debates between the novelist Helen Reed and her lover, Ralph Messenger, director of a center of cognitive science, putting literature and cognitive science literally into bed together.[3] Ian McEwan, in *Enduring Love* (1999), places the science writer, Joe Rose, currently immersed in evolutionary psychology and brain-based notions of mind, into conflict with his girlfriend Clarissa, a literature professor and Keats specialist whose name pays tribute to one of the great early exemplars of the novel form.[4] Most spectacularly of all, Richards Powers, in *Galatea 2.2* (1995), throws a novelist (named Richard Powers) headfirst into the fractious world of cognitive neuroscientific research, as he accepts the challenge of a brilliant and obsessive Artificial Intelligence researcher, Philip Lentz, to help program a neural network that could credibly pass a comprehensive exam in English literature.[5] Each of these books takes the science very seriously—Powers in particular shows an astounding command of cognitive theory and an exemplary awareness of rival positions and debates among cognitive researchers—and each argues in its own way that novelists have long had subtle and powerful techniques for pursuing the very questions—about the self, about consciousness, about the interpenetration of cognition and emotion, of mind and body—that cognitive scientists have increasingly come to ask.

In the long, wide-ranging title essay of his recent collection *Consciousness and the Novel*, Lodge has also explored these issues as a respected literary critic, staking out some of the rich and productive ground for interdisciplinary exchange between literary theory and the sciences of mind and brain.[6] (In the process, Lodge also gives students of his work crucial information on some of the philosophical and neuroscientific sources behind *Thinks*.) Among much else, Lodge brings up two topics of special relevance here: the signal role of Jane Austen in the history of fictional representations of consciousness and the crucial importance for novelists and narrative theorists of what is called "Theory of Mind" theory (40–42, 46–49).

In this chapter, I bring these two topics together, arguing that in *Emma*, the novel that features her most deft and penetrating social observation, Austen represents a repertoire of interpersonal behaviors that can best be described and understood in relation to theories of Theory of Mind. Placing her characters in situations that force them to guess and guess again at one another's intentions, beliefs, and emotional states, Austen shows how pervasively they rely on social-cognitive strategies closely analogous to those that cognitive neuroscientists currently study under the rubric of "theory of mind."

In order to "read" one another's minds, Austen's characters must pay special kinds of attention to one another's bodies—the eyes, facial expressions, gestures, vocal tones, and the movements of blood under the skin—as well as monitoring their own "gut" feelings (interoception) as they gauge the effect and validity of emotional displays that may always be downplayed or outright faked. Along with the novel's well-known emphasis on verbal puzzles and linguistic confusion runs an equally significant concern with the ambiguities and pitfalls inherent in monitoring the intentions and emotions of others through the medium of the body. Bodily displays, no less than words, can prove ambiguous or deceitful. Yet they can also betray the conscious subject into self-revelation, and the most successful mindreaders of *Emma* exhibit their own theories of mind in action as they negotiate the claustrophobic and treacherous social environment of Highgate, seeking to exploit moments of "embodied transparency" exhibited by others while trying themselves to remain studiously illegible.[7] The narrative attention and descriptive clarity that Austen brings to these intersubjective transactions and the sense of conscious purpose that her characters at times bring to the effort of "mind reading" invite us to consider Austen herself as an early theorist of what is now called Theory of Mind, a connection that appears less anachronistic once one has identified comparable trends in the philosophical and rhetorical writings of Austen's time.

Theory of Mind (or "ToM") theory, with its obvious relevance not only to the representation of consciousness in narrative works but also to characterization, character interaction, and the reading process, has sparked a great deal of interest among literary scholars, who have already done much to flesh out Lodge's suggestive hints in "Consciousness and the Novel." Lisa Zunshine, in her important book *Why We Read Fiction: Theory of Mind and the Novel*, argues persuasively that we can only understand literary characters as humanlike entities, with intentions and emotions, because we automatically bring our mind-reading capacities to bear on relevant literary representations. In this way, "ToM makes literature as we know it possible."[8] Indeed, for Zunshine the appeal of fiction has a great deal to do with its capacity to exercise and titillate our cognitive hunger for such stimulation, since our "cognitive adaptations for mindreading are promiscuous, voracious, and pro-active" ("Transparency" 68). Blakey Vermeule, working independently, delineates a distinct novelistic lineage especially devoted to such cognitive stimulation, the "high theory of mind tradition" running from Henry Fielding and Samuel Richardson through Austen, George Eliot, and Henry James to McEwan's *Atonement*.[9] In *Fictional Minds*, his lucid introduction to the value of cognitive approaches for understanding representations of mind in novels, films, and other narrative forms, Alan Palmer outlines the usefulness of several competing versions of ToM theory for narrative poetics.[10] Significantly, both Zunshine and Palmer follow Lodge in crediting Austen with the development (if not the discovery) of crucial new narrative techniques for representing consciousness, although Lodge emphasizes Austen's use of free indirect discourse rather than her representations of Theory of Mind behaviors. Building on these precedents, and on my own previous work on Austen's representation of embodied subjectivity in *Persuasion*, I want to place Austen's innovative portrayal of "deep intersubjectivity" more firmly in its Romantic-era context, while acknowledging that Austen's achievement in this area would be much harder to appreciate and critically describe without the framework and terminology offered by ToM theory.[11] I provide, however, only a brief overview of cognitive theories of Theory of Mind, referring readers to Zunshine, Vermeule, and Palmer, as well as to the relevant citations from cognitive science and psychology, for fuller accounts.

According to ToM theory, the traditional philosophical problem of other minds really isn't a problem, at least, not of the everyday sort. Human beings are adaptively designed, as highly (and when need be, deviously) social animals, to search for and identify signs of intentionality, emotions, and belief states in others, primarily as revealed by the face and eyes, although blind people readily develop a sense of other minds through voice and touch. Innately equipped with what Simon Baron-Cohen calls a "mindreading instinct," human subjects, given sufficient exposure to a social environment, ordinarily develop a remarkable ability to identify intentions and emotional states, to make complex judgments concerning the relation of intentions to belief states, and to make fine discriminations between genuine and feigned emotional displays.[12] (The qualifier "ordinarily" is needed because Baron-Cohen, in company with many other researchers, understands autism in terms of a ToM deficit—hence, the title of his provocative book, *Mindblindness*.) Although our ToM capacity is innate and found across diverse cultures, it does not develop full blown or in isolation. Rather, like another inherently social adaptation, the language instinct, its normal development requires social interaction throughout a critical developmental period. Children develop ToM only gradually, from about ten months to five or six years old, although very young children exhibit a marked curiosity about the mental states of others and even newborns exhibit what Colin Trevarthan calls "primary intersubjectivity."[13]

Like many areas within the cognitive neurosciences, ToM theory has proven a contentious as well as exciting area for research, and several competing models have been proposed. Baron-Cohen (in common with Jerry Fodor and Alan Leslie) takes a modular approach: his Theory of Mind Mechanism (ToMM) constitutes a discrete mental module, localizable in the brain and thus susceptible to the type of selective impairment he sees in autism. It works in concert with a network of related modules that emerge one after the other in a normal developmental sequence. First comes an intention detector (ID) that allows one to discriminate agents from objects and track the intentions of the former. Next there is an eye-direction detector (EDD) that follows the eye movements of other intentional agents in order to pick out their intentional objects. (I see the teacher looking at me; I see the cat looking at a mouse.) Then comes a shared attention mechanism (SAM) using information passed along from the first two submodules to enter into a "triadic" representational relation (I "stay with" the cat as it continues to hunt the mouse, watching the cat as it watches its prey). Finally, the Theory of Mind Mechanism (ToMM) builds on information from the first three submodules to posit a state of mind behind the perceived behaviors. (The teacher is looking at me because she thinks I'm daydreaming again; the cat is watching the mouse because she's hungry and wants to eat it, or bored and wants to play with it, or both. And because she's evolutionarily adapted to do so, just as I'm adapted to notice, take interest in, and make assumptions about the mental states behind her intentional behavior.)

In competition with the modular and evolutionary account best known from *Mindblindness*, cognitive psychologists have proposed a "simulation" approach to ToM and still a third alternative, prominently advocated by Alison Gopnik, that posits a much more capacious and flexible cognitive domain dedicated to theory making. Gopnik, who calls her view "theory theory," does recognize the innate predisposition toward sociality and the developing child's inborn propensity to seek out faces and gazes that play key roles in Baron-Cohen's evolutionary account.[14] Where Baron-Cohen posits a network of information-processing modules, however, Gopnik sees the growing child as itself a theorist, developing theories to account for the social behaviors around it and discarding them and replacing them with new hypotheses, again in a roughly predictable sequence, in the face of increasingly acute empirical observations. (A younger child might assume that when she can't see the mouse, the cat can't either. An older, more sophisticated child will discard and replace the theory behind this assumption to better take into account what she's learned about differences in perspective: the cat has an online mental representation of the mouse under the couch, even though I can't see it there and thus have no such representation myself.) According to the rival simulation approach, however, human subjects do *not* rely on stored theories or hypotheses in order to make sense of social behavior. Rather, as Robert Gordon writes, they "use the resources of their own minds to simulate the psychological etiology of the behavior of others, typically by making decisions within a 'pretend' context."[15] Now, if I were that cat, watching that mouse, what would I be thinking?

Most theory of mind researchers concur, however, in accepting certain well-established observations, even if they interpret the empirical data differently.[16] It is commonly agreed, for example, that interest in other minds emerges "strikingly early" in human infants, indicating that at least some rough precursor to ToM is innate; that ToM helps account for the persistence of what philosophers call "folk psychology" (our "common" sense that other human beings have minds, intentions, perceptions, and emotions commensurate with our own); and that autism represents a ToM deficit (although "autism" represents a spectrum of cognitive disorders and therefore generalization remains controversial). Most researchers agree as well that "mind reading" of the sort studied by ToM researchers is part of a universal core human cognitive endowment and that the sorts of deficits seen in autism can be found across cultures and in all social classes. They also agree in accepting a number of experimental findings indicating that ToM develops in predictable (and therefore testable) ways. Newborns show a marked preference for human faces and voices; by nine months an infant will follow the gaze of a caregiver and point out objects; between two and three years, children begin using mental-state verbs like "see," "think," and "know" and by three they can engage with others in pretend play, mutually sustaining a belief ("this red block is a dog, the orange one is a kitty") that both players know to be false. At four to five years, a major threshold is passed when a child can attribute false beliefs to others while maintaining a contrary belief. ("My brother thinks the candy is all gone, but I know I hid the last piece under the cushion when he wasn't looking.") Other mind-reading feats develop still later: only at six years, for example, can a child make a distinction between another's real emotions and false emotional displays. ("You look like you're mad at me but, I know you're just kidding.") Although "mind reading" does not involve telepathy, it does involve a quite amazing repertoire of cognitive abilities that few other animals can even approximate and that can be selectively impaired, yet can continue to function in the face of other, more global impairments such as early Alzheimer's disease. These abilities have drawn the attention of fiction writers at least since the eighteenth century, with Austen's novels marking a new level of subtlety and sophistication in the representation of mind reading that has proved difficult to surpass since.

Before continuing, one should note that the behaviors described by Austen and other writers in the "high Theory of Mind" tradition do not map precisely onto the behaviors theorized and empirically examined by recent ToM researchers. Matthew Belmonte, an autism researcher who has read and generously commented on the relevant literary criticism, remarks that neuroscientific work on ToM has largely been concerned with the attribution of beliefs rather than the larger spectrum of mental life (intention, volition, and emotion as well as belief) evoked by the term *mind reading*.[17] The neuroscientist's conception of theory of mind may thus prove to be narrower than that of the literary scholar, and the latter may hold on to models (such as the modular ToM "mechanism") that are losing their purchase in the world of laboratory science. These are serious caveats, and Belmonte's article is essential reading for any literary researcher interested in ToM. Still, it can be argued that the emphasis on beliefs arose in the scientific literature mainly because this area most readily lent itself to empirical testing (as in a whole series of ingenious "false belief" tests).[18] A number of scientific researchers have continued to include a much larger range of mental contents in their discussions of ToM even as they have focused their investigations on belief attribution. Gopnik, for example, broadly defines "theory of mind" in terms of "our understanding of the minds of ourselves and others" and includes experimental studies of beliefs, desires, differences in perspective, pretense and imagination, and emotions (real and simulated) in her 1999 overview of the topic.[19] Gordon, in the same reference work (the *MIT Encyclopedia of Cognitive Science*, or *MITECS*) also writes broadly of "everyday human competence in predicting and explaining human behavior, including the capacity to ascribe mental states."[20] Baron-Cohen, surveying fifteen years of ToM research in an overview published in 2000, also proffers a generous definition: "By theory of mind we mean being able to infer the full range of mental states (beliefs, desires, intentions, imagination, emotions, etc.) that cause action."[21] Such inclusive definitions have persisted well into the first decade of the twentieth century. A group of neuropsychological researchers writing in the journal *Science* in 2007, for example, define "theory of mind" as "taking other persons' perspectives and inferring other people's thoughts, feelings, and intentions," a definition as broad as any found in cognitive literary studies.[22] At the very least, cognitive and neuroscientific work on Theory of Mind has inspired literary scholars to notice and describe a range of literary representations, concerning states of consciousness in particular and nonverbal character interaction in general, that had long remained largely invisible to literary criticism and narrative poetics, and yet now seem integral to any robust understanding of what Palmer calls "fictional consciousness."

If "mind reading" is indeed (as the neuroscientific researcher Rebecca Saxe puts it), "innate, universal, and species-specific," then the contextual factors that would have helped select for it, over evolutionary time, must be sought for in the social environment.[23] Human beings, with their uniquely complex and flexible social arrangements, require insight into the intentions and emotions of others for their own self-preservation and for reproductive success. And yet the minds of others are notoriously closed to direct access, as Austen's Emma herself points out in a conversation with Frank Churchill. "Oh! do not imagine that I expect an account of Miss Fairfax's sensations from you, or from any body else. They are known to no human being, I guess, but herself."[24] (Here, as elsewhere, Austen's characters not only engage in attempts at "reading" other characters' minds but they comment on these activities as well.) Given what might be called the inaccessibility problem, then, social agents must make do instead with forming reasonable interpretations based on indirect evidence, as Emma and Frank in fact are doing in relation to Jane throughout the middle part of the novel. On account of the reticence and indirection required by the social mores of the time in relation to erotic matters and "courtship" in general, much of this evidence is by default nonverbal—looks, blushes, facial expressions—or verbal but nonsemantic (vocal tones that may tell more than the words themselves). Making things more complicated, as well as more interesting, is that Frank, for the most part, does *not* really need to "read" Jane, for he already knows much more than he lets on to Emma; in fact, a good deal of his "mind reading" is feigned, a matter of social manipulation, and thus all the more noteworthy. Emma, in contrast, by this point in the novel has already been exposed as a spectacularly unreliable interpreter of social cues—even when these bear directly on the fortunes of Emma and those she holds dear. Hapless in her prior attempts to read the mind of so transparent a character as Mr. Elton, Emma can hardly hope to prove a match for an archmanipulator like Frank.

Emma's comic misunderstanding of Mr. Elton's romantic intentions—comic to the reader, less so to Emma and her protégée Harriet Smith—has often been read in ways that highlight the disparity between the ease with which Emma solves verbal riddles and her difficulty in grasping obvious social cues. Her considerable verbal intelligence contrasts with a striking lack of what would now be termed social intelligence. Less attention has been given, however, to what constitutes the social cues in question and to why readers feel these cues *are* obvious, given the indirection mandated by the bourgeois courtship rules of the period. These cues turn out to be, in fact, just the kinds of behavior of interest to ToM theorists: expressive glances, vocal inflections, gazes directed in one direction and not in another, feigned and genuine emotional displays. Emma, "too busy and eager in her own previous conceptions and views," can neither "hear" Elton "impartially" nor "see him with clear vision" (93); she misses, in other words, crucial nonverbal messages no less than verbal ones. John Knightley, in contrast, can read Elton's face and eyes with an accuracy that would seem uncanny if readers did not implicitly take human "mind-reading" skills for granted. His (correct) theory that Elton desires Emma derives from such evidence as Elton's nonverbal behavior on being offered a ride in the same carriage as the clever, handsome, and rich young lady in question: "Mr. Elton was to go, and never had his broad face expressed more pleasure than at this moment; never had his smile been stronger; nor his eyes more exulting than when he looked at her" (93). John Knightley's adept mind-reading abilities (a trait he shares with his brother) stand out, however, in relation to Elton's and Emma's notable failures in the scenes to follow. Finally getting a clue as to Elton's intention, Emma gives him "such a *look* as she thought must restore him to his senses" (105, my emphasis). It doesn't. Told by Emma, shortly after, that she has attributed his advances to an interest in Harriet, Elton refuses to believe her: "No! . . . I am sure you have *seen* and understood me" (109, again my emphasis). Emma's shocked and troubled silence gives rise to another glaring failure of social interpretation: "Charming Miss Woodhouse! allow me to interpret this interesting silence. It confesses that you have long understood me" (109–10). Once again, Elton gets things exactly backwards. Yet the irony cuts still deeper for Emma, who must realize that she has seen and *mis*understood all along.

Emma's and Elton's explicit failures to read each others' minds through observing one another's faces and bodies—sensational though these failures are—come late in their relation and receive fairly little narrative attention. In contrast, Frank Churchill's entry into the plot brings with it a pronounced focus on acts of mind reading, no more so than in two chapters—volume 2, chapter 8, and volume 3, chapter 2—that showcase a stunning variety of such behaviors. The classic (and indeed constitutive) mind-reading "mechanisms" described by Baron-Cohen—monitoring other social agents for signs of intentions, watching their eyes and following the direction of their gazes, sharing their attention as it flits from one object (or agent) to another, and extrapolating hypotheses regarding their beliefs and other mental states—all come notably into play. So do some equally interesting feats of social cognition that Baron-Cohen neglects, such as looking for blushes and similar signs of heightened cardiovascular activity or using one's eyes more aggressively to provoke certain behaviors or emotional displays in others. These two chapters give a good sense of what Austen is up to throughout the double marriage plot that will eventually bring Frank together with Jane and Emma with Mr. (George) Knightley.

Making all this much more interesting, of course, is that Frank and Jane, having something to hide, actively resist the interpretive efforts of others, Jane relying mainly on circumspection, Frank on active (and fiendishly clever) deception, including fostering the general assumption that his love interest is not Jane but Emma. Emma herself notices early on how hard Frank is to read: "She must see more of him to understand his ways" (160). To the contrary, the more she sees, the less she understands. Being Emma, however, she actively participates in her own deception, to a degree that eventually makes Frank wonder if *she* is misleading *him*. At the dinner party at the Coles' (the setting for volume 2, chapter 8), however, Frank plays brilliantly to Emma's weaknesses, not only through verbal deception but through nonverbal manipulation as well.

Here are some of the important social puzzles Emma wants to solve that evening: Does the mysterious gift of a piano, delivered to the house where Jane is staying with relatives, mean that Jane is involved with a married man and thus that much less a threat to the local marriage market? Has Harriet recovered socially from the fiasco with Elton? Does Knightley regard Jane as marriageable material? Has Emma jeopardized her own social standing by agreeing to dine with the Coles, whose fortune comes from "trade"? Most importantly, in Emma's mind, the party brings an opportunity of "judging of" Frank's "general manners, and by inference, of the meaning of his manners toward herself"; of "guessing" whether he loves her, and "of fancying what the observations of all those might be," who would see them together in a large social group for the first time (176). News of the piano, however, soon becomes the talk of the evening and draws attention toward Jane, potentially casting suspicion on her secret lover, Frank (who has just returned from a sudden trip to London). But Frank uses a facial expression—a smile—to deftly turn Emma's suspicions toward Jane's alleged married admirer, Mr. Dixon, instead. "Why do you smile?" Emma asks him, and Frank answers, "I smile because you smile, and shall probably suspect whatever I find you suspect," tacitly encouraging her to think the worst of Jane and Mr. Dixon (179). His first real coup of the evening comes when he harnesses a genuine display of emotion—his secret love for Jane—to seemingly prove the sincerity of his concurrence with the Dixon story he has just helped to fix in Emma's mind: "And now I can see it in no other light than as an offering of love" (181). As Emma scans Frank's face, attempting to read his mind, the "conviction seemed real; he looked as if he felt it." Because, having himself bought the piano in London to send to his beloved, he does feel it.

Encouraged by Frank's flattery (which, quite economically, confirms Emma in her misjudgments while passing for flirtation), Emma starts to believe that she "divined what everybody present must be thinking," deriving proof of Frank's interest in herself from his pointed preference of her, deducing confirmation of Mr. Dixon's dalliance with Jane from the latter's "blush of consciousness," and exchanging "smiles of intelligence" with Frank on "first glancing towards" Jane, though "it was most prudent to avoid speech" (182). Speech is readily avoided, thanks to what Baron-Cohen calls the SAM (shared attention mechanism), mutually deployed by Emma and Frank in their knowing looks toward Jane. The SAM, however, proves easier to set in motion than to control, and Frank almost betrays himself when Emma deploys her EDD (eye-direction detector) to catch Frank gazing at Jane. "When Mr. Cole had moved away, and her attention could be restored as before, she saw Frank Churchill looking intently across the room at Miss Fairfax, who was sitting exactly opposite." When Emma rather pointedly asks Frank, "What is the matter," Frank improvises, again playing the fop (his dubious excuse for the London trip was getting his hair cut properly) and nearly overplaying it: "I believe that I have been very rude; but really Miss Fairfax has done her hair in so odd a way—so very odd a way—that I cannot keep my eyes from her. I never saw anything so outrée! Those curls!" (184). Having regained his balance, Frank improvises a second and more stunning coup of social cognitive manipulation, first claiming he will go and "quiz" (tease) Jane on her hair and, moreover, drop in an allusion to Dixon, and then explicitly inviting Emma to engage in further mind reading as he does so: "and you shall see how she takes it;—whether she colours." But when Emma follows Frank's instructions, she finds herself suddenly unable to see Jane's face and eyes, as Frank "had improvidently placed himself exactly between them, exactly in front of Miss Fairfax, she could distinguish nothing" (184). By first inviting Emma to read Jane's body ("and you shall *see* how she takes it") in order to confirm a hypothesis concerning Jane's mental state (Jane's supposed belief that the piano comes from Dixon along with her guilty consciousness of the illicit nature of her relation to him), and then intentionally blocking Emma's view, Frank makes the salience of mind-reading activities in *Emma* manifest in the very act of short-circuiting them.[25] (He also gives himself a chance to exchange knowing looks with Jane while screened from Emma's EDD and SAM.) Or rather, Austen, in representing these activities, helps render her characters more psychologically compelling while stimulating the reader's own mind-reading mechanisms. Here, as so often in *Emma*, mind reading becomes most noticeable in its temporary collapse.

Since everyday mind reading is *not* telepathy but a sort of inspired (or, in cognitive scientific terms, productively constrained) guesswork based on sensory evidence that can be obscured (as here), faked (as in playacting or social deception such as Frank's), or just plain misinterpreted, one should expect it to frequently get things wrong.[26] To quote Frank himself on the subject, "sometimes one conjectures right, and sometimes one conjectures wrong" (200). Yet what keeps social manipulators like Frank on edge is the constant threat that their true intentions will after all prove legible to someone else's mind-reading capabilities, even if that someone's ToMM goes comically awry as often as does Emma's. On the verge of leaving Highgate for a time, Frank stops for a quick farewell to Emma, and—for this once—misled by certain ambiguous signs, he begins to suspect that Emma indeed knows the truth about his intentions toward Jane. Almost (again, just this once) true to his name, Frank comes close to openly confessing all:

> "In short," said he, "perhaps Miss Woodhouse—I think you can hardly be without suspicion"—
> He looked at her, as if wanting to read her thoughts.

As must by now be evident, that is exactly what Frank is trying to do. True to form, however, Emma assumes that Frank must want to confess his love, not for Jane but for Emma. When she replies in a defensively clipped, still ambiguous manner, Frank remains prudently silent for a time: "She believed he was looking at her; probably reflecting on what she had said, and trying to understand the manner" (215). Then Frank, his mind-reading abilities safely back on track, simply sighs. This sigh remains tantalizingly unexplained in the narrative, inviting readers to deploy their own mind-reading mechanisms to interpret it. I read it not only as a sigh of relief—Frank hasn't been found out after all—but simultaneously as a sigh of disappointment: something in Frank *wants* to confess, to stop manipulating Emma, to make things right with her, to finally get to talk with someone, especially an intelligent and sympathetic friend, about his love for Jane. The moment passes, and Frank departs, returning several months later just in time to attend another high visibility social gathering.

The ball that forms the setting for volume 3, chapter 11, stands in a pendant relation to the party held by the Coles. It reunites many of the same characters, again placing them in a kind of social fishbowl, everyone eyeing everyone else in attempts to gauge social standing, to guess at the progress of various romances, and even, in this case, to follow attempts at social revenge. The most prominent addition to the cast is Mrs. Elton, Elton's new wife, whose upstart manners gall Emma to no end and who is in turn galled by her knowledge of Emma's prior attempt to match Elton with Harriet. Again the chapter begins by underscoring the role of gestures, the face, and especially the eyes in conveying mental states and intentions: "though he [Frank] did not say much, his eyes declared that he meant to have a delightful evening" (264). Austen primes this theme again a bit later, as the irrepressible voice of Miss Bates leaves Emma to rely solely on her eyes as she tracks Mrs. Elton's lapses in etiquette: "Her gestures and movements might be understood by anyone who looked on like Emma, but her words . . . were soon lost under the incessant flow of Miss Bates" (266).

The set of dances duly begins, along with an unchoreographed but equally elaborate dance of looks, expressions, and pointed glances. Even before the music starts, characters begin showing a preference for "looking" their meanings rather than stating them. After Frank has chosen to begin the dance with Emma, "his father looked his most perfect approbation of" the gesture (269). As the dancing starts in earnest and the music and footsteps grow louder, glances begin to fly, not only between the partners but throughout the room and across the divide between dancers and lookers-on. Emma, irked that Knightley chooses not to dance, tries to provoke him with her eyes—"Whenever she caught his eye, she forced him to smile"—while Knightley in turn "seemed often observing her" (269). (Their strong ocular connection says something about their hidden feelings for one another, by this point in the novel hidden not so much from the wary reader as from the characters themselves.) Then Emma turns her attention to Harriet only to find her suddenly without a dance partner, in this context a socially awkward position. Emma sees in addition that Mr. Elton, the sole male dancer not on the floor, is making a point of leaving Harriet squarely in her embarrassing dilemma. Worse, Emma must watch Elton and Mrs. Elton blatantly exchange gloating looks over Harriet's discomfort, as they tacitly count on Emma's gaze direction detection and shared attention capacities to make sure she shares Harriet's embarrassment and pain. So

Emma sees, and is meant to see, Mrs. Elton "encouraging" the slight "by significant glances" and must watch in dismay as "smiles of high glee" pass between Elton and his wife. Finally, Emma can take no more and begins to fear that her own body may reveal more of her mental state than she might wish: "She would not look again. Her heart was in a glow, and she feared her face might be as hot" (270–71).

In a preview of the alliance that will help bring the novel to an end, Knightley—whose social status cannot be called into question—chivalrously comes to Emma's aid by condescending to dance with Harriet, thus confounding the Eltons' attempts at further humiliation. Emma, filled with "pleasure and gratitude," cannot wait to acknowledge his kindness, and thanks to Knightley's mind-reading abilities, she doesn't have to: "though too distant for speech, her countenance said much, as soon as she could catch his eye again" (271). Finally, the dancing and supper over, Emma has a chance to converse with Knightley, but the return to verbal communication is facilitated by one last powerful nonverbal exchange: "her eyes invited him irresistibly to come to her and be thanked" (273). Why do Austen's readers automatically accept that eyes alone can convey intentions so accurately, and even so "irresistibly"? Because Austen has endowed her characters with what are now called "Theory of Mind" capacities, and readers unconsciously rely on their own implicit theories of ToM to understand such passages. Who, after all, has ever put the novel down at this point to ask, "Wait! How did Emma just do that? Is she psychic or something?"

In "Consciousness and the Novel," Lodge suggests that the "ability novelists have to create characters, characters often very different from themselves, and to give a plausible account of their consciousnesses, is a special application of Theory of Mind" (42). Austen's *Emma* demonstrates that one of the ways to make a character's consciousness seem real or "plausible" is to represent that character putting his or her own theory of mind to work. Drawing, no doubt, on the example of Samuel Richardson (whose pioneering representation of mind reading in *Clarissa* has been described in detail by Zunshine), Austen delineates some of the ways human beings extrapolate information regarding the mental states and emotional dispositions of others from observing their gesture, expressions, and especially their eye movements.[27] In doing so, Austen makes common cause with some of the most influential psychological thinking of her time, most significantly, perhaps, with the "common sense" philosophy of Thomas Reid. In his *Essays on the Intellectual Powers of Man*, Reid had argued in 1786, much as theory of mind theorists would two centuries later, that even young children, "long before they can reason," manifest an innately driven social intelligence, seeking for and understanding signs of intention and emotion in those around them.[28] They assume that those with whom they interact are "intelligent beings" like themselves: that is, they early develop a theory of mind. The preverbal child, Reid states, "can, by signs, ask and refuse, threaten and supplicate. It clings to its nurse in danger, enters into her grief and joy, is happy in her soothing and caresses, and unhappy in her displeasure: that these things cannot be without a conviction in the child that the nurse is an intelligent being, I think must be granted" (633–34).

Reid goes on to argue that human beings rely throughout their lives on this innate propensity to attribute intentions and emotions to others based on facial expressions, gestures, and extrasemantic vocal tones: "certain features of the countenance, sounds of the voice, and gestures of the body, indicate certain thoughts and dispositions of mind" (635). The postulate of such a nonverbal language of "natural signs," innate and universally understood, played a key role not only in "common sense" philosophy but in a number of early neuroscientific accounts of mind as well, including those of Matthew Baillie and Charles Bell in England and Pierre-Jean-Georges Cabanis and F. J. Gall on the Continent.[29] These Romantic-era brain scientists not only make the "natural language" of expression integral to their accounts of pervasive mind-body interaction (if not identity), but they give it a neurological basis. Baillie, for example, holds that distinct human emotions are "conveyed along nerves" to various muscle groups in the body, "producing a change in the countenance and attitude, which is expressive of emotion. This becomes a natural language," innate and universal ("not connected with any arbitrary customs of society").[30] This natural, nonverbal language becomes, in turn, a key component of the dramatic theory of Baillie's sister, Joanna Baillie, who in her introduction to the *Plays on the Passions* calls for a smaller, more intimate theater enabling a more "natural" acting style, one taking advantage of the innate language of expression rather than the overdrawn, artificial stage gestures demanded by the cavernous theaters of the time.[31]

If emotions, intentions, and states of mind can be interpreted from their bodily manifestations, then could mimicking the bodily signs oneself give one special insight into another's thought process? This intriguing inversion of ToM theory, and with it a special variant of mind reading, can by found in Edmund Burke's *Philosophical Enquiry into the Sublime and Beautiful.* Burke, whose "physiological" aesthetics presume extensive mind-body interaction and look forward to the embodied psychologies of the Romantic era, suggests in the *Enquiry* that "when the body is disposed . . . to such emotions as it would acquire by the means of a certain passion; it will of itself excite something very like that passion in the mind."[32] He cites the example of the "celebrated physiognomist Campanella," whose researches into human expression helped make him a brilliant mimic. "When he had a mind to penetrate into the inclinations of those he had to deal with, he composed his face, his gesture, and his whole body, as nearly as he could, into the exact similitude of the person he intended to examine, and then carefully observed what turn of mind he seemed to acquire by this change." Using his own body to read the embodied minds of others, Campanella could "enter into the dispositions and thoughts of people, as effectually as if he had been changed into the very men" (162). Austen's contemporary James Hogg gives this special version of mind reading a fictional twist (and demonic aura) in *The Private Memoirs and Confessions of a Justified Sinner*, published a few years after *Emma* in 1824. Hogg's character Gil-Martin, a stand-in for the devil, claims powers at least equal to those of Campanella. "If I contemplate a man's features seriously, mine own gradually assume the very same appearance and character. And what is more, by contemplating a face minutely, I not only attain the very same likeness, but, with the likeness, I attain the very same ideas as well as the same mode of arranging them, so that, you see, by looking at a person attentively, I by degrees assume his likeness, and by assuming his likeness I attain to the possession of his most secret thoughts."[33] Here mind reading does become infallible, perhaps understandably, given Gil-Martin's occult powers. Significantly, however, even Hogg's devil does not engage in outright telepathy but instead employs his own highly specialized version of reading the mind through the medium of the body.

Austen's representation of the more quotidian sort of mind reading throughout *Emma* may also be read in terms of her distinctive experience as a woman writer in an era that placed inordinate social burdens on female subjects. In addition to the example of Richardson's *Clarissa*, "natural language" theories like Reid's and Bell's, and her own famously keen observation of social behaviors, Austen could have drawn on her experience as a "middling class" woman of the times. Conduct book writers are now notorious for having enjoined their young female readers to maintain a "meek and silent" demeanor in public and to communicate nonverbally instead.[34] According to John Gregory, in his *Father's Legacy*, women should remain "silent in public" but make use of meaningful looks and facial expressions instead of speaking: "One may take a share in conversation without uttering a syllable."[35] James Fordyce, in the *Sermons to Young Women*, counsels women to "read" the men around them, the better to please them without unnecessary verbal exchange: "Your business chiefly is to read Men, in order to make yourself agreeable and useful."[36] Rousseau, in book 5 of *Emile*, holds that women's true language is a bodily, nonverbal one: "Why do you consult their mouth when it is not the mouth which ought to speak? Consult their eyes, their color, their breathing, their fearful manner, their soft resistance."[37] Women writers did not need to discover the importance of mind reading and nonverbal communication on their own; these behaviors were prescribed to them as part of their official social duty.[38]

What does it mean, then, to read *Emma* in light of recent Theory of Mind theory? Certainly not that Austen, relying on a mysterious and unexamined faculty called "intuition," somehow "anticipated" a body of scientific work on largely unconscious mental mechanisms that cognitive researchers would not posit for at least another 150 years. Nor yet that Austen single-handedly recruited her deservedly famous powers of social observation to discriminate and represent social behaviors invisible to her contemporaries and to most everyone else up until the late 1970s and the publication of Premack and Woodruff's paper "Does the Chimpanzee Have a Theory of Mind?"[39] Earlier models of activities closely aligned to, if not wholly identifiable with, what would later be called mind reading made part of the "natural philosophy" of Austen's own time and could be found in well-known and readily available works like Burke's *Enquiry* and Reid's *Essays*. Novelists had already begun to explore this area, most strikingly Richardson in *Clarissa*, and the significance of reading mental events through their bodily manifestations had become a topic for literary and dramatic theory by the publication of Baillie's "Introductory Discourse" in 1798. The conduct book tradition, in addition, focused the attention of women writers like Baillie and Austen on the very activities—meaningful looks, unspoken displays of interest and assent in conversation, silently "reading" others through tracking their nonverbal behaviors—that would encourage the discrimination and representation of theory of mind phenomena.

Why not, then, explicate these phenomena in *Emma* entirely in terms that would have been familiar or at least available to Austen herself; why bring in recent ToM theory at all? In a case like this, a model (or set of related models) from cognitive science can act as a new lens with which to focus on material—including aspects of Austen's fictional technique and trends in her contemporary intellectual culture—that have long eluded critical attention. It can as well provide useful terms for describing such freshly perceived effects. These terms prove no less useful for criticism because Austen would not have used or recognized them—she would no more have recognized terms from narrative poetics or feminist theory equally valuable in describing her distinctive literary achievement. Indeed, some of these terms may enable the discrimination and enhance the discussion of specific instances where Austen's artistic observation and technique allow for greater nuance and particularization than what one finds in the psychological discourses of her era. Consider, as a final instance, how much more readily one could analyze and describe the intersubjective drama of a passage like the following once one has been apprised of how tracking gaze direction and sharing another's attention contribute to attempts at mind reading.

> They were entering the hall. Mr. Knightley's eyes had preceded Miss Bates's in a glance at Jane. From Frank Churchill's face, where he thought he saw confusion suppressed or laughed away, he had involuntarily turned to her's; but she was indeed behind, and too busy with her shawl. Mr. Weston had walked in. The two other gentlemen waited at the door to let her pass. Mr. Knightley suspected in Frank Churchill the determination of catching her eye—he seemed watching her intently—in vain, however, if it were so—Jane passed between them into the hall, and looked at neither. (287)

Looking, looking at looking, looking down to avoid being looked at, "catching" another's eye, or trying to, and looking on at the whole exchange of looks given and withheld: such nonverbal behaviors are just as crucial to the social dynamics and psychological drama of *Emma* as the verbal exchanges and linguistic puzzles that earlier criticism has made so much of. Moreover, since Austen explores these behaviors using the flexible medium of fictional representation and technique, rather than the necessarily limiting means of the controlled experiment, she can place them within a more holistic account of nonverbal social cognition, one that includes psychophysiological phenomena such as blushing, the proactive use of the eyes to create (not just observe) responses, and attempts at concealment (like Jane's sudden interest in her shawl), in addition to the mind-reading behaviors described by cognitive researchers today. Building on, extending, and refining Romantic-era understandings of nonverbal interaction and social cognition, Austen creates a complex, nuanced picture of mind reading that only gains in richness by comparison with current Theory of Mind theory.

CHAPTER SIX

Romantic Incest

Literary Representation and the Biology of Mind

Incest—or rather, the avoidance of incest—has struck a number of influential thinkers as providing the key to understanding human culture. J. G. Frazer made the universality of the incest prohibition central to his demonstration of deep similarities among so-called primitive and modern cultures alike in his 1910 study, *Totemism and Exogamy*. Sigmund Freud went further and made the repression or sublimation of incestuous desires crucial both for the development of individual psychic life and for the rise of human society in works like *Totem and Taboo* (1913). Claude Lévi-Strauss, in *Elementary Structures of Kinship* (1949), made the incest prohibition the "fundamental step because of which, by which, but above all in which, the transition from nature to culture is accomplished."[1] Over the past decade, the ubiquity of incest avoidance has proved no less significant for those seeking to establish the biological foundations of culture or to call radically into question the distinction between nature and culture. In *Human Universals* (1991), Donald E. Brown presents the Darwinian approach to the universality, "or near-universality," of the incest taboo as an exemplary case of how biological anthropology should best be theorized and empirically tested.[2] Steven Pinker, distilling the new field of evolutionary psychology for popular consumption in *How the Mind*

Works (1997), includes an anti-Freudian account of incest avoidance that covers much of the same ground as does Brown.[3] Illustrating his theory of "gene-culture co-evolution," E. O. Wilson, the founder of "sociobiology," presents still another, updated version of the evolutionary theory of incest avoidance in his ambitious book *Consilience* (1998).[4]

Creative artists too have long recognized the universality of the incest prohibition and its role in defining the difference—or congruence—between humans and other animals. The incestuous brother in Francis Beaumont and John Fletcher's *A King and No King* (1611) claims that to "cure" his lovesickness, one must first "Orethrow Divinity, all morall Lawes,/And leave mankinde as unconfinde as beasts."[5] Literary violations of the incest taboo—at least outside of pornography—are anything but casual: they broach the fundamental laws of human society and raise the question of a shared human nature. In Coleridge's metaphorical terms, the incest prohibition is the "Citadel, that contains the very *Palladium* of the Human Race," its tutelary shrine and safeguard.[6] Although the stakes are uniformly high, however, the representation of incest takes on different forms in different cultural moments. As James Twitchell remarks in *Forbidden Partners*, his extensive study of incest in modern culture, the Romantic era (especially in Britain) stands out both for the "frisson" and the self-consciousness that it adds to the portrayal of incestuous desire.[7] Many pre-Romantic literary treatments do not speak of conscious desire for incestuous intercourse. In *Oedipus Rex*, in the *Nibelungenlied*, in eighteenth-century novels like Daniel Defoe's *Moll Flanders* and Fanny Burney's *Evelina*, the incestuous love (actual or apparent) is inspired *before* the revelation of any kinship bond. The same holds true for the British Gothics that feature incestuous couplings for their shock value and to further intensify an atmosphere of moral squalor. Ambrosio, in Matthew Lewis's *The Monk* (1796), learns that Antonia is his sister only after raping and murdering her. Edmund in Horace Walpole's Gothic drama *The Mysterious Mother* (1768) also learns only after the fact that he has coupled with his sister (who, thanks to an earlier and, on his side, unknowingly incestuous encounter, also happens to be his daughter).

In contrast to these examples of what is called "unconscious" or, better, "unwitting" incest, the incestuous heroes and heroines of the Romantic tradition quite knowingly pursue their forbidden loves. This is especially true of portrayals of sibling incest which, as several critics have remarked, stands as the quintessential form of Romantic incest.[8] It is not only the conscious pursuit of prohibited relations, however, that sets the Romantic representation of sibling incest apart from eighteenth-century and Gothic treatments like Defoe's or Lewis's. A second and equally crucial difference is that Romantic writers present sibling incest not as a perversion or accidental inversion of the ideal sibling relation but as an extension and intensification of it.[9] As opposed to the unwittingly incestuous siblings of most earlier traditions, who have grown up apart and do not meet before the age of sexual maturity, Romantic incestuous couples tend instead to share a history going back to infancy (although it may be temporarily disrupted during early adolescence). Indeed, so strong is the power of shared childhood experiences that adopted siblings, or foster siblings, or even neighbors who grew up together tend to have the same valence in Romantic narratives as do siblings by blood. The rootedness of incestuous desire in early childhood experience, in fact, makes a psychobiological reading of Romantic sibling incest all but irresistible, although to date no extended treatment of the subject has even considered such an approach.

"More than" Siblings: Romantic Incest and Childhood Bonds

Fictional texts in the British Romantic tradition feature various kinds of sibling (or quasi-sibling) relationships, all tending to follow the same narrative trajectory, from a shared childhood to a tragic end. The relation can involve full siblings (as in Percy Shelley's *Laon and Cythna* [1817] and implicitly in Byron's *Manfred* [1817]), half siblings (as in Byron's *Bride of Abydos* [1813] as originally planned), first cousins (the published *Bride of Abydos* and the 1818 version of Mary Shelley's *Frankenstein*), adopted siblings (Robert Southey's *Thalaba* [1801], the 1831 *Frankenstein*, and Percy Shelley's revision of *Laon and Cythna* as *The Revolt of Islam* [1818]), or neighbors raised as virtual brother and sister (the "Vaudracour and Julia" episode from Wordsworth's 1805 *Prelude*). In all of these cases, the siblings or quasi siblings are reared together, become erotically involved, and are separated by death. It is remarkable that, in the three texts that were revised or redesigned under editorial pressure, the weakening of the kinship tie does not alter the couple's fate or much diminish the aura of an incestuous relation. In a series of related texts, including Wordsworth's *White Doe of Rylstone* (1815) and Walter Scott's *Waverley* (1814), a brother and sister share an unusually intense sibling bond and, although they do not become erotically entangled, are nevertheless separated by death at a point when they would otherwise be left together in exile or isolation. Mary Shelley's "The Brother and Sister" (1832) follows the same pattern up to the tragic denouement, then veers away from the brother's imminent death by giving the sister an appropriate (that is, exogamous) erotic object. For Romantic writers, sibling attachment fuses with sexual desire to constitute an idealized erotic love, yet death disrupts or closely follows upon the consummation of that love.

Childhood attachment, going back to the infancy of one or both lovers, typically gets highlighted rather than downplayed. In the published *Bride of Abydos*, Selim and Zuleika are raised as half siblings; although worries about censorship ("the times") induced Byron to "alter their consanguinity & confine them to cousinship," they remain siblings in effect as well as (for the great part of their childhood and youth) in belief.[10]

> What other hath Zuleika seen
> From simple childhood's earliest hour?
>   What other can she seek to see
> Than thee, companion of her bower,
>   The partner of her infancy?
> These cherish'd thoughts with life begun.[11]

When Selim reveals their true relationship along with his erotic feelings, he becomes for Zuleika not something different from her brother but something more: "no more—yet now my more than brother" (II.22.502). Victor Frankenstein similarly describes Elizabeth as "my more than sister—the beautiful and adored companion of all my occupations and my pleasures."[12] In Southey's *Thalaba*, the hero feels a more than sibling love for his adopted sister: "Oneiza called him brother; and the youth / More fondly than a brother loved the maid."[13] Wordsworth's Vaudracour and Julia, though kin neither by blood nor adoption, are raised together "from their cradles up"—"Friends, playmates, twins in pleasure."[14] As Wordsworth's metaphor implies, a shared childhood promises to collapse difference into sameness. Laon describes Cythna as his "shadow," a "second self";[15] Manfred describes Astarte obsessively in terms of likeness—in appearance, in voice, in her pursuits, her "wanderings," her "mind."[16] Whether or not building on innate similarities, common childhood associations within a shared environment promote virtual identity despite sexual difference.

That result is just what one would expect according to associationist psychology, the influential social constructionist theory of the time. As David Hartley had written in *Observations on Man* (1749), "If beings of the same nature . . . be exposed for an indefinite time to the same impressions and associations, all their particular differences will, at last, be over-ruled, and they will become perfectly similar, or even equal" (1: 82).[17] Since the mind is considered most "ductile" in early childhood, siblings—sharing the same basic "nature" and the same early environment and exposed to the same series of "impressions"—stand the greatest chance of becoming "perfectly similar." Since (according to sympathy theory, an outgrowth of associationist psychology) sympathy relies on a prior sense of identification, those who share early experiences and perceive one another as "like" have the best foundation for a loving relationship. "A basis this for deep and solid love," Wordsworth writes of Vaudracour and Julia's shared childhood associations, "And endless constancy, and placid truth" (9.576–77). By extension, it becomes all but impossible to replicate this effect among lovers who meet at an age of sexual maturity. "The companion of our childhood always possesses a certain power over our minds," Victor Frankenstein explains of his bond with Elizabeth, "which hardly any later friend can obtain" (212). Intensifying the bond of shared associations and resulting likeness, moreover, the Romantic writer adds the innumerable mental traces of a budding mutual affection itself. "And still of every dream," Southey writes of Thalaba, "Oneiza formed a part,/And hope and memory made a mingled joy" (IV.4). The shared isolation—from the rest of the family and from the world—that characterizes so many of these sibling or quasi-sibling couples only intensifies the effect of early associations. As Fergus tells Waverley, shortly before the execution that prevents him from joining his sister in exile, "you can never know the purity of feeling which combines two orphans, like Flora and myself, left alone as it were in the world, and being all in all to each other from infancy."[18]

Yet "purity" does not very well convey the sexual element of affectionate feelings predicated on likeness, intensified by a history of mutual love, and heightened by the tensions and desires set into play by sexual difference. There is something distinctly prurient in Southey's description of the growing love between Thalaba and Oneiza:

> She call'd him Brother; was it sister-love
>   For which the silver rings
> Round her smooth ankles and her tawny arms
>   Shone daily brightened? for a brother's eye
>   Were her long fingers tinged?   (III.25)

Adopting an associationist language of "irradicable" impressions, Mary Shelley declares of Flora's near-fatal love for Lorenzo, in "The Brother and Sister," that "reverence and love for him had been moulded into the substance of her soul from infancy." But "reverence" does not obstruct the emergence of a "more than" familial affection on either side: "and yet there was mingled a something beyond, pertaining to their difference of sex."[19] This "something beyond," when allowed to fully develop, paradoxically comes to represent the ultimate fulfillment of sibling love and yet equally to demand its disruption, through the death, often quite violent and sometimes ritualistic, of one or both partners.

In *Thalaba*, "Azrael, the Angel of Death" takes Oneiza on her wedding night, just at the point when the foster siblings would consummate their technically licit desire. The Sultan to whom Thalaba confides his story, however, opines that "for some untold crime / Judgement had thus stricken him," leaving the implication that the union of virtual siblings indeed had a criminal taint (VIII.1). Victor Frankenstein feels "horror and dismay" at the idea of his (already long deferred) "union" with Elizabeth, and they too find their wedding night tragically interrupted (151). Vaudracour and Julia manage to consummate their love and produce a child out of wedlock, but Vaudracour gets thrown into prison, Julia is "immured" in a convent, and the infant, restored to Vaudracour, mysteriously dies "by some mistake, / Or indiscretion of the father" (9.839, 908–9). Both Byron and Shelley, who seem to hold up incestuous love as an ideal union transcending "artificial opinions or institutions," bring their sibling lovers to tragic ends as well, a glaring inconsistency noted by Twitchell.[20] "I loved her, and destroy'd her," Manfred darkly pronounces of Astarte (II.2.117); Selim is gunned down the night he reveals his desire to Zuleika—by her (and his adoptive) father. Laon and Cythna, separated after a single night of dizzying passion, are reunited only to be burnt on an expiatory pyre, consumed together on a "couch of snakes, and scorpions, and the fry / Of centipedes and worms" (X.38.8–9). Shelley also alludes to the death by fire of a sibling-lover in *Rosalind and Helen* (1819), a poem that narrates the unwitting incestuous love between Rosalind and her half brother, who conveniently drops dead with horror when he learns the truth about their blood relation on their wedding day.[21]

Trying to make sense of the tragic element of Romantic incest, critics (myself included) have tended to fall back on Freudian models, resorting to notions of subliminal "guilt" or the "unconscious" horror of incest.[22] It's difficult to understand, however, why creative artists should be able to put aside their guilt or horror long enough to idealize sexual love between siblings but not sufficiently to give the lovers the happy endings they seem so richly to deserve. Freud's notion that the "primitive" ritual punishments described by Frazer (and uncannily evoked by Percy Shelley) survive in the "horror of incest" felt in modern psychic life depends, moreover, on accepting some version of Freud's racial unconscious, a step very few critics, even those psychoanalytically inclined, would now explicitly want to take.[23] Worse, it's still harder to see why such unconscious guilt or horror, assuming it exists, would apply to relations between foster siblings or to first-cousin unions (licit in many cultures and featured unproblematically in Romantic-era novels like Jane Austen's *Mansfield Park* and Susan Ferrier's *Marriage*), much less to unions between unrelated children like Vaudracour and Julia. A rival theory, however, developed contemporaneously with those of Freud and Frazer, does offer to account, to begin with, for the equivalence found in these texts between sibling and quasi-sibling sexual relations. This theory, which remains today foundational to biological understandings of human incest aversion, was first proposed in 1891 by the Finnish anthropologist Edward Westermarck in his *History of Marriage*.

Incest, Evolution, and the Return to Westermarck

In his analysis of the incest prohibition, Westermarck took an approach directly opposite to Freud's. Instead of beginning by assuming the inevitability of sexual attraction between family members, Westermarck was instead struck with the "remarkable absence of erotic feelings between persons living very closely together from childhood," for whom "sexual indifference is combined with the positive feeling of aversion when the act is thought of."[24] He saw this as an "innate tendency" most likely inherited from the "lower animals" (2: 195–97), a psychological mechanism with a "deep biological foundation" and with the adaptive purpose of minimizing the "detrimental" effects of "in-breeding" (2: 218, 236). For Westermarck, this mechanism, whatever its precise character, was evoked by early association rather than by the intuitive recognition of a blood-tie; it was found among "housemates" whether or not they were siblings by blood (2: 193). Where half siblings share a father, and therefore are brought up by their respective mothers in different households, no aversion would be expected; among "foster-siblings," on the other hand, whose "social relations . . . have been exactly similar to those of blood-relatives of corresponding degree," sexual indifference should hold and marriage should seem "unnatural and objectionable" (2: 199, 206). Attacked by both Frazer and Freud, Westermarck stood his ground through successive editions of his book, but his account of incest aversion caught on only briefly before becoming eclipsed by theories grounded in psychoanalysis and cultural anthropology.

At a time when Charles Darwin's star has been rising almost as fast as Freud's has been sinking, however, Westermarck's notions have come due for a major revaluation. As Brown points out, Westermarck had presented a "straightforward Darwinian view" of the matter, assuming "continuity" among humans and other animals rather than the fundamental divergence hypothesized by Freud, reasoning that mating habits would evolve to maximize fitness and seeking a biological explanation for a specieswide psychological characteristic.[25] Moreover, by the time Brown and others came to reconsider Westermarck, biological anthropologists had claimed to find new evidence for his theory. As critics (and responsible adherents) of evolutionary approaches to anthropology and psychology like to point out, most evolutionary hypotheses cannot be tested among humans, as they can among fruit flies or macaques. It just doesn't seem ethical, say, to rear significant numbers of prospective sexual partners together and then see what happens when they are free, or even encouraged, to marry. Yet in several culturally distinct cases, in Taiwan, Lebanon, and in the early phase of the kibbutz movement in Israel, that is precisely what was tried.

In the *sim-pua* form of marriage, for example, found in Taiwan and various districts in South China, children are contracted to one another in early childhood; the bride, often still in her infancy, is adopted into the groom's family to grow up at his side. As Arthur Wolf has exhaustively demonstrated in research conducted over twenty-five years, these marriages exhibit a classic "Westermarck effect." In cases when the bride is adopted by three years of age, the contracted couples try to back out of the destined marriage, their unions have a low fertility rate compared to control groups, and a surprisingly high number end in divorce, given the strong social pressures to remain married.[26] The practice of *bint 'amm* marriage in certain parts of the Arab world, studied most thoroughly in Jordan, involves marrying first cousins who have grown up as virtual siblings. These marriages too inspire resistance, have high rates of breakup, and produce comparatively few offspring. In the early days of the Israeli kibbutzim, unrelated children of both sexes were raised together from infancy. None brought together in the first few years of life ever married, or, it is claimed, engaged in mature sexual relations, despite the lack of any taboo against it and the opportunities presented by proximity and familiarity.[27] According to Westermarck, of course, "proximity" is just the problem (2: 205).

Other investigators have looked at clinical and epidemiological studies of incest in light of the Westermarck hypothesis. (Westermarck himself readily acknowledged that incestuous sexual relations sometimes took place; he was interested in accounting for their relative infrequency, not in demonstrating their impossibility.) If early and regular domestic exposure triggers some sort of negative sexual imprinting in young children, and perhaps a corresponding protective response in caregivers as well, one would expect occurrences of incest to occur most frequently where one finds the least early contact (and, since incestuous sex is often unwilling, where differences in social power are greatest as well). As the psychiatrist Mark Erickson has pointed out in a review of the relevant studies, stepfathers are far more likely to pursue incestuous relations than biological fathers, and biological fathers involved in care giving are less likely to commit incest than biological fathers who have had little early exposure to their daughters.[28] (Stepfathers who *have* taken a large role in raising their infant stepdaughters, on the other hand, are no more likely to commit incest than biological fathers.) Step-siblings brought together after both have grown out of early childhood are much more likely to form incestuous couples than siblings raised together from infancy, and full siblings who have been separated are more likely to become sexually involved than those who have remained together. Incest between children and their mothers (where early exposure is assumed to be greatest) turns out to be the rarest form of all. Interestingly, the two biographical cases most often cited in studies of Romantic incest, Byron's involvement with his half sister Augusta and the alleged (but never conclusively documented) sexual feelings between William and Dorothy Wordsworth, both fit this pattern neatly. William and Dorothy, who certainly had an intense loving relationship but never seem to have become sexually involved, lived together in their early years, were then separated, and became housemates and travel companions at the time of Dorothy's late adolescence: almost a recipe for an overheated sibling relationship stopping somewhere short of actual incest.[29] Byron and Augusta, on the other hand, who do seem to have engaged in sexual relations, grew up in separate households. As Byron himself (somewhat archly) explained, "Never having been much together, we are naturally more attached to each other."[30]

Could one apply the Westermarck hypothesis retrospectively to the "data" provided by fictive portrayals of sibling love in the British Romantic period? The prospect is certainly tempting. Mary Shelley comes close to suggesting such a hypothesis herself as Alphonse Frankenstein, Victor's long-suffering father, seeks to account for his son's seeming coolness to Elizabeth. "You were attached to each other from your earliest infancy; you studied together, and appeared, in disposition and tastes, entirely suited to one another. But so blind is the experience of man, that what I conceived to be the best assistants to my plan, may have entirely destroyed it. You, perhaps, regard her as your sister, without any wish that she might become your wife" (150–51). The chastened foster father of a *sim-pua* bride could scarcely put it better. One critic seeking to reground literary studies on evolutionary principles, Joseph Carroll, has in fact cited the Westermarckian revival in considering the relation of Catherine and her adoptive brother Heathcliff in *Wuthering Heights*, a coupling that bears distinct similarities to Romantic depictions of sibling incest.[31] Encouraged by the "findings" presented by "recent evolutionary research" on incest avoidance, Carroll concludes that Heathcliff and Catherine, "raised as brother and sister, are not engaged in a primarily sexual liaison as adults" and that critics who see their relation in steamier terms can only be "erroneously importing" an incestuous reading into an innocent (if "histrionic") text.[32]

Unfortunately for Carroll—or for any simplistic attempt to uncover literary "Westermarck effects"—fictional representations just don't work that way. Like dreams, fictive works can bear any number of possible relations to the rules and regularities of daily experience, sometimes giving us the inverse of the lived world.[33] If Emily Brontë is at liberty to people the Yorkshire moors with ghosts, why not incestuous foster siblings as well? If one can imagine a sphinx, why not a wittingly incestuous Oedipus, however "unnatural" either might appear to an evolutionary biologist? Carroll tries to get around this by surmising that Brontë has "displaced" (a curious term for an avowed anti-Freudian) her conflicted asexual relationship with her brother Branwell onto her imagined quasi siblings. (Carroll needs to take this step in any case because Catherine and Heathcliff have passed the critical period for negative imprinting when Mr. Earnshaw brings the latter into the household—both children are at least six at the time.) But if Brontë can reimagine her brother as a mysterious, passionate gypsy, she can fantasize their relationship as a sexual one just as readily. Does Carroll think that human beings avoid sex with family members *in their dreams*? If anything, the fictive imagination, with its (adaptive?) capacity to generate counterfactual situations and scenarios without number, would seem still less constrained than the dreaming brain in generating possibilities (however improbable) and impossibilities alike.[34]

There is the added problem—still assuming that there *is* some psychological mechanism that under the right conditions tends to produce a Westermarck effect—that the human mind notoriously lacks insight into its own workings. Most cognitive scientists and neurophilosophers agree with Freud's emphasis on the nonconscious character of much mental experience and the limitations of conscious introspection—if anything, Freud is thought to have underestimated how much mental life must remain unconscious. One could experience Westermarckian imprinting and behave accordingly without ever being conscious of a Westermarck effect. For that matter, one could consciously believe the opposite, as did several generations of psychoanalysts and many of their patients, who were taught to believe that they had once desired and continued subliminally to desire to copulate with their opposite-sex parents, although their behavior probably suggested otherwise. Carroll tries to address this problem with the claim, itself highly Romantic, that literary works manifest "intuitive" knowledge that "often outruns scientific understanding."[35] Reviving the Shelleyan notion of literature as prophecy hardly seems the way to broach a more "scientific" account of the literary imagination. In any case, why do the intuitions of writers like Southey, Wordsworth, Byron, and Shelley fail so abysmally, when (in contrast to the ambiguous treatment in *Wuthering Heights*) they represent "cosocialized" children explicitly feeling sexual desire for one another?

Given its prominent placement as the first major example in his book, Carroll's discussion of incest and *Wuthering Heights* proves misleading in another way. The Westermarck effect, assuming there is one, far from typifies the way that human minds ordinarily function in negotiating social life. As Westermarck argued, incest avoidance almost certainly constitutes an "inheritance" from other mammalian species—comparable to the innate face preference and snake avoidance responses exhibited by infants—and cannot serve as a good example of species-specific human cognitive behavior (2: 237). One important point lost sight of in the 1990s debates on Darwinian "fundamentalism"—in which the "pluralist" Stephen Jay Gould subjected the evolutionary biologist Richard Dawkins, the philosopher Daniel Dennett, and the whole tribe of evolutionary psychologists to the same sweeping criticism—is that Dawkins and Dennett both agree with Gould in stressing the importance of human culture and the exceptional character of human cognition.[36] Evolutionary psychologists, their popularizers (like Pinker), and their literary followers (like Carroll), though featuring Dawkins's "selfish gene" theory as one of their key tenets, ignore Dawkins's claim that human behavior, including sexual behavior, is generally motivated not by detailed, hard-wired or "instinctive" programs (as in some other animals) but by innate "learning strategies" that allow for many different ways to reach the same target values. So in place of the elaborate mate-selection program assumed by evolutionary psychology, for Dawkins human beings are born destined to find orgasms pleasurable but also to develop any number of ways to obtain them. The advantage, Dawkins writes, is that such programming is simpler to genetically engineer and more flexible in response to changes in the environment. (The disadvantage is that the "possibilities of . . . masturbation are not anticipated.")[37] For Dennett, too, whereas "animals are rigidly controlled by their biology, human behavior is *largely* determined by culture, a *largely* autonomous system of symbols and values, growing from a biological base, but growing indefinitely away from it."[38] The Westermarck effect, which would seem to arise from a genetically hard-wired, blindly functioning imprinting program, proves an exception to the generally complex and frequently unpredictable character of human behavior—and it is as an exceptional case that Dawkins himself discusses it.[39] Even if one could locate Westermarck effects at work in fictive texts, this discovery would be anything but exemplary of how evolutionary theory might inform literary analysis.

Since fictive texts by their very nature could not be expected to manifest the effects of a psychological mechanism like that hypothesized by Westermarck, what can one make after all of the coincidence between Westermarck's account and the Romantic portrayal of sibling incest? For these texts do manifest something very like a Westermarck effect, with sexual unions between cosocialized pairs—siblings, half siblings, foster siblings, cousins, and close neighbors alike—repeatedly ending in disaster. In the second half of this chapter, I argue that British Romantic writers did come up with a model for representing sibling incest with remarkable parallels to Westermarck's hypothesis, but not because they were blindly responding to unconscious impulses or intuitions. Rather, it is in the unique and historically specific character of Romantic-era culture and discourse that an interpretation of the literary Westermarck effect must be sought.

Minute Particulars and Human Universals

The early nineteenth century in Britain saw the convergence of a set of social trends and intellectual developments that, taken together, help make sense of the odd narrative trajectory followed by the "more than" siblings of the Romantic imagination: from childhood association, through adolescent romance, to separation and death. Some of these have been noted in earlier studies of Romantic literary incest.[40] Over the course of the eighteenth century, the family unit had become tighter and more affectionate, while childhood (for the middle and upper classes) became more of a protected, playful phase of life. Especially in early childhood (before brothers went off to school), sibling relations were given the opportunity to become warmer, more exclusive, and more intense, as many autobiographical records of the time attest. Associationist theory encouraged Romantic writers to think of early sibling relations as developmentally crucial, forged over a period when impressions would be most intense, their effects most lasting, and their consequences for later social and psychological development most powerful. At the same time, notions of femininity were being revalued and relations between the sexes thrown into crisis; both trends are especially evident in the feminist movement of the 1790s and the backlash that followed. Male writers began to see their sisters (or sister figures) not only as ideal affectionate partners but as sources of inspiration and icons of sensibility, as ideal intellectual companions and ethical guides. (The depictions of Astarte, of Cythna, of Elizabeth Frankenstein, and of Dorothy in "The Sparrow's Nest" all spring to mind.) Like and yet crucially unlike, a locus for egocentric self-reflection and a resource for androgynous self-transformation ("She gave me eyes," William writes of Dorothy), intimately familiar yet provocatively other, sisters may well have seemed ideal erotic partners—at least on paper. For the male Romantic writer or his fictional representative, or for the female writer at once emulating and criticizing the masculine Romantic mode, the love between opposite-gender siblings (or otherwise "cosocialized" pairs) could seem a model and even foundation for mature sexual love rather than its opposite.

When these seemingly ideal unions are imaginatively represented, however, the acknowledgment of their aversive nature comes in the shape of tragedy and separation, preventing, closely following, or nearly coinciding with their consummation. "I shall be with you on your wedding-night," as Frankenstein's monster luridly declares (168). For the reasons given above, it is not especially helpful to view this as the sign of an unconscious recoil, much less as the intuitive expression of a blind psychological mechanism unavailable to consciousness. Romantic-era writers could, however, have become aware of the universal aversion to incest with childhood associates in the same way Westermarck did later in the nineteenth century—through a combination of direct observation and reading in early ethnographies shaped by conducive habits of thought. The portrayal of an idealized erotic sibling relation, that is, gets disrupted by a conflicting but conscious acknowledgment that such relations just don't work, resulting in the fractured, self-canceling narrative pattern outlined above. The passage in *Frankenstein* in which Victor's father articulates something very like the Westermarck hypothesis, in a novel that at other times idealizes the "more than" sibling relation, manifests such inconsistency (or perhaps, in this case, irony) quite starkly.

The same associationist habits of thought that encouraged Romantic writers to imaginatively fuse the sibling and sexual relations could also inspire the contrary notion that cosocialized children would resist sexual unions. As Westermarck notes, his hypothesis had been partly anticipated by Jeremy Bentham in the *Theory of Legislation*, a work first published in a French redaction of Bentham's notes in 1802. Without idealizing the sibling relation in a Romantic manner, Bentham relies on associationist logic in arguing, regarding incest aversion, that housemates would find one another sexually unexciting. "It is very rare that the passion of love is developed within the circle of individuals to whom marriage ought to be forbidden. There needs to give birth to that sentiment a certain degree of surprise, a sudden effect of novelty . . . Individuals accustomed to see each other and to know each other, from an age which is neither capable of conceiving the desire nor of inspiring it, will see each other with the same eyes to the end of life."[41] The same countless associated impressions and remembered feelings, that is, that ground the affection between siblings or other housemates also keep that affection from becoming sexualized. "Their affections," Bentham concludes, "have taken another course, like a river which has dug its bed, and which does not change it." Passion flows at right angles to familiarity.

The Romantic era also saw a renewed interest in universal human characteristics and innate or instinctive behaviors, as well as a novel, politically loaded discourse on the dangers of inbreeding. Enlightenment writers, promoting an abstract conception of human nature based on shared capacities for reason and reflection, tend to downplay concrete universals like incest aversion. To the contrary, writers like Bernard Mandeville and Henry Bolingbroke view incest prohibitions in terms of parochial (if widespread) customary practices with no basis in "natural" law.[42] Montesquieu paints an idealized picture of erotic sibling love in *Lettres persanes* (1721), pitting an affectionate Persian brother and sister against the dominant "Mahométan" society that harshly condemns their union, although (as was widely believed at the time) sibling incest is quite licit for Zoroastrians like Aphéridon and Astarté.[43] In contrast to her namesake in *Manfred*, Astarté eventually manages (after various misadventures) to marry and live happily with her brother.[44] The seeming universality of incest avoidance becomes a special target for Enlightenment writers, who feel that equally rational thought processes can lead, for accidental reasons, to a variety of customary and natural-*seeming* practices.

Although the transition from Enlightenment and Romantic discourse is often—and for good reason—presented in terms of a shift from universals to particulars, from shared human qualities to human differences, another and equally important strain within Romanticism reaffirms certain universals in a more grounded, embodied, ecological fashion.[45] Romantic thinkers tend to devalue abstract conceptions of human reason and to instead view human universals in light of the consequences of a shared basic body plan (and nervous system) attuned to certain basic human experiences and widespread environmental constants. Several influential writers, including J. G. von Herder, Erasmus Darwin, and William Lawrence, give adaptationist arguments for universal human characteristics and, minimizing the distance between humans and other animals, tend to see as instinctive behaviors crucial to survival and procreation. Although none of these writers (to my knowledge) discusses incest aversion, both Darwin and Lawrence note the harmful effects of inbreeding, Lawrence taking as his prime example the degeneration found among the aristocracy.[46] In a notable instance of inconsistency, Percy Shelley (a careful reader of Darwin and for a time Lawrence's patient) condemns the aristocracy as "inbred monsters" in *Laon and Cythna* (XI.22.7), his radical politics momentarily clashing with his idealization of sibling incest. All of these notions were readily available to the writers discussed above, but they rarely feature explicitly in the relevant fictional texts. If, however, a substantial theoretical discussion of incest by a British Romantic writer were extant somewhere, one would expect it to include both associationist reasoning and a respect for concrete human universals, to at least touch on the question of innate avoidance and the biology of inbreeding, and to show an acquaintance with the ethnographical literature both in establishing the rule and noting exceptions to it. Happily, such a document exists, although it has long been overlooked in studies of Romantic incest.

"Nobody Marries Their Sisters": Coleridge on Sibling Incest

Coleridge devoted a long notebook entry in November 1803 to the topic of "Incest" in relation to "Brotherly and Sisterly Love," adding a coda inspired by a dispute on the subject with Southey.[47] Coleridge begins by dismissing William Paley, who had included a brief section on incest in his *Principles of Moral and Political Philosophy* (1785). Paley, reacting to Enlightenment arguments against a natural law prohibiting incest, develops a functionalist approach to the question. He argues that, given the opportunities and temptations presented by the "unreserved intimacy" characteristic of mixed-sex households, chastity could only be preserved within families by a learned and legally enforced "abhorrence of incestuous conjunctions."[48] The incest taboo helps underwrite paternity and the institution of marriage in addition to the stability of the family. For Coleridge, however, the aversion to incest is a matter of far more than legal and utilitarian significance, broaching issues central to understanding attachment, love, and human nature. Sibling affection, "greatly modified by the difference of Sex, made more tender, graceful, soothing, consolatory, yet still remaining perfectly pure," would constitute a "glorious fact *for* human Nature," even if comparatively rare; as a near universal ("being, as it is, only not universal"), chaste sibling love constitutes instead a "glorious fact *of* human Nature." It demonstrates how the passions can be disciplined by the "power of Education," gives the "human Heart" two modes of love by "dividing the sisterly

& fraternal from the conjugal affection," and purifies and strengthens the latter by the prior and "habitual" practice of the former. Precisely because sibling love is asexual, it provides an alternative model for human love and attachment and thus even renders married love a less exclusively (and crudely) physical affair than it might have proved otherwise.

Coleridge gives two complementary explanations for incest aversion, one psychological and one historical, both depending on the "common Laws of association." The psychological explanation closely resembles the one independently developed by Bentham the year before. "Nature & Providence" have conspired to keep sibling and conjugal affection separate chiefly "by making the *age of Puberty* a distinct revolutionary Epoch in the human mind & body—/ a new feeling best & most certainly coalesces with a new Object, the idea of this becoming *vivid*, which an habitually familiar object scarcely can become." As the Hartleyan terminology ("coalesces") suggests, this is a more enthusiastic version of Bentham's association-ist argument that novelty, rather than habituation, best inspires mature sexual passion. As Coleridge goes on to point out, however, this argument would explain sexual apathy between siblings but not the "great religious *Horror* attached to Incest," even if a vague "sort of *ominous* Feeling" might proceed from its very infrequency. To explain the positive feeling of horror or aversion, Coleridge supposes that some early group or "Tribe" such as the "Magi" (Montesquieu's Zoroastrians) had capriciously encouraged sibling marriages. The next step in the argument assumes that inbreeding would have deleterious effects, a notion Coleridge would have encountered in reading Buffon and (Erasmus) Darwin, although this remains implicit. The "consequences of this in a few Generations became so marked & so terrific, as to attract the attention of mankind then few in number comparatively, so as to be wisely regarded by them as a proof of divine Vengeance on the Practice." The "terrific" aura of incest would persist not in some racial unconscious but by means of a historical tradition passed down from one generation to the next, a horror of incest remaining when the "physical Fact, that first occasioned it" had long been forgotten.

Once this horror of incest had become culturally established, it would then be internalized by children (again, via "common Laws of association") as an incidental but powerful feature of the socialization process. As happens, a "little child will say—that it will marry his Sister—& is instantly with shake of the Head and serious Look told, O no!—nobody marries their Sisters—According from the age of Three, at which time a child may be supposed capable of observing, to the age of 14 or 15, at which time his sexual Instincts begin to disquiet him, he hears of a thousand marriages, but never one of a Brother & Sister." The cultural prohibition thus takes on the "precise feeling of *Necessity*." Having established grounds both for sexual indifference between housemates and a culturally instituted horror of incest on associationist principles, Coleridge finds an "Instinct" for incest avoidance needlessly "*recondite*." Moreover, given his Creationist bias, Coleridge finds it illogical: If there were such an instinct, Edenic man's "first act by the necessity of the case must have been to act in contradiction to it." Even though Coleridge resists the notion of inherited animal traits posed by protoevolutionary thinkers like Erasmus Darwin and William Lawrence, however, he still relies on the new biological thinking of the time in assuming the harmful effects of inbreeding and in allowing for "sexual Instincts" whatsoever. He draws on early ethnographical literature both in establishing the rarity of incestuous unions and allowing for the exceptional cases found among the "copper Indians, or Otaheitans," but he characteristically puts off discussion ("a hateful Task") to an indefinite "elsewhere." The coda to the entry argues, against Southey's objection, that a moral feeling can be "traditionary" even when its historical cause has been "every where forgotten."

Coleridge's theory of sibling incest avoidance cannot be equated, of course, with Westermarck's hypothesis of an innate aversion to incest triggered by proximity during a critical period of childhood. Nevertheless, Coleridge assumes (as does Bentham) that children brought up together, whether or not biologically related, would ordinarily feel sexual indifference toward one another, and he anticipates Westermarck in establishing the near universality of incest aversion on a combination of ethnographical, biological, and empirical grounds. Coleridge's notebook entry shows that at least one British Romantic writer broke with Enlightenment views in recognizing a near-universal aversion to incest and in positing something very like the Westermarck effect, giving it an associationist rather than psychobiological explanation. Moreover, Coleridge develops this argument despite having portrayed an idealized erotic relation between foster siblings a few years earlier in *Osorio* (1797), whose hero and heroine were "Born on one day, like twins" and "Nursed in one cradle."[49] Not surprisingly, their union is deferred (and nearly prevented) by the machinations of the hero's brother, although they do (unlike most of their Romantic counterparts) manage to narrowly avoid a tragic separation at the end. Nevertheless, Coleridge's intellectual inconsistency on the subject suggests how other Romantic writers could be predisposed to imagine an eroticized sibling relationship and yet still view that same ideal as an unnatural and even horrific one. This paradoxical view of sibling incest as both ideal and aversive would account for the narrative ambivalence characteristic of Romantic representations of sibling and "more than" sibling passion.

Conclusion: Locating Human Universals

The study of human universals has been making a remarkable comeback in a number of fields, including linguistics, psychology, anthropology, and throughout the cognitive sciences. Literary studies, on the contrary, have shown a great deal more interest in "difference" than in universals, treating the latter with suspicion or outright hostility. As Patrick Colm Hogan cogently argues, however, literary scholars can find sound methodological, theoretical, and even political reasons for reconsidering the issue and adding the study of literary universals to the wider cognitivist project.[50] But this pursuit will fare badly if it becomes a matter of simplistically mapping the human universals posited by evolutionary psychology or sociobiology onto the content of fictive texts. Rather, the study of literary universals will prove more convincing if it concentrates on formal features and constraints, rhetorical and prosodic devices, and questions of genre and narrative, treating specific thematic elements or other aspects of local content more sparely and with special caution.[51] Such studies, as Hogan emphasizes, will need to pay careful and informed attention to the historical and cultural situatedness of a given text or tradition, if the discrimination of universals is not to become confused with the chauvinistic projection of currently dominant cultural norms.

The case of Romantic incest can be seen as exceptional in that, unexpectedly, a thematic issue does gain clarity from comparison with a model borrowed from biological anthropology. By taking the evolutionary theory of incest avoidance seriously, and working from the assumption that something like the Westermarck effect does hold over time and across cultures, one can make sense of the two features of Romantic incest that critics have had great trouble accounting for: that incestuous desire, though idealized, nearly always ends tragically; and that this pattern holds equally for biological siblings, foster or adopted siblings, and various other cosocialized pairs. But the significant parallels between the Westermarck hypothesis and the recurrent narrative pattern of Romantic incest reflect not intuitive insight into a universal cognitive mechanism but rather a historically contingent coincidence. British Romantic writers just happen to have represented sibling incest in a manner consistent with the evolutionary approach currently back in favor, although in other times and places writers could—and did—come up with alternative representations of incest having little or nothing to do with cultural universals or biopsychological mechanisms. The revived study of human universals may hold real promise for literary critics and theorists, but not if universals are baldly asserted as norms or givens. Rather, their applicability to a given text or practice must be cautiously demonstrated in the context of a specific cultural and historical milieu. Far from freeing the critic from the burden of historical contextualization, the discrimination of cultural universals only adds to that burden by significantly raising the stakes of literary interpretation.

CHAPTER SEVEN

Language Strange

Motherese, the Semiotic, and Romantic Poetry

British writers of the Romantic era—scientists, poets, and natural philosophers alike—developed their own early biological understandings of cognition and culture, from brain-based or "corporealist" accounts of mind to an embodied universalism that fundamentally revised Enlightenment conceptions of human nature.[1] Some of these accounts bear remarkable affinities with cognitive, neuroscientific, and evolutionary models currently in vogue, although such affinities do not always signal a particularly deep relation between Romantic-era speculation and theories developed or reformulated in recent years. In some cases, as with Romantic representations of and speculation on incest avoidance, the parallels between recent and Romantic paradigms, intriguing as they are, may reflect quite different approaches to understanding cultural universals. (That Romantic-era writers *do* show an interest in such universals remains highly significant in itself.) In other cases, such as representations in early nineteenth-century fiction of what is now called Theory of Mind, the affinities seem far more robust, especially in light of the larger discursive context, including Edmund Burke's physiological rhetoric and Thomas Reid's "common sense" philosophy. In every instance, as I have argued throughout this study, perceived resemblances between then and now mark the beginning, not the end, of cognitive cultural inquiry. Rather than resort to notoriously vague terms (sometimes known as "weasel words") like *intuition* and *anticipation*, the critic's task is to explore such parallels without collapsing historical and cultural difference into superficial similarity.

Yet such affinities or resonances between the Romantic era and our own historical period remain extremely valuable *as* starting points. They can help us to reexamine well-known phenomena, such as the Romantic sublime, with different eyes or to thoroughly rethink influential critical models that have worn thin, such as the poststructuralist approach to the Romantic figure of apostrophe. They can reorient thinking on perennial issues, such as the Romantic ambivalence toward the visual sense and the self-evident yet puzzling connection between the creative imagination and the image in the mind's eye. Bringing a fresh set of intellectual interests, an array of new models, and an expanded critical vocabulary to the work of critical investigation, the literary scholar stands not only to reopen old questions and revitalize ongoing debates but to ask fundamentally new questions and to discriminate certain literary and cultural patterns that earlier criticism has simply failed to notice.

In this final chapter, I explore just such a previously "hidden" pattern, examining a motif in British Romantic poetry that has never been identified as such (although a few specific instances have received a good deal of individual attention). Centrally concerned with the female voice and with meaningful, affecting, yet nonsemantic utterances, the motif touches on several areas discussed in previous chapters: Romantic notions of a "natural" human language, a protobiological, "embodied" Romantic understanding of human universals, and a widespread Romantic interest in the importance of early childhood experience in the development of mind. In addition, these poetic representations of "strange" female vocalizations bring out as well a larger Romantic-era revaluation of the feminine and a (by now) well-known set of male Romantic anxieties regarding female speech and maternal power. I want to begin, then, by reviewing some of the issues involved in Romantic representations of and attitudes toward the feminine.

Students of British Romantic-era literature were relatively slow to take up feminist criticism, perhaps because their field had for some time been focused on an unusually small and exclusively male poetic canon. As a result, the deployment of "feminist critique"—revaluation of the male-authored canon from a feminist reader's perspective—and "gynocritics"—the study of women as writers—to rethink Romantic literature took place almost simultaneously rather than in sequence.[2] Among the foundational works of feminist Romantic criticism, studies of Dorothy Wordsworth, Mary Shelley, and Mary Wollstonecraft all figure prominently. As this particular selection of representative names suggests, however, the residual dominance of "six-poet Romanticism" significantly affected the early development of gynocritics in the field.[3] Dorothy Wordsworth and Mary Shelley lent themselves to critical attention not least because their works, and scholarly works devoted to them, were readily available, thanks in large part to their affiliation with (and ancillary status in the study of) canonical male poets. Contemporary women novelists, most notably Jane Austen, having long been dissociated from "Romanticism," played almost no role in these early studies. (Even Shelley's *Frankenstein* had to prove its "endurance" before gaining serious attention in the field.)[4] Most contemporary women poets remained, for the time, scarcely known. These (understandable) exclusions had important consequences for the first wave of feminist work on Romantic-era women's writing.

With the advantages of hindsight, early descriptions of Romantic-era women's writing seem to respond as much to the diminished (and now exploded) Romantic canon of the 1980s as to the historical situation of women writers in the late eighteenth and early nineteenth centuries. Put differently, a feminist poetics of exclusion and silencing, advanced in the 1980s by several influential critics, might now strike one as a better reading of what twentieth-century Romantic literary history had made of the literary archives at its disposal rather than of the archives themselves. Pioneering feminist studies of Dorothy Wordsworth, for example, built on her reluctance to publish, her willing subservience to her brother, and the self-abnegating aspects of her private journal writing to develop broader descriptions of "female Romanticism" that, for a new critical generation working avidly on the era's published women writers, now seem unduly bleak.[5] Viewing Dorothy Wordsworth's "reticence" as normative rather then exceptional (Alexander 58), early feminist critics of Romanticism developed exclusionary models of women's relation to language (not just literary language) that have since lost much of their purchase. After a decade or so of sustained critical attention to Anna Barbauld and Charlotte Smith, Hannah More and Maria Edgeworth, Felicia Hemans and Letitia Elizabeth Landon, notions of women's "exclusion from speaking subjectivity" or of "conventional" language as a "male" property no longer seem adequate to the expanded field.[6] Critics who have worked to revive the study of the women poets, dramatists, and fiction writers of the period tend in contrast to stress the woman poet's readier command of the ascendant "vernacular" language, to acknowledge the growing dominance of women novelists within the literary marketplace, or to point to the male writer's envy of the "conventional" facility and commercial success of Hemans and Landon.[7] If William Wordsworth, as Margaret Homans once argued, helped codify a "myth" of female objectification and silence, he did so in the face of his debts to and competition with the comparatively fluent and popular women writers of his time.[8]

The male poet's projection of his "anxiety of authorship" onto "feminine figures"—a characteristic Romantic practice first discussed by Sonia Hofkosh—lies at the uneasy center of the recurring literary motif I discuss in this chapter.[9] Critics who drew on Jacques Lacan to code "symbolic language" as a masculine prerogative also drew on Julia Kristeva to broach a "semiotic" discourse as a feminine alternative. Homans terms this (confusingly enough) a "literal or nonsymbolic" language that reconnects the woman writer to the "literal or presymbolic language" marking the transition from infancy to speaking childhood, an alternative discourse that, according to Homans, Dorothy Wordsworth sought to recapture in her journal writing ("Representation" 13, 29). Susan Levin also relates Dorothy Wordsworth and "the women of Romanticism" generally to a "semiotic discourse" that "bespeaks an infantile fusion with the mother" (163–64). Meena Alexander, another important early feminist critic of the Romantic tradition, similarly finds a "rhythmic, presymbolic function" at work in Dorothy Wordsworth's prose, epitomized by her transcription of her nephew John's baby talk: "Man Mam Ma—Dad dad—da pap pap—sometimes—ta ta—often nan, nan nan. Na na, da da nong" (59–60). The example, striking as it is, stands out now not for its representativeness but for its distance from most contemporary women's writing. Joanna Baillie's "A Mother to Her Waking Infant" succeeds not by imitating presymbolic discourse (something Baillie does not think to attempt) but thanks to its deft handling of the nascent poetic vernacular, addressed over the infant's head to a new readership being shaped by Robert Burns, Mary Robinson, Barbauld, Smith, and More.

Male poets of the Romantic era, however, *do* attempt to convey in verse a "nonsymbolic" speech, characterized by the extrasemantic "rhythms and intonations" attributed by Kristeva to the "first echolalias of infants" and reactivated for her in "poetic language" as well.[10] Male Romantic poets, however, attribute such rhythmic, sussurant, strange language not to helpless infants but to dangerous, seductive, powerful women. Female figures—immortal, demonic, witchlike, otherworldly— in poems by S. T. Coleridge, Walter Scott, John Keats, Thomas Love Peacock, and Walter Savage Landor, variously hiss and murmur, "make sweet moan" or "bubble like honey," sing in bewitching tones or "lull" in "language strange"; they even hum like bees. Why do these semantically empty but rhythmic, melodic noises have the power to turn the male characters who listen to them love struck and passive, supine and spellbound?

In pursuing this question, I look for help to what may at first seem an unlikely source: evolutionary aesthetics. In her important book on the developmental and evolutionary basis of artistic behavior, *Art and Intimacy*, Ellen Dissanayake has attributed a leading role in the formation of social bonds and in the genesis of the arts to early interaction between infants and their primary caregivers (usually their mothers).[11] A repertoire of stylized, patterned, quasi-ritualistic behaviors characterize mother-infant interaction across cultures, facilitating the child's social as well as cognitive development and establishing a foundation for social bonding generally in the loving intimacy that distinguishes the infant's relation with its primary caregiver. The patterned and dynamic character of such behaviors, beginning with intense eye-contact exchanges and including the playful and repetitive rituals that grow around rocking, snuggling, swinging, approach-avoidance games, joint handling of rattles and other toys, singing, and early verbal exchanges also set templates for the rhythmic, iterative, theme-and-variation aspects of the temporal arts, including music, dance, ritual drama, song, and poetry.

Like Kristeva, that is, Dissanayake posits important continuities between the rhythmic verbal experiences of infancy and mature poetic expression, marked, Kristeva writes, by an "instinctual, maternal element" (136). Whereas Kristeva, however, shows most interest in the vocalizations of the infants themselves, Dissanayake follows a number of developmental psychologists and psycholinguists in attending more closely to the unusual verbal behaviors exhibited by mothers (and other nurturers) toward the infants in their care.[12] In *Art and Intimacy* and in related essays published since, Dissanayake points to the special role that a "high-pitched, undulant, breathy, patterned, repetitive" mode of speech plays, genetically, in introducing the child to spoken language and, in the evolution of human cultures, in forming a kind of template for metered verse (336).[13] This unusual speech mode has been variously termed *motherese, parentese, baby talk* (Dissanayake's preferred term) and *infant-directed speech*.[14] Although *infant-directed speech* (IDS) is the term most likely to prevail, I have featured *motherese* in this chapter's title because it enshrines the tacit assumption of researchers (who began studying IDS in the 1970s) that women would perform the work of primary infant caregiving—an assumption borne out in relation to most traditional societies, including Romantic-era Britain.

Anyone, however—including fathers and older children—who spends a good deal of time caring for and interacting with infants can become adept at motherese, most likely guided unconsciously by innate preferences manifested in the infant's behavior. (Parents and other intimate caregivers will generally do most anything it takes to quiet, amuse, engage, and earn affection from infants, who have pronounced biases and make for remorseless teachers.) Daniel Stern, one of the first developmental psychologists to view motherese as an important subject for research, sometimes calls it "infant-elicited speech," perhaps the most useful term of all.[15] For, although motherese is spoken by the caregiver to a preverbal infant, it nevertheless makes part of a dyadic exchange in which the infant plays its part with glances, smiles, head movements, and preverbal sounds such as cooing, all of which may be imitated and varied by the caregiver. So for Dissanayake, baby talk is best considered as a *"multimedia performance."*[16] She stresses as well that infants do not play a passive or even subordinate role in these performances but in fact direct them: "Because infants let us know by their own positive and negative reactions which movements, expressions, and sounds they prefer, they can be said to actively elicit, shape, and otherwise influence the pace, intensity, and variety of signals that adults present to them."[17]

A good deal of research suggests that the infants' preferences are driven by innate biases, at least some of them species specific—that is, unique and universal to humans.[18] Although motherese can vary according to different cultural settings, linguists and psychologists have long been impressed by the recurrence of certain key features across diverse cultures and languages. These "universal" features include elevated pitch (sometimes more than an octave higher than in habitual speech), repetition, and exaggerated intonation contours and rhythms, lending motherese a "melodic and singsongy" quality.[19] Another cross-cultural feature noted by Stern is the inclusion of "nonsense sounds," with phrases consisting of "squeaks and squeals mixed in with some words."[20] Dissanayake remarks that, in a few societies, motherese becomes altogether nonsemantic and musical, the more widespread rhythmic and musical speech replaced by "other rhythmically regular noises such as tongue-clicking, hissing, grunting, or lip-smacking" (*Art* 30). Even semantically meaningful utterances spoken in motherese—semantically meaningful, of course, to the mother but not to the preverbal infant—show a marked exaggeration of "poetic" features such as stresses and accents, dynamic pauses and changes of rhythm, alliteration and assonance, parallelism, and even a "repetitive regulating meter."[21] In this way, IDS (or motherese or baby talk) can be seen as protoaesthetic, "foundational" for later participation in poetic discourse.[22]

Linguists tend to emphasize the features of IDS most likely involved in facilitating language acquisition, including heightened prosodic contours that may promote syntactic learning, the repertoire of distinctive "melodies" readily associated with "particular affective meanings" and thus preparing the child to acquire sound-meaning pairings, and the elongated vowels that isolate and pedagogically exaggerate the vowel sounds of a particular language.[23] This last feature makes an especially good case for the presumed role of IDS in facilitating language acquisition; although adults deploy many of the features of motherese in talking to pets, they do not hyperarticulate vowels for their dogs and cats.[24] This emphasis on the role of motherese in facilitating language acquisition again provides a contrast with Kristeva's superficially similar notion of the "maternal, semiotic processes" that also "prepare the future speaker for entrance into meaning and signification" but must be repressed—along with the primary relation to the mother—as the price of that entrance. "But the symbolic (i.e., language as nomination, sign, and syntax) constitutes itself only by breaking with this anteriority . . . Language as symbolic function constitutes itself at the cost of repressing instinctual drive and continuous relation to the mother" (*Desire* 136).[25] Kristeva has in fact been charged with a "massive disavowal of the tutelary role the mother classically assumes with respect to the child's linguistic education—of her function as language teacher, commentator, storyteller."[26] In contrast, one could say of work on motherese in general what Barbara Charlesworth Gelpi says of Stern's approach to language acquisition in particular: "Infants of both genders move into language in the company of their mothers."[27] Stern, Dissanayake, and linguists like Anne Fernald all emphasize the intimate, affective character of motherese, and child development researchers include "high affect" among the universal features of infant-directed speech.[28]

High affect may sound like a vague and subjective term, but experimenters measure it by rating the prevalence of what they call "low-pass-filtered speech," in which the "intonation and rhythm can be heard but the words cannot be understood."[29] The notion of low-pass-filtered speech, if not the term, may well strike a familiar chord with readers of John Keats. Most notably in "La Belle Dame sans Merci," a poem that stages an encounter between a socially dominant male—a knight— and an otherworldly, perhaps demonic female—the beautiful, pitiless lady of the title—Keats describes the woman's speech as an incomprehensible "language strange," high in affect (she "made sweet moan"), rhythmic ("a fairy's song"), and overtly linked to maternal behavior ("And there she lulled me to sleep").[30] Less well known but no less to the point is Keats's representation of the seduction of Glaucon by the witch Circe in *Endymion*: "Thus she link'd / Her charming syllables, till indistinct / Their music came to my o'er-sweeten'd soul" (III.443–45).

"Who could resist?" Glaucon continues: "She took me like a child of suckling time" (III.453, 456). And as Lamia, yet another of Keats's dangerous, otherwordly temptresses, addresses her seductive rhetoric to Hermes, the "words she spake,/Came, as through bubbling honey" (*Lamia* I.64–65). When language grows indistinct or "strange," when musical rhythms and affective accents crowd out sense, the female speaker for Keats becomes most dangerous, most alluring, most irresistible—and most maternal.

The conjunction of an otherworldly woman, rhythmic and emotive (low-pass-filtered) vocalization, seduction, danger, and maternal overtones does not belong solely to Keats. A group of poems published in the early nineteenth century feature the same constellation of motifs: Scott's "Glenfinlas" (1801), Coleridge's "Christabel" (1816), Peacock's *Rhododaphne* (1818), and Landor's "The Hamadryad" (1842) can all be added to the three examples from Keats. Landor's Hamadryad (a wood nymph whose existence is attached to a certain tree) might be called "La Belle Dame *avec* Merci"; she initially pities the mortal, Rhaicos, who falls in love with her, and Rhaicos meets an ill end only through a sort of accident (283).[31] Like the belle dame of Keats, the nymph engages in maternal behaviors, bathing Rhaicos's feet, feeding him honey, telling him a story ("Tell me some tale about them," Rhaicos asks when she mentions hamadryads; "May I sit/Beside thy feet?" [120–21]). Her first speech to Rhaicos, in fact, might be taken as a microparable of language acquisition from the infant's perspective:

> He heard a buzz
> At first, and then the sound grew soft and clear,
> And then divided into what seem'd tune,
> And there were words upon it, plaintive words.
>
> (49–53)

Rhaicos's relation with the nymph retains an ambivalent and forbidden character, however, and he brings about both of their deaths by thoughtlessly wounding the messenger bee she has dispatched to his father's house (where he remains in a kind of prolonged childhood) to bring her assurance of Rhaicos's love. Even though Rhaicos's father provisionally agrees to spare the wood-nymph's tree, the hamadryad and the paternal sphere remain fundamentally at odds.

Other poets develop the "language strange" motif in relation to an outright contest or struggle between the illicit and threatening discourse of a female speaker and the defensive resort of a male speaker to officially sanctioned forms of speech (such as prescribed prayers). In "Christabel," for example, the seductive, powerful, apparently demonic Geraldine initially gains Christabel's attention through an uninterpretable moaning, not clearly human or even animate: "It moaned as near, as near can be,/But what it is she cannot tell" (39–40).[32] When Geraldine speaks, her "voice was faint and sweet"; when she takes Christabel to bed, she "holds the maiden in her arms" as would "a mother with her child" (72, 299–301). Casting a spell that she describes to Christabel as "lord of thy utterance," Geraldine leaves her now literally unable to "tell" what has happened, except through a mimetic acting out (268). Significantly, when she tries to speak of Geraldine, Christabel can give voice only to a nonsemantic "hissing sound," twice repeated (459, 591). In opposition to Geraldine's witchlike spells and indecipherable moaning, the poem introduces a licensed poet, the "minstrel bard" Bracy, who wishes to "clear" the wood of "thing unblest" through "music strong and saintly song" (529, 561). In this case, the contest between official, male "saintly song" and illicit, female "spell" becomes indefinitely deferred, but other poems, including *Rhododaphne* and "Glenfinlas," stage similar contests that leave male culture at least partly victorious.

"Glenfinlas or Lord Ronald's Coronach," a literary ballad set in the forest that gives the poem its title, is based on a "simple tradition" concerning two Highlanders who spend the night in a hunter's *bothy* (or hut) and rashly wish for female companionship. "The words were scarcely uttered," Scott writes in the head note, "when two beautiful young women, habited in green, entered the hut, dancing and singing" (4: 138).[33] One of the singing women takes her victim into the forest, where he is "torn in pieces and devoured"; the other hunter, less easily seduced, protects himself from the "Green Women" by playing "some strain, consecrated to the Virgin Mary." In the ballad itself, the two hunters become the "matchless" chief Lord Ronald and his friend Moy, a prophetic "seer" from the isle of Columba, long associated with a firmly entrenched monastic Christian culture. Moy, moreover, is (like Coleridge's Bracy) a minstrel, well equipped with "many a spell" (4: 141). It is Ronald, of course, who makes the wish for woman's "panting breath and melting eye," abandoning Moy and the *bothy* to wander into the forest where he is duly ripped apart, presumably by one of the Green Women. Her accomplice, entering the hut disguised as a "huntress maid," evokes Coleridge's sexy, vulnerable, maternal Geraldine with her "Chill'd" cheek and "bosom bare"; even the "moaning howl" of the hunting dogs suggests the close affinities between the two supernatural ballads (4: 147–48). (These affinities do not seem to be a matter of borrowing, as Scott first heard "Christabel" recited only in 1802, a year after "Glenfinlas" was first published.)[34] Much as Christabel asks Geraldine (in vain) to pray—but here more pointedly and forcefully—Moy instructs his would-be seducer to "three times tell

each Ave-bead,/And thrice a Pater-noster say" (4: 150). The resort to Latin intensifies the masculine, patriarchal character of Moy's Christian discourse; as Gelpi
points out, one way of stressing women's alienation from the official, dominant
discourse is to "make the use of a 'dead' or 'learned' language—a language that is
no longer a 'mother tongue' anywhere in the world—purely a male prerogative."[35]
When the witch woman refuses to pronounce the Latin prayers, Moy recites "thrice
St. Oran's rhyme" (St. Oran, Scott's note tells us, was known for "rigid celibacy"
[4: 155]) and "thrice St. Fillan's powerful prayer" (4: 151). His "more than mortal"
enemy is reduced to a language of pure sound, a "wild yell" that mingles with
the "howling gale," transmuting into "ghastly laughter" as she disappears into the
weirdly rhythmic storm—"Rain beats, hail rattles" (4: 151–52). Moy finishes what
Coleridge's Bracy only begins, driving from the woods the demonic female with
her ungodly vocalizations.

The significant web of connections among these texts has long evaded scholarly
attention, but Romanticists have not failed to notice the interrelated thematics of
language, gender, and eroticism in such high profile works as "La Belle Dame sans
Merci" and "Christabel." Psychoanalytical readers of "Christabel," in particular,
have paid close attention to the significance of Geraldine's maternal behaviors, and
some have related these to the poem's thematic concerns with language, poetry,
and the silencing or disruption of the speaking voice.[36] In "The Mother Tongue:
Christabel and the Language of Love," for example, Margery Durham develops a
Kleinian reading that relates Geraldine's power over Christabel's "utterance" to
the mother's role in the "development of speech," demonstrating how Coleridge's
notebooks reveal a concern with these very issues near the time of the poem's
composition.[37] "Hart[ley] seemed to learn to talk by touching his mother," reads
one revealing notebook entry, which Durham convincingly relates to Geraldine's
"spell": "In the touch of this bosom there worketh a spell,/Which is lord of thy
utterance, Christabel!" For a psychoanalytical critic like Durham, however, the
child's acquisition of symbolic language serves at once to displace and to com-
pensate for the mother-infant bond rather than being facilitated by and indeed
grounded in continuing mother-infant interaction, as it is in cognitive developmental, psycholinguistic, and evolutionary accounts of infant-directed speech.
The maternal vocalization that Coleridge writes out of his brief notebook entry on
speech acquisition reasserts itself, I would argue, in the eerie moaning that begins
Geraldine's romance with Christabel and the imitative hissing that seeks to end
it. The male poet's indirect acknowledgment, that is, of the central role of rhythmic, highly patterned, affect-laden, "low-pass filtered" maternal speech—which

can lose its semantic import without losing its meaning—helps account for the salience of the "language strange" motif in the poetry not only of Coleridge but of Keats, Scott, Landor, and Peacock as well.

Peacock's *Rhododaphne: Or the Thessalian Spell* comes closest to directly articulating this connection, after first establishing between the Thessalian witch of the title and the poem's hero, Anthemion, a complex relation that is (again) at once erotic, maternal, and "unnatural."[38] Rhododaphne initially approaches Anthemion, her intended victim, with the "soft sweet accents," "musically sweet," that evoke what linguists will later call *motherese*; significantly, she compares Anthemion to an "infant" in her very first speech to him (7: 13–14). Anthemion is warned that, as a Thessalian maid, his temptress may well be subjecting him to "unnatural spells" and "unholy song"—that her "tones so sweetly wild" are in fact conveying "words of power" (7: 14, 22–23). Even though Anthemion already loves another, however, he finds Rhododaphne's voice irresistible:

> Oh! there was passion in the sound,
> Intensest passion, strange and deep;
> Wild breathings of a soul, around
> Whose every pulse one hope had bound,
> One burning hope, which might not sleep.
> But hark! that wild and solemn swell!
> And was there in those tones a spell,
> Which none may disobey!   (7: 33–34)

Rhododaphne's pulsing, passionate, musical voice (she is singing, at this moment in the narrative, to the music of her own lyre), like a mother's voice, asks not just for love but also for obedience. Anthemion escapes for the moment but, fatally, his "eyes and ears had drank the charm" (7: 37). He will return to Rhododaphne, despite intuiting that the "magic maid" has caused his beloved's death, to find his own voice lost in a second infancy: "his accents fell / Perplexed, confused, inaudible" (7: 65); shortly afterward, he will passively follow her "like a child" (7: 70).

P. B. Shelley, an early fan of *Rhododaphne*, found it "most remarkable," not least for its "Greek and Pagan" sensibility.[39] No less remarkable, however, is the poem's extended treatment of the female voice and its uncanny power, as well as its development of a perspective on erotic love (the presiding deity of *Rhododaphne* is "Uranian Eros") that bears comparison with the high cultural value attributed by Dissanayake to early experiences of "intimacy." The introduction to Canto IV begins by seeming to relegate powerful female speech to a mythical past:

"Magic and mystery, spells Circean, / The Siren voice," Peacock writes, have "passed away," "chased" off by Truth and Reason, a linkage of scientific progress and disenchantment that similarly informs the decline theory of poetry that Peacock will develop two years later in his essay "The Four Ages of Poetry."[40] Here, however, Peacock immediately reverses himself: "Yet deem not so." "The Power of Spells," he continues,

> Still lingers on the earth, but dwells
> In deeper folds of close disguise,
> That baffle Reason's searching eyes:
> Nor shall that mystic power resign
> To truth's cold sway his webs of guile,
> Till woman's eyes have ceased to shine,
> And woman's lips have ceased to smile,
> And woman's voice has ceased to be
> The earthly soul of melody.
>
> (7: 41–42)

The conjunction here of shining eyes, smiling lips, and melodic voice, recalling the "multimedia" character of mother-infant interaction, suggests that the "power" of the female voice has everything to do with the primacy of the mother-infant bond. "Unnatural spells" and "unholy" songs like Rhododaphne's gain their power not from magical art but from "woman's voice," the sweet, thrilling, passionate, semantically meaningless, yet psychologically meaningful voice that most every male poet, like most every human subject, would have heard throughout infancy.

This voice, for Dissanayake, remains triply powerful, for it ushers the child into language, provides (as is evident) a template for mature erotic exchange, and builds a foundation not only for later artistic behaviors but for the social bonds that the temporal arts facilitate and help maintain as well. In his lines on Eros (at the beginning of Canto VII, the poem's concluding section), Peacock sketches out a myth of human socialization that depends on the same connections among love, "social bonds," and the arts:

> Love first in social bonds combined
> The scattered tribes of humankind,
> And bade the wild race cease to roam,
> And learn the endearing name of home.
> From Love the sister arts began,

That charm, adorn, and soften man.
To Love, the feast, the dance, belong,
The temple-rite, the choral song;
All feelings that refine and bless,
All kindness, sweetness, gentleness.

(7: 77)

From a perspective that, like Dissanayake's, stresses the central place of the
mother-infant bond in this civilizing process, however, the conclusion of Peacock's
poem develops in a decidedly warped manner. For Peacock introduces "Uranian
Eros" not as an ally but as an enemy of Rhododaphne. By "Uranian Eros" Peacock could (and partly does) mean something like celestial love (as opposed to
sexual passion). In this sense, Milton takes Urania as his celestial muse in *Paradise Lost*. But Peacock would have been acutely aware that in Plato's *Symposium*,
"Uranian" love refers to a "higher" erotic bond that exists only between men, as
opposed to heterosexual love. Pausanius, the speaker who introduces this distinction, goes so far as to declare that Uranian Aphrodite, the mother of Uranian Eros,
though a goddess has solely male attributes.[41] Nor would Peacock (or for that
matter Shelley, who defended the Greek practice of male homosexual love in his
"Discourse on the Manners of the Ancient Greeks") have been all that surprised to
learn that, later in the nineteenth century, *Uranian love* would become a term for
male homoeroticism.[42] In *Rhododaphne*, the intervention of Uranian Eros (who,
like Appolonius in *Lamia*, comes to disenchant an illusory erotic paradise) leads
to the miraculous revival of Anthemion's first, mortal beloved and thus displaces
an illicit heterosexual union with a licit one. But in order to do so, Uranian Eros
must destroy Rhododaphne and all she has come to represent—the magical female
voice, the maternal power and quasi-maternal eroticism that account for its force,
along with the "impious" "murmured spells" that give it direct expression here (7:
79, 85).

Why does "woman's voice" become so sinister in poems like *Lamia* and *Rhododaphne*, "Christabel," "La Belle Dame sans Merci" and "Glenfinlas," and why
do poets come to demonize it at this particular moment in cultural history? Why
does one poem after another stage a contest between official male and "unholy"
or "impious" female voices? It hardly seems incidental that Rhododaphne is slain
by Uranian Eros with an arrow "borrowed from Apollo's quiver" or that Eros calls
upon "all-ruling Jove" in destroying her (7: 85). Psychoanalytical readers of the
more widely anthologized poems tend to trace the male poet's interest in sinis-

ter female figures to a deep-rooted ambivalence toward the mother. As a Kleinian, for example, Durham relates Geraldine, with her magical, horrific bosom, to the "split" mother (170). Feminist revisions of psychoanalytic theory point to a culturewide ambivalence—or worse—toward the mother and toward the feminine in general, what Karen Horney terms the "dread of woman," and one can readily find evidence for such anxiety throughout the literature and mythology of the Western tradition.[43] To better understand why ambivalence toward maternal figures and male anxieties concerning the female voice take the specific form they do in this particular group of texts, however, one might consider their location at the junction of a near-universal phenomenon of nurturing and a specific moment in cultural history. The primary nurturer—all but invariably a mother, nurse, or other female figure for Romantic-era society—promotes and eases the child's entry into language with a rhythmic, repetitive, emotive—that is, protopoetic—form of speech.[44] Although male poets sometimes write the maternal voice out of their portrayals of mother-infant interaction, as Wordsworth does in the famous "Blest babe" passage of *The Prelude*, or Coleridge in relating language acquisition to *touching* the mother, they know better.[45] The 1799 *Prelude* begins, after all, with Wordsworth recalling how "one, the fairest of all rivers, loved / To blend his murmurs with my Nurse's song" (2–3). That singing, murmuring, nurturing female voice reasserts itself in poems like "La Belle Dame," but in a highly ambivalent manner. By suggesting that language, and poetic language above all, does not substitute for the mother but rather finds its basis in her rhythmic utterances, the image of the murmuring, chanting, or moaning female disturbs the male poet's sense of a privileged or exclusive relationship to the "real language of man" and its prosodic cadences.

If Wordsworth tends to repress, or rather mute, the mother's role in language acquisition—"I held mute dialogues with my mother's heart"—other poets of the period underscore it instead.[46] Byron, at times the most aggressively masculine of male Romantic poets, gives these lines to Myrrha in *Sardanapalus*:

> "The very first
> Of human life must spring from woman's breast,
> Your first small words are taught you from her lips,
> Your first tears quench'd by her . . ."   (I.2.509–12)

Sardanapalus replies, appropriately enough, "My eloquent Ionian! thou speak'st music" (I.2.516).[47] Anne Yearsley, in her verse child-rearing manual "To Mira, on the Care of Her Infant," describes a developmental sequence—from the newborn's initial confusion to its interest in the "cadence" of maternal speech to the first apprehension of verbal meaning—that bears a surprising but distinct kinship to Fernald's thinking on the role of IDS in speech acquisition.[48]

> Sound strikes at first on her new-organ'd ear
> As if far off; monotonous comes near.
> Her taste yet sleeps, no melody she owns,
> Nor wakes to joyous, or to thrilling tones:
> Dull indiscrimination blinds her views;
> But still, the sound once caught, the ear pursues,
> Till cadence whispers o'er the eager thought,
> And human accents strike, with meaning fraught;
> Then gentle breathings in the babe inspire
> Joy, pleasure, sympathy, new-born desire.
>
> (145–54)

Human accents first become meaningful not simply through a loving relation with a maternal figure but by means of the musical "cadence" that a female caregiver is likely to give her infant-directed speech. The mother-infant dialogues Yearsley describes are anything but mute; they make speech meaningful (and thus proto-symbolic) by investing it with emotionally salient cadences or rhythms.

Any generation of poets confronted with the widespread practice of "mother-ese," despite wanting to view language and the poetic tradition as male preserves (as the Romantic poets so often did), might conceivably have developed a motif comparable to the "language strange" pattern I've outlined here. Given their pronounced interest in infancy and childhood and in early psychological development, however—interests that inspired the sort of sustained, empirical observation of infants that Coleridge records in his notebooks—Romantic-era writers may have been especially aware of the female nurturer's role in language acquisition or less prone to dismiss it as the cloying prattle of nursemaids. Certainly, they noticed the nonsemantic, prosodically rich vocalizations of infants and could describe them with a seriousness hard to imagine in earlier poetry, as in this striking passage from Wordsworth's "Michael":

> Never to living ear came sweeter sounds
> Than when I heard thee by our own fire-side
> First uttering, without words, a natural tune;
> When thou, a feeding babe, didst in they joy
> Sing at thy Mother's breast.   (345–49)[49]

The same passage touches as well on the high valuation placed on maternal nurturing in the period, a time when many authorities followed Jean-Jacques Rousseau's *Emile* in recommending that women nurse their own children and in placing responsibility for early education squarely on the mother: the "first education belongs incontestably to women."[50]

Indeed, as Gelpi and other scholars have demonstrated, the role of the biological mother was accorded an unprecedented importance in Romantic-era theories, practices, and ideologies of child rearing.[51] Displacing wet nurses and nursery maids as primary caregivers, mothers, according to James Fordyce, were now expected "not barely to supply their [infants'] bodily wants, but chiefly to watch the gradual openings of their minds."[52] Thomas Gisborne, in one of the better-known conduct books of the era, reiterates Fordyce's conception of the mother-educator, tasking mothers with the duty of "modelling the human mind during the early stages of its growth."[53] Similarly, for Lord Kames the "education of children is the mother's peculiar province," especially the early "culture of the heart."[54] Female writers across the ideological spectrum concurred with these influential male prescriptions, from the conservative Hannah More, who informs mothers that the "great object to which you . . . are called is the education of your children," to the radical feminist Mary Wollstonecraft, for whom the "care of children in their infancy" remains "one of the grand duties annexed to the female character by nature."[55] More adds that her primary role in forming her children's mind gives the mother a "power wide in its extent, indefinite in its effect, and inestimable in its importance"; most educational writers of the era would readily agree.[56]

The new cultural salience of motherhood was not, of course, altogether a good thing for women; heightened attention to motherhood meant heightened surveillance and anxieties as well. One such anxiety concerned the alleged dangers of female volubility: "What words," Fordyce huffs, "can express the impertinence of a female tongue let loose into boundless loquacity?"[57] Romantic-era mothers, as Julie Kipp has shown in compelling detail, were frequently placed on trial in the educational, medical, legal, and literary discourses of the time.[58] The mother's central role in childrearing could be celebrated, idealized, or rendered suspect, but it could not be ignored.

Early Romantic theories of language, emphasizing as they do the emotive and extrasemantic qualities of human speech, may also have contributed to the cultural conditions that encouraged the "language strange" motif to emerge when it did. Both Johann Gottfried Herder and Rousseau, although they do not discuss anything one could safely identify with "motherese," do posit crucial, indeed primal, links between language and passion in their accounts of the origins of language. They also hypothesize continuity rather than an absolute break between human speech and the nonsymbolic but meaningful cries of animals and prelinguistic humans. Herder, in his *Essay on the Origin of Language*, posits an original "language of feeling" that human beings have "in common with animals," although each species develops its own distinctive version.[59] This "maternal language," composed of nonsemantic "sighs and sounds," makes quasi-musical use of universally intelligible "accents" and "tonal modes" (88–89). Remnants of this natural proto-language remain in all human languages, but can be most easily detected in the "flow and rhythm" of the "poems and songs" of the ancients and in those of "all savages" in the present. If all this sounds reminiscent of Kristeva's notion of the "semiotic" vocalizations of infants, Herder poses the same connection, equating the first human languages with the "babbling vocabulary of the nursery" (135).

Rousseau, in his own *Essay* on the same subject, also roots linguistic expression in the natural and universally affecting "accents" of the human "passions."[60] The first human languages would have been "sung, rather than spoken," relying mainly on "sounds, accents, and number, which are natural" (by "number," Rousseau means metrical "quantity and rhythm") (15). Poetry, music, and ordinary language all share a common origin, and the first languages were both musical and poetic: "The first tales, the first speeches, the first laws, were in verse," something "bound to be, since feelings speak before reason" (50–51). A rhythmic, tonally expressive, universally intelligible, "natural" language of feeling becomes a commonplace in Romantic-era discourse on language, particularly in the "common sense" school of Thomas Reid and other Romantic-era philosophers and in the neuroscientific speculation of pioneering brain scientists like Matthew Baillie and Charles Bell.[61] In *Emile*, Rousseau's treatise on education, this "language natural and common to all men" becomes explicitly connected to the vocalizations and gestures of preverbal children. "Doubtless there is such a language, and it is the one children speak before knowing how to speak" (65). Though not "articulate," this language is meaningful: "accented, sonorous, intelligible." The female "nurses" of young children can understand and respond to this language, making themselves understood through accent rather than semantic meaning. Although nurses "pronounce words, these words are perfectly useless; it is not the sense of the word that children understand but the accent which accompanies it" (65). Rousseau verges here on a description of infant-directed speech but only if one ignores the absence of "nonsense" sounds and interprets "accent" to include the rhythms, melodic pitch

contours, and other features associated with motherese—and with certain temptresses found in British Romantic poetry.

Did Romantic-era writers recognize, more explicitly than had Rousseau, the
links between the emotive "natural language" of rhythms, tones, and accents and
the special manner in which mothers and other primary caretakers speak to preverbal children? If so, one might expect to find at least one early description of infant-
directed speech in the "natural philosophy" of the era, one that would moreover
credit the mother with thus helping to guide her infant into speech rather than
criticizing her in classic antifeminist fashion for excessive female volubility. That
is precisely what one does find in William Smellie's *Philosophy of Natural History*,
published in two volumes in 1790 and 1799, although I have never seen it credited
as an early account of motherese.[62]

Smellie's two volumes touch on a number of the issues that, I have argued,
coalesce in the "language strange" motif: "natural" language theory, emotionally
expressive tones and rhythms, the critical role of the mother in early education and
the child's initiation into speech, and a pronounced interest in the child's own early
development and preverbal vocalizations. In the first volume, he rehearses (and
quotes extensively from) Reid's argument that, without the foundation of a "natural language" of "particular sounds and gestures," no artificial language could ever
have arisen (1: 171–72). In the second volume, Smellie notes that human infants,
like "brute" animals, can understand "gestures and inarticulate sounds" and can
communicate in the same manner (the "inarticulate language of the child") long
before they learn to speak (2: 157–58). Later in the same volume, in a noteworthy
chapter on the "Language of the Beasts," Smellie returns to the postulate of a "*natural* language common to man and to most of the inferior animals," here explicitly
linked with the emotions: "such vocal *sounds* as are expressive of different feelings,
wants, and desires" (2: 413–14). Unlike the arbitrary sound/meaning pairings of
artificial languages, these naturally expressive sounds are "uniformly the same"
across the globe, suffering "no variation from climate or institution" (2: 414).

Before ending his discussion of animal communication, Smellie pauses to note
one remarkable difference between human beings and most other species: while
the "*females* of the inferior animals are no so *loquacious* as the *males*," in the "human
species . . . the *females* are much more talkative" (2: 437, 440). He even claims that
"*female* children," though raised in the same family and "receiving the same instructions and example," often acquire the "faculty of speech" a year or two "sooner
than the *male*" (2: 440). Whether these observations reflect Romantic-era social

realities or social myths, they suggest that femininity could be associated with excess of speech as well as with silence and that girls could be seen as more linguistically adept than their brothers, at least in the early years. Smellie's explanation for these data (factual or not) begins with noting that, throughout human history and across known cultures, "the early education and management of children have necessarily devolved upon the mothers" (2: 440). The maternal role begins prebirth, in the relatively long human period of gestation in the womb, and mothers continue to nurture their offspring postbirth through the "wonderfully complicated system of vessels" that enable lactation and breastfeeding (2: 441). At two to three months, or as soon as the infant is capable of attending to "particular objects," the "exertions of the mother" become "almost perpetual" as she seeks to stimulate and assist the development of the child's "weak, but gradually augmenting" mental capacities (2: 441). To this end, mothers make use of what Dissanayake terms a "multi-media" performance, addressing both the eyes and ears, the latter attracted by nature to "any loud *noise*" (2: 442). Then comes Smellie's description of something that could well be termed infant-elicited speech:

> The mother, who wishes to appease the fretfulness, or even to keep up the chearfulness of the child, tosses it about in her arms, sings, and talks alternately; and, on such occasions, it is astonishing to observe the quickness of her transitions from one species of incomprehensible jargon to another. Still, however, she goes on either *rattling* with her *tongue*, or making a *rattling noise* on tables, chairs, &c. A person who had never attended to these scenes, which are so often exhibited by a sprightly mother and a sprightly child, would be apt to conclude, that both were proper inmates for a bedlam. These are well known to be universal facts.
>
> (2: 442)

Far from evincing hereditary madness, these "universal facts" stem from the "best and wisest purposes of Nature," which has endowed women with that "loquacity which is requisite for amusing and teaching young children to *speak*" (2: 443). Replying to those who, like Fordyce, "blame women for *speaking much*," Smellie counters that women "ought to *speak much*," that "Nature compels them to *speak much*," and that, "when they do so, they are complying religiously with one of her most sacred and useful laws" (2: 443).

Unlike Herder and Rousseau, Smellie does not relate the "natural" language of feeling to poetry or music. Links among passion, an emotionally charged language, metrical rhythm, and the "earliest poetry of all nations" (1: 160) can, however, be detected throughout the poetic theory of Wordsworth, as I have argued at length in *British Romanticism and the Science of the Mind* (74–82).[63] Indeed, Wordsworth's "Preface" to *Lyrical Ballads* is difficult to fully comprehend without assuming some active interest in natural language theory at work behind his connections among linguistic expression, pleasure, poetic meter, and the "great and universal passions of men."[64] A further link between these issues and the "language of the nursery" is patent in Herder and Rousseau and implicit in Wordsworth's "Michael," while Smellie's chapter on animal communication shows how readily speculation on natural language could become attached to the new cultural centrality of the mother-educator-linguistic mentor and to the intimately related phenomenon of infant-elicited speech. This network of connections informing Romantic-era discourses on language, poetry, mothering, and early child development do much to elucidate the "language strange" motif in Romantic poetry. Yet the close (and patently obvious) relation between the mother or other female primary nurturer and what Kristeva calls the "semiotic" can only be articulated, by male Romantic poets like Coleridge, Keats, Landor, and Wordsworth himself, indirectly and in highly ambivalent fashion.

Male poets of Romantic-era Britain had professional as well as ideological reasons for registering anxiety in relation to "woman's voice." As Hofkosh, Marlon Ross, and other critics have discussed, the profession of authorship could no longer be considered a masculine monopoly by the early nineteenth century.[65] Not only did the number of publishing women writers continue to grow, but female-coded forms, such as the novel; modes, such as "sensibility" writing; and genres, such as the Gothic, were gaining cultural centrality despite the criticism (when not outright hostility) of male reviewers and rivals. How much more threatening, then, might the woman writer seem if the role of the mother's voice or "Nurse's song" in language acquisition—and in helping to establish the template for mature poetic activity—were fully acknowledged? This role could most readily be acknowledged, the "language strange" pattern suggests, under the sign of the witch, the demon, the fairy, or the lamia: the woman of powerful spells, seductive voice, maternal lulling, whose irresistible utterance can be countered only by the bards and priests of official male culture. The otherworldly woman with her strange language turns dreams into nightmares, although her victims wake long enough to tell their tales and to reassert their poetic voices.

I want to end, however, by briefly considering two well-known poems that stage the relation between the male poet and the powerful but enigmatic discourse of the female other in terms that suggest daydream more than nightmare. The first,

Wordsworth's "Solitary Reaper," comes close to what once would have been termed a "wish-fulfillment" dream. It puts into play several of the elements characteristic of the "language strange" topos: an exotic female figure performing verse in musical tones and in an enigmatic language; her enchanting effect on the male speaker, here identified with the poet; and the "thrilling" tonalities of the female voice. In this case, however, the anxiety that marks the "language strange" poems is missing or residually present only in that the solitary reaper, *as* a reaper, would inescapably be associated with death (and she does wield Death's conventional "sickle"). The predominant tone of the poem, in contrast, remains confidant and even proprietary: "The music in my heart I bore, / Long after it was heard no more." There is really no contest here; confronted with a rival female singer, the poet drinks deep ("I listen'd till I had my fill") and moves on, possessed of the alien "music." The "language strange" motif in this case gives way to another masculine Romantic motif or discursive move, which I have elsewhere discussed as the absorption or "colonization of the feminine" and that Diane Hoeveler has explored more extensively in *Romantic Androgyny*.[66]

Coleridge's "Kubla Khan" presents a more ambiguous case, somewhere in between nightmare and wishful fantasy. In this case the muse figure is split, as Hoeveler writes, between the "woman wailing for her demon-lover," an anxious projection of untamed sexuality and destructive female otherness, and the "damsel with a dulcimer," a comparatively "muted" and "desexed" (209–10) version of the wailing woman. *Damsel* would seem to be performing the work that the analogous term *Maiden* does in "The Solitary Reaper"—disavowing any association between the singing muse figure and the mother by presenting her as a young, unmarried woman. Yet the speaker of "Kubla Khan" proves notoriously unable to internalize the voice of the female other. "Could I revive within me / Her symphony and song" remains forever fixed in the limbo of the conditional tense, in stark contrast to the sense of completion conveyed by the past tense in Wordsworth's poem: "Her music in my heart I bore." The "Abyssinian maid" represents a most tantalizing possibility—that the idealized male poet might harness the incantatory, illicit power of the "wailing" woman, yet another version of the "faery song," "sweet moan," or "Thessalian spell" central to the "language strange" motif, by rendering her a less threatening "maid" and internalizing her "song." It doesn't work, of course. If it did, however, the male poet would gain enormous creative power ("I would build that dome in air"), and would become a virile yet also androgynous figure with "flashing eyes" and "floating hair." It might be irresponsible to interpret these last details in relation to the mother involved in dyadic infant play, her brightened eyes

seeking out contact, her hair tossed by the rhythmic head movements that typically accompany maternal vocalization. Yet the reference to the "milk of Paradise"
a few lines on signals that the mother cannot be too far off at this moment in the
poem.

Mary Robinson, Coleridge's senior by fourteen years and an established poet
when he was still young and obscure, herself played the role of Coleridge's maternal muse for a time and likely would have recognized the motif when she saw it.
I conclude, then, by suggesting that her poem "To the Poet Coleridge" represents
not only an early and prescient interpretation of "Kubla Khan" (as other readers
have noted) but a critical riposte to it as well.[67] The first four stanzas, each ending
with the word *blended*, shower Coleridge with praise and his poem with appreciation, in tones that could be taken variously as flirtatious, sisterly, or maternal ("I'll
gather wild flow'rs, dew besprent,/And weave a crown for THEE").[68] The fourth
stanza goes further than Coleridge himself does in "Kubla Khan," indulging him
in the fantasy that the male poet can successfully internalize the incantatory power
of the female muse:

> While, op'ning to my wond'ring eyes,
> Thou bidst a new creation rise,
> I'll raptur'd trace the circling bounds
>   Of thy RICH PARADISE extended,
> And listen to the varying sounds
> Of winds, and foaming torrents blended.

What the fourth stanza gives, however, the final stanza gently takes away. The idealized, romanticized male poet ("I'll listen to the minstrel's lay") yields without fan-
fare, without struggle, to the powerfully singing woman and her "sweet" "cadence,"
one that inspires answering "ecstatic measures" not in the poet Coleridge but in
the poetess Robinson:

> And now, with lofty tones inviting,
> Thy NYMPH, her dulcimer swift smiting,
> Shall wake in me ecstatic measures!
> Far, far remov'd from mortal pleasures!
> In cadence rich, in cadence strong,
> Proving the wondrous witcheries of song!
>   I hear her voice! thy *sunny dome*,
> Thy *caves of ice*, loud repeat,
> Vibrations, madd'ning sweet

Calling the visionary wand'rer home.
She sings of THEE, O favour'd child
Of Minstrelsy, SUBLIMELY WILD!

The Poet Coleridge becomes, in the end, a child, one, moreover, being called home—by a mother's voice? The "witcheries of song" belong, once more, to the female muse and to the female poet who can best reproduce her "cadence," a cadence that should sound familiar, however dimly, to all of us.

Notes

Preface

1. Interested readers might begin with Mary Thomas Crane and Alan Richardson, "Literary Studies and Cognitive Science: Toward a New Interdisciplinarity," *Mosaic* 32 (1999): 123–40; Richardson, "Cognitive Science and the Future of Literary Studies," *Philosophy and Literature* 23 (1999): 157–73; Richardson, "Studies in Literature and Cognition: A Field Map," *The Work of Fiction: Cognition, Culture, and Complexity*, ed. Richardson and Ellen Spolsky (Aldershot: Ashgate, 2004), 1–29; Patrick Colm Hogan, *Cognitive Science, Literature, and the Arts: A Guide for Humanists* (New York: Routledge, 2003).

2. Linda Hutcheon and Michael Hutcheon, "A Convenience of Marriage: Collaboration and Interdisciplinarity," *PMLA* 116.5 (Oct. 2001): 1364–76.

3. Ellen Spolsky, "Darwin and Derrida: Cognitive Literary Theory as a Species of Post-Structuralism," *Poetics Today* 23.1 (2002): 43–62, and "Cognitive Literary Historicism: A Response to Adler and Gross," *Poetics Today* 24.2 (2003): 161–83.

4. Lisa Zunshine, editor's introduction to *Introduction to Cognitive Cultural Studies*, ed. Zunshine (Baltimore: Johns Hopkins University Press, forthcoming).

5. Richardson, *British Romanticism and the Science of the Mind* (Cambridge: Cambridge University Press, 2001); for the first use of *neural historicism*, see Crane and Richardson 137.

6. Semir Zeki, *Inner Vision: An Exploration of Art and the Brain* (Oxford: Oxford University Press, 1999), 1. For the contrasting claims of the "consilience" program, see Edward O. Wilson, *Consilience: The Unity of Knowledge* (New York: Knopf, 1998).

7. V. S. Ramachandran and Sandra Blakeslee, *Phantoms in the Brain: Probing the Mysteries of the Human Mind* (New York: William Morrow, 1998), 5.

CHAPTER ONE: Introduction

1. Howard Gardner, *The Mind's New Science: A History of the Cognitive Revolution* (New York: Basic Books, 1985).

2. See Michael S. Gazzaniga, ed., *The New Cognitive Neurosciences*, 2nd ed. (Cambridge: MIT Press, 2000), and *The Cognitive Neurosciences 3* (Cambridge: MIT Press, 2004).

3. For an introduction to cognitive approaches to film studies, see the introduction and relevant essays in David Bordwell and Noel Carroll, eds., *Post-Theory: Reconstructing Film Studies* (Madison: University of Wisconsin Press, 1996). For two important contributions to art history in light of the cognitive neuroscience of vision, see Semir

Zeki, *Inner Vision: An Exploration of Art and the Brain* (Oxford: Oxford University Press, 1999), and Margaret Livingstone, *Vision and Art: The Biology of Seeing* (New York: Abrams, 2002). On music and cognition, see Fred Lerdahl and Ray Jackendoff, *A Generative Theory of Tonal Music* (Cambridge: MIT Press, 1983), and David Temperley, *The Cognition of Basic Musical Structures* (Cambridge: MIT Press, 2004).

4. I discussed this dilemma a decade ago in "Cognitive Science and the Future of Literary Studies," *Philosophy and Literature* 23 (1999): 157–73.

5. Peter Stockwell, *Cognitive Poetics: An Introduction* (London: Routledge, 2002), and Patrick Colm Hogan, *Cognitive Science, Literature, and the Arts: A Guide for Humanists* (New York: Routledge, 2003). Hogan provides the better introduction.

6. On cognitive approaches to rhetoric and figurative language, see chap. 4. Two important recent contributions to the cognitive study of narrative are David Herman, *Story Logic: Problems and Possibilities of Narrative* (Lincoln: University of Nebraska Press, 2002), and Suzanne Keen, *Empathy and the Novel* (Oxford: Oxford University Press, 2007).

7. Peter Brooks, "Aesthetics and Ideology: What Happened to Poetics?" *Critical Inquiry* 20.3 (1994): 509–23. For cognitive approaches to poetics, see Reuven Tsur, *Toward a Theory of Cognitive Poetics* (Amsterdam: North-Holland, 1992), and David S. Miall, *Literary Reading: Empirical and Theoretical Studies* (New York: Peter Lang, 2006).

8. See, in particular, Elaine Scarry, *Dreaming by the Book* (New York: Farrar, Strauss, and Giroux, 1999); Ellen Esrock, *The Reader's Eye: Visual Imagining as Reader Response* (Baltimore: Johns Hopkins University Press, 1994); and Patrick Colm Hogan, *The Mind and Its Stories: Narrative Universals and Human Emotion* (Cambridge: Cambridge University Press, 2003).

9. Judith F. Duchan, Gail A. Bruder, and Lynne E. Hewitt, *Deixis in Narrative: A Cognitive Science Perspective* (Hillsdale, NJ: Lawrence Erlbaum, 1995); Ellen Semino and Jonathan Culpeper, eds., *Cognitive Stylistics: Language and Cognition in Text Analysis* (Amsterdam: J. Benjamins, 2002); Reuven Tsur, *What Makes Sound Patterns Expressive: The Poetic Mode of Speech Perception* (Durham: Duke University Press, 1992).

10. I am thinking especially of the work of Hogan and Scarry (cited above) and Mark Turner, particularly *Reading Minds: The Study of English in the Age of Cognitive Science* (Princeton: Princeton University Press, 1991) and *The Literary Mind* (New York: Oxford University Press, 1996).

11. Don Byrd, *The Poetics of the Common Knowledge* (Albany: State University of New York Press, 1994), 330.

12. Ellen Spolsky, "Cognitive Literary Historicism: A Response to Adler and Gross," *Poetics Today* 24.2 (2003): 164. Hereafter cited in the text.

13. For "constructivist interactionism," see Spolsky, "Darwin and Derrida: Cognitive Literary Theory as a Species of Post-Structuralism," *Poetics Today* 23.1 (2002): 43–62. Hereafter cited in the text.

14. F. Elizabeth Hart, "The Epistemology of Cognitive Literary Studies," *Philosophy and Literature* 25.2 (2001): 331, 320. Hereafter cited in the text.

15. N. Katherine Hayles, "Constrained Constructivism: Locating Scientific Inquiry in the Theater of Representation," in *Realism and Representation: Essays on the Problem of Realism in Relation to Science, Literature, and Culture*, ed. George Levine (Madison: University of Wisconsin Press, 1993), 32. Hereafter cited in the text.

16. See also Donna Haraway's discussion of "situated knowledges" in the context of a "feminist empiricism" that would combine a recognition of "radical historical contingency" with a "no-nonsense commitment to faithful accounts of a 'real' world" in "Situated Knowledges: The Science Question in Feminism and the Privilege of Partial Perspective," *Simians, Cyborgs, and Women: The Reinvention of Nature* (New York: Routledge, 1991), 187–88.

17. See, e.g., Brian Boyd, "Jane, Meet Charles: Literature, Evolution, and Human Nature," *Philosophy and Literature* 22 (1998): 1–30.

18. Mary Crane, *Shakespeare's Brain: Reading with Cognitive Theory* (Princeton: Princeton University Press, 2001), 7. Hereafter cited in the text.

19. Mark Turner, "The Cognitive Study of Art, Language, and Literature," *Poetics Today* 23.1 (2002): 18. Hereafter cited in the text.

20. Gary Snyder, "Entering the Fiftieth Millennium," in *The Gary Snyder Reader: Prose, Poetry, and Translations, 1952–1998* (New York: Counterpoint, 1999), 390–94. For a lucid exploration of the concept of "deep history" (without reference to Snyder) from a historian's disciplinary perspective, see Daniel Lord Smail, *On Deep History and the Brain* (Berkeley and Los Angeles: University of California Press, 2007).

21. David Perkins, *Is Literary History Possible?* (Baltimore: Johns Hopkins University Press, 1992), 128–29.

22. Ellen Spolsky, *Gaps in Nature: Literary Interpretation and the Modular Mind* (Albany: State University of New York Press, 1993), 19–41. Hereafter cited in the text.

23. Ellen Spolsky, *Word vs. Image: Cognitive Hunger in Shakespeare's England* (Basingstoke: Palgrave Macmillan, 2007).

24. Ellen Spolsky, *Satisfying Skepticism: Embodied Knowledge in the Early Modern World* (Aldershot: Ashgate, 2001).

25. J. M. Balkin makes a similar point in his valuable study, *Cultural Software: A Theory of Ideology* (New Haven: Yale University Press, 1998), 77.

26. Mary Crane, "'Fair is Foul': *Macbeth* and Binary Logic," *The Work of Fiction: Cognition, Culture, and Complexity,* ed. Alan Richardson and Ellen Spolsky (Aldershot: Ashgate, 2004), 110. Hereafter cited in the text.

27. Lisa Zunshine, "Rhetoric, Cognition, and Ideology in A. L. Barbauld's *Hymns in Prose for Children* (1781)," *Poetics Today* 23.1 (2002): 9–20.

28. Again, compare Balkin, who argues that "we are by nature cultural creatures" but not therefore "infinitely malleable" (*Cultural Software,* 5).

29. Chantal Mouffe, "Hegemony and New Political Subjects: Toward a New Conception of Democracy," *Marxism and the Interpretation of Culture,* ed. Cary Nelson and Lawrence Grossberg (Urbana: University of Illinois Press, 1988), 89–90.

30. Richardson, *British Romanticism and the Science of the Mind* (Cambridge: Cambridge University Press, 2001).

31. John R. Searle, *The Rediscovery of the Mind* (Cambridge: MIT Press, 1992), 175–96; for the "mind is what the brain does," see Stephen Kosslyn and Olivier Koenig, *Wet Mind: The New Cognitive Neuroscience* (New York: Free Press, 1992), 4.

32. For a useful contrast between the Freudian unconscious and the cognitive or "adaptive" unconscious, see Timothy D. Wilson, *Strangers to Ourselves: Discovering the Adaptive Unconscious* (Cambridge: Belknap Press of Harvard University Press, 2002), 1–16.

CHAPTER TWO: The Neural Sublime

1. This first self-experiment is taken from Jerry A. Fodor, *The Modularity of Mind: An Essay on Faculty Psychology* (Cambridge: MIT Press, 1983), 66–67.

2. I owe this self-experiment and the accompanying diagram to Daniel C. Dennett, *Consciousness Explained* (Boston: Little, Brown, 1991), 323–24.

3. The Kanizsa triangle was included by Gaetano Kanizsa in his article "Subjective Contours," *Scientific American* 234 (April 1976): 48–52, and in his book *Organization in Vision* (New York: Praeger, 1979). It is frequently reproduced and discussed, as, e.g., in Donald D. Hoffman, *Visual Intelligence: How We Create What We See* (New York: Norton, 1998), 48–49 (hereafter cited in the text), and Francis Crick, *The Astonishing Hypothesis: The Scientific Search for the Soul* (New York: Simon and Schuster, 1995), 27–28.

4. Another illusion designed by Kanizsa (see note 3, above). Reproduced and discussed in Crick, *The Astonishing Hypothesis*, 38–39.

5. Sometimes attributed to Ludwig Wittgenstein, the "duck-rabbit" figure was designed by the psychologist Joseph Jastrow and first published in his essay "The Mind's Eye," *Popular Science Monthly* 54 (1899): 299–312, based on an earlier drawing published in *Harper's Weekly* in 1892, after a similar drawing published in a German magazine, *Fliegende Blätter*, the same year. It is reproduced and discussed in (to name only two examples) Hoffman (95) and Paul M. Churchland, *The Engine of Reason, the Seat of the Soul: A Philosophical Journey into the Brain* (Cambridge: MIT Press, 1995) 107–9.

6. Designed by Louis Albert Necker and first published in his "Observations on Some Remarkable Phenomena Seen in Switzerland: And an Optical Phenomenon Which Occurs on Viewing a Figure of a Crystal or Geometrical Solid," *London and Edinburgh Philosophical Magazine and Journal of Science* 3 (1832): 329–37. It is reproduced and discussed in, e.g., Hoffman, *Visual Intelligence*, 19–24, and Crick, *Astonishing Hypothesis*, 29–30.

7. The best introduction to Hoffman's work is his book *Visual Intelligence*, cited above. At present, change blindness demonstrations can readily be found on the Internet. As Internet addresses frequently change, the interested reader is invited simply to do an Internet search with the phrase "change blindness."

8. For an introduction to Banaji's work, see her Web pages at Harvard University: www.people.fas.harvard.edu/~banaji/. Motion blindness demonstrations can also easily be found on the Internet via a whole phrase search for "motion blindness."

9. E. H. Gombrich, *Art and Illusion: A Study in the Psychology of Pictorial Representation*, 2nd ed., revised (Princeton: Bollingen, 1969), 5–6.

10. Guy Sircello, "How Is a Theory of the Sublime Possible?" *Journal of Aesthetics and Art Criticism* 51.4 (Fall 1993): 545. Hereafter cited in the text.

11. James H. Austin, *Zen-Brain Reflections: Reviewing Recent Developments in Meditation and States of Consciousness* (Cambridge: MIT Press, 2006), xxvi (hereafter cited in the text). Buddhist meditation practices (and the resources of Buddhist writings on mind, self, and consciousness, often directly based on insights gleaned from such practices) have been recommended by an influential trio of cognitive researchers as a useful methodological supplement to empirical and theoretical work in cognitive neuroscience. See Francisco J. Varela, Evan Thompson, and Eleanor Rosch, *The Embodied Mind: Cognitive Science and Human Experience* (Cambridge: MIT Press, 1991), 21–33.

12. Longinus, "On the Sublime," as excerpted in Andrew Ashfield and Peter de

Bolla, *The Sublime: A Reader in British Eighteenth-Century Aesthetic Theory* (Cambridge: Cambridge University Press, 1996), 24. The volume is hereafter cited in the text as *Sublime*.

13. For a survey, see Kenneth Holmqvist and Jaroslaw Pluciennik, "A Short Guide to the Theory of the Sublime," *Style* 36.4 (2002): 718–41.

14. Cynthia A. Freeland, "The Sublime in Cinema," in *Passionate Views: Film, Cognition, and Emotion*, ed. Carl Plantinga and Greg M. Smith (Baltimore: Johns Hopkins University Press, 1999), 83.

15. Immanuel Kant, *Critique of Judgment*, trans. Werner S. Pluhar (Indianapolis: Hackett, 1987), 138–40. Hereafter cited in the text.

16. Samuel Holt Monk is clear enough on this point: "The direction of this growth" in a progression of eighteenth-century theories of the sublime "is toward the subjectivism of Kant" (*The Sublime: A Study of Critical Theories in 18th-Century England* [Ann Arbor: University of Michigan Press, 1960], 4). The teleological character of Monk's study has been critically noted by Ashfield and de Bolla in their helpful introduction to *The Sublime Reader* (2) and by Vanessa L. Ryan in "The Physiological Sublime: Burke's Critique of Reason," *Journal of the History of Ideas* 62.1 (April 2001): 265 (hereafter cited in the text).

17. Anne K. Mellor, *Romanticism and Gender* (New York: Routledge, 1993), 88. See also Frances Ferguson, who remarks that "the sublime has, like higher idealism, recurrently been conceived as a transcendence of experience," in *Solitude and the Sublime: The Romantic Aesthetics of Individuation* (New York: Routledge, 1992), 37.

18. In her essay "Toward a Female Sublime," e.g., Patricia Yeager speaks of a "mock sublime" (193), a female "sublime of nearness" (195), a deliberately "failed sublime" (201), and claims that women writers must "re-invent" the sublime (195). Patricia Yeager, "Toward a Female Sublime," in *Gender and Theory: Dialogues on Feminist Criticism*, ed. Linda Kauffman (London: Blackwell, 1989), 191–212. For the ecological sublime, see below in this chapter.

19. Edmund Burke, *A Philosophical Enquiry into the Origin of Our Ideas of the Sublime and Beautiful and Other Pre-Revolutionary Writings*, ed. David Womersley (London: Penguin, 1998), 101. Hereafter cited in the text.

20. On "theory of mind" theory, see chap. 5.

21. Mary Wollstonecraft, *Mary and The Wrongs of Women*, ed. Gary Kelly (Oxford: Oxford University Press, 1980), 83–84.

22. Holmqvist and Pluciennik note that the contributions of Burke and Kant can be seen as "incomparable paradigms of talking about" the sublime (718–19).

23. Thomas Weiskel, *The Romantic Sublime: Studies in the Structure and Psychology of Transcendence* (Baltimore: Johns Hopkins University Press 1986), 23–24.

24. In *British Romanticism and the Science of the Mind*, 148–49.

25. For a recent overview of Shelley's interest in medicine and medical science, see Sharon Ruston, *Shelley and Vitality* (Houndmills: Palgrave Macmillan, 2005), 74–101.

26. Percy Bysshe Shelley, *Shelley's Prose, or, The Trumpet of a Prophecy*, ed. David Lee Clark (Albuquerque: University of New Mexico Press, 1954), 177. Hereafter cited in text.

27. Quotations from Shelley's poems (cited by line, *Mab* cited by book and line) follow the texts in *Shelley's Poetry and Prose*, ed. Donald H. Reiman and Sharon Powers (New York: Norton, 1977).

28. Quotations from *The Revolt of Islam* (not included in Reiman and Powers), cited by line, follow *Shelley: Poetical Works*, 2nd ed., ed. Thomas Hutchinson and G. M. Matthews (London: Oxford University Press, 1970).

29. Angela Leighton traces Shelley's image of the waves washing over and erasing marks on the sand, conveying "a writing that is deserted and emptied of the gods" (47), throughout her study of Shelley and the sublime; see esp. her discussion of this image as it occurs in "The Triumph of Life" (*Shelley and the Sublime: An Interpretation of the Major Poems* [Cambridge: Cambridge University Press, 1984], 170–73).

30. For an important and lucid discussion of the syntax and imagery by which Shelley conveys experiences of dissolving and erasure, though without reference to the sublime, see William Keach, *Shelley's Style* (New York: Methuen, 1984), 118–53.

31. William Wordsworth, the "Two-Part *Prelude*" 1: 176–82, *The Prelude 1799, 1805, 1850*, ed. Jonathan Wordsworth, M. H. Abrams, and Stephen Gill (New York: Norton, 1979).

32. For a neuroscientific account of such "aftereffects" at the neuronal level, see Horace Barlow, "Adaptation by Hyperpolarization," *Science* 276 (9 May 1997): 913–14. Briefly, neuronal adaptation to a repeated stimulus reduces the number of action potentials causing a given array of neurons to "fire," by means of a gradual increase of "the negative intracellular potential of [each relevant brain cell], so that a diminished fraction of each cycle of modulation rises above the cell's firing threshold, and fewer impulses occur with each cycle as adaptation progresses" (914). When the stimulus suddenly ends or attention is turned to a different but related stimulus, the effect persists for a few moments.

33. Christopher Hitt, "Toward an Ecological Sublime," *New Literary History* 30.3 (1999): 615.

34. V. S. Ramachandran and Sandra Blakeslee, *Phantoms in the Brain: Probing the Mysteries of the Human Mind* (New York: William Morrow, 1998), 58. Hereafter cited in the text.

35. Gerald M. Edelman, *Bright Air, Brilliant Fire: On the Matter of the Mind* (New York: Basic Books, 1992), 17 (exclamation in original).

36. Churchland, *The Engine of Reason*, 5.

37. I wrote this paragraph, with the allusion to Dickinson, for a lecture given at Princeton University in March 2007, about a year before I had a chance to read Richard Powers's brilliant novel, *The Echo Maker* (2006). I was the more amused, then, to find that Powers had contrived his own pastiche of the (mathematical) neural sublime trope to be included in the first book of his fictional neuroscientist, Gerald Weber: "Mental space is larger than anyone can think. A single brain's 100 billion cells make thousands of connections each. The strength and nature of these connections changes [*sic*] every time use triggers them. Any given brain can put itself into more unique states than there are elementary particles in the universe." The title of Weber's (imaginary) first book? *Wider Than the Sky* (Richard Powers, *The Echo Maker* [New York: Picador, 2006], 93).

38. "And they inclos'd my infinite brain into a narrow circle": *Visions of the Daughters of Albion*, plate 2, line 32, in William Blake, *The Complete Poetry and Prose of William Blake*, rev. ed., ed. David V. Erdman (Garden City: Anchor, 1982).

CHAPTER THREE: The Romantic Image, the Mind's Eye, and the History of the Senses

1. Thomas Hobbes, *Leviathan: Or the Matter, Forme and Power of a Commonwealth Ecclesiasticall and Civil*, ed. Michael Oakeshott (New York: Collier, 1962), 175.

2. John Locke, *An Essay Concerning Human Understanding*, ed. Peter H. Nidditch (Oxford: Clarendon Press, 1975), 363.

3. For an overview, see Alan Richardson, *Literature, Education, and Romanticism: Reading as Social Practice* (Cambridge: Cambridge University Press, 1994), 44–64.

4. Jean-Jacques Rousseau, *Emile: or, On Education*, trans. Allan Bloom (New York: Basic Books, 1979), 170, 116.

5. Edmund Burke, *A Philosophical Enquiry into the Origin of Our Ideas of the Sublime and Beautiful and Other Pre-Revolutionary Writings*, ed. David Womersley (London: Penguin, 1998), 187. Hereafter cited in the text.

6. Samuel Johnson, *Lives of the English Poets*, ed. Arthur Waugh (London: Oxford, 1952), 1: 27. Hereafter cited in the text.

7. The philosophical resemblances between the associationist psychology of the seventeenth and eighteenth centuries and connectionism in cognitive psychology and artificial intelligence theory are discussed at length in John Sutton, *Philosophy and Memory Traces: Descartes to Connectionism* (Cambridge: Cambridge University Press, 1998).

8. W. J. T. Mitchell, "Visible Language: Blake's Wond'rous Art of Writing," in *Romanticism and Contemporary Criticism*, ed. Morris Eaves and Michael Fischer (Ithaca: Cornell University Press, 1986), 48–49. Hereafter cited in the text.

9. William H. Galperin, *The Return of the Visible in British Romanticism* (Baltimore: Johns Hopkins University Press, 1993), 19, 31.

10. William Wordsworth, *Selected Prose*, ed. John O. Hayden (Harmondsworth: Penguin, 1988), 400. Hereafter cited in the text.

11. F. A. Pottle, "The Eye and the Object in the Poetry of Wordsworth," in *Romanticism and Consciousness: Essays in Criticism*, ed. Harold Bloom (New York: Norton, 1970), 273–87. Hereafter cited in the text.

12. Elaine Scarry, *Dreaming by the Book* (New York: Farrar, Strauss, and Giroux, 1999), 162–66. Hereafter cited in the text.

13. See, esp., Stephen M. Kosslyn, *Image and Brain: The Resolution of the Imagery Debate* (Cambridge: MIT Press, 1994).

14. Martha J. Farah, "The Neural Bases of Mental Imagery," in *The New Cognitive Neurosciences*, ed. Michael S. Gazzaniga, 2nd ed. (Cambridge: MIT Press, 2000), 970, 972.

15. Stephen M. Kosslyn and William L. Thompson, "Shared Mechanisms in Visual Imagery and Visual Perception: Insights from Cognitive Neuroscience," in *The New Cognitive Neurosciences*, 982.

16. See "Lines Composed a Few Miles above Tintern Abbey," lines 106–7, and the "Two-Part *Prelude*" of 1799, 2: 268–310. My text for the shorter poems is *William Wordsworth: The Poems*, ed. John O. Hayden, 2 vols. (Harmondsworth: Penguin, 1977), and, for *The Prelude*, Wordsworth, *The Prelude 1799, 1805, 1850*, ed. Jonathan Wordsworth, M. H. Abrams, and Stephen Gill (New York: Norton, 1979).

17. Samuel Taylor Coleridge, *Biographia Literaria or Biographical Sketches of My*

Literary Life and Opinions, ed. James Engell and W. J. Bate, 2 vols. (Princeton: Princeton University Press, 1983), 1: 304.

18. Discussed in chapter 2.

19. M. H. Abrams, *Natural Supernaturalism: Tradition and Revolution in Romantic Literature* (New York: Norton, 1971), 356–72.

20. Diane Ackerman, *A Natural History of the Senses* (New York: Random House, 1990); Michel Foucault, *Discipline and Punish: The Birth of the Prison*, trans. Alan Sheridan (New York: Vintage, 1995), 195–228.

21. Robert Jütte, *A History of the Senses: From Antiquity to Cyberspace*, trans. James Lynn (Cambridge: Polity Press, 2005), 10. Hereafter cited in the text.

22. I adapt the term *biosocial* from Paul Ekman, afterword to Charles Darwin, *The Expression of the Emotions in Man and Animals*, 3rd ed., ed. Paul Ekman (New York: Oxford University Press, 1998), 393.

23. Boris Eichenbaum, "The Theory of the 'Formal Method,'" in *Russian Formalist Criticism: Four Essays*, ed. Lee T. Lemon and Marion J. Reis (Lincoln: University of Nebraska Press, 1965), 106–11.

24. Roman Jakobson, "Closing Statement: Linguistics and Poetics," *Style in Language*, ed. Thomas A. Sebeok (Cambridge: MIT Press, 1960), 375.

25. Reuven Tsur, *What Makes Sound Patterns Expressive: The Poetic Mode of Speech Perception* (Durham: Duke University Press, 1992), 52–53, 111–35.

26. Frank Kermode, *Romantic Image* (New York: Vintage, 1957), 43.

27. On Coleridge, the "mind's eye," and the poetic salience of the visual image, see Frederick Burwick, "Romanticism as Cognitive Process," *Prism(s): Essays in Romanticism* 15 (2007): 7–32. For example, Burwick quotes Coleridge stressing the "advantages of one who has been from Childhood accustomed to make *Images* the symbols of Things, instead of resting on mere Words," and extolling Shakespeare's ability "by a single word to produce the picture in the imagination" (12–13). Coleridge's writings show no less ambivalence on this issue than do Wordsworth's, however. Coleridge too speaks of the "despotism of the eye" (Abrams 366), and he seconds, in a comment on the sublime, Burke's valuation of verbal associations over images: "The grandest efforts of poetry are where the imagination is called forth, not to produce a distinct form, but a strong working of the mind . . . the result being what the poet wishes to impress, namely, the substitution of a sublime feeling of the unimaginable for the mere image" (*The Romantics on Milton: Formal Essays and Critical Asides*, ed. Joseph Anthony Wittreich Jr. [Cleveland: Case Western Reserve University Press, 1970], 201).

28. Louise Vinge, *The Five Senses: Studies in a Literary Tradition* (Lund: CWK Gleerup, 1975), 166.

29. "The Aeolian Harp," line 28. Quotations from Coleridge's poems follow *The Complete Poems*, ed. William Keach (London: Penguin, 1997).

30. Gabrielle G. Starr, "Multi-Sensory Imagery," in *Introduction to Cognitive Cultural Studies*, ed. Lisa Zunshine (Baltimore: Johns Hopkins University Press), forthcoming.

31. For a pioneering argument along these lines, with special relevance to literary studies, see Allan Paivio, "The Mind's Eye in Arts and Science," *Poetics* 12 (1983): 1–18. Paivio has recently updated his "dual coding" approach in *Mind and Its Evolution: A Dual Coding Theoretical Approach* (Mahwah, NJ: Erlbaum, 2007). For "multiple coding," see Wilma Bucci, *Psychoanalysis and Cognitive Science: A Multiple Code Theory* (New York: Guilford, 1997).

32. See chapter 1.

33. See the discussion of Shelley's "Alastor" in chapter 2.

34. Charles Bell, *Idea of a New Anatomy of the Brain: A Fascicle of the Privately Printed Edition of 1811* (London: Dawsons, 1966) 5, 8–9.

35. Ibid., 9–10.

36. François Joseph Gall, *On the Functions of the Brain and of Each of Its Parts: With Observations on the Possibility of Determining the Instincts, Propensities, and Talents, or the Moral and Intellectual Dispositions of Men and Animals by the Configuration of the Brain and Head*, trans. Winslow Lewis, 6 vols. (Boston: Marsh, Capen, and Lyon, 1835), 1: 92.

37. Pierre-Jean-Georges Cabanis, *On the Relations between the Physical and Moral Aspects of Man*, trans. Margaret Duggan Saidi, ed. George Mora, 2 vols. (Baltimore: Johns Hopkins University Press, 1981), 1: 92, 163.

38. Sir Walter Scott, *Waverley*, ed. Andrew Hook (Harmondsworth: Penguin, 1972), 53.

39. William Hazlitt, *Lectures on the English Poets and The Spirit of the Age*, ed. Catherine MacDonald Maclean (London: Dent, 1967), 154. Hereafter cited in the text.

CHAPTER FOUR: Romantic Apostrophe

1. See Andrew Ortony, ed., *Metaphor and Thought*, 2nd ed. (Cambridge: Cambridge University Press, 1993), and Yesahyahu Shen, "Cognitive Aspects of Metaphor," *Poetics Today* 13 (1992): 567–74, for helpful introductions to this topic.

2. Robert P. Abelson, "Artificial Intelligence and Literary Appreciation: How Big Is the Gap?" in *Literary Discourse: Aspects of Cognitive and Social Psychological Approaches*, ed. László Halász (Berlin: de Gruyter, 1987), 39.

3. George Lakoff and Mark Johnson, *Metaphors We Live By* (Chicago: University of Chicago Press, 1980).

4. George Lakoff and Mark Johnson, *Philosophy in the Flesh: The Embodied Mind and Its Challenge to Western Thought* (New York: Basic Books, 1999), 47.

5. Mark Turner, *Death Is the Mother of Beauty: Mind, Metaphors, and Criticism* (Chicago: University of Chicago Press, 1987), 9–10.

6. Mark Turner, *The Literary Mind* (New York: Oxford University Press, 1996), v.

7. Raymond Gibbs, *The Poetics of Mind: Figurative Thought, Language, and Understanding* (Cambridge: Cambridge University Press, 1994), 1.

8. Paul de Man, "The Epistemology of Metaphor," *Critical Inquiry* 5 (1978): 13–30, reprinted in *On Metaphor*, ed. Sheldon Sacks (Chicago: University of Chicago Press, 1979), 28 (hereafter cited in the text); Jacques Derrida, "White Mythology: Metaphor in the Text of Philosophy," *Margins of Philosophy*, trans. Alan Bass (Chicago: University of Chicago Press, 1982), 253.

9. Paul de Man, "Semiology and Rhetoric," *Allegories of Reading: Figural Language in Rousseau, Nietzsche, Rilke, and Proust* (New Haven: Yale University Press, 1979), 10. Hereafter cited in the text.

10. Jonathan Culler's 1975 discussion of how the "overheard" status of lyric poetry complicates the "communicative circuit" of ordinary discourse anticipates his later work on apostrophe, although the term itself does not come up in the earlier context (*Structuralist Poetics: Structuralism, Linguistics, and the Study of Literature* [Ithaca:

Cornell University Press, 1975], 164–66). All references to Culler in the text refer to his essay "Apostrophe" *The Pursuit of Signs: Semiotics, Literature, Deconstruction* (Ithaca: Cornell University Press, 1981), 135–54.

11. Mary Jacobus, "Apostrophe and Lyric Voice in The Prelude," *Lyric Poetry: Beyond New Criticism*, ed. Chaviva Hosek and Patricia Parker (Ithaca: Cornell University Press, 1985), 171; Cynthia Chase, "'Viewless Wings': Intertextual Interpretation of Keats's 'Ode to a Nightingale,'" *Lyric Poetry: Beyond New Criticism*, 211. For another significant essay on apostrophe from this period, see Barbara Johnson, "Apostrophe, Animation, and Abortion," *A World of Difference* (Baltimore: Johns Hopkins University Press, 1987), 184–99.

12. For the sake of convenience, given the multiplicity of examples, all quotations of Romantic-era poetry in this chapter are taken from David Perkins, ed., *English Romantic Writers*, 2nd ed. (Fort Worth: Harcourt Brace, 1995). Line numbers are given only for longer poems.

13. Anne Yearsley, *A Poem on the Inhumanity of the Slave-Trade* (London: Robinson, 1788), ii, 1. J. Douglas Kneale, in arguing against Culler's reading of apostrophe, claims that addresses (such as the examples here from Yearsley and from Wordsworth's "Ode to Duty") constituting a poem's opening lines cannot be considered apostrophes. For Kneale, apostrophe, as a turning away, requires the "pretext" of an addressee, established earlier in the poem, that can be turned from ("Romantic Aversions: Apostrophe Reconsidered," *Rhetorical Traditions and British Romantic Literature*, ed. Don Bialostosky and Lawrence D. Needham [Bloomington: Indiana University Press, 1995], 151, 154). I agree instead with Culler's counter-argument, in his talk "Apostrophe Revisited," that there is a "default option of lyric address" and that such apostrophes turn from "unmarked lyric address to something distinctive" even in the first lines of poems ("Apostrophe Revisited," talk given during the special session "The Overhearing of Lyric," Modern Language Association Convention, New Orleans, 29 December 2001). Quintilian, in fact, includes an opening address in his classical discussion of apostrophe, the famous opening line ("Quousque tandem abutere . . .") of Cicero's attack on Catiline (Quintilian, *Institutio Oratoria*, trans. H. E. Butler, 4 vols. [Cambridge: Harvard University Press, 1921], 2: 42–43).

14. Richard J. Gerrig, *Experiencing Narrative Worlds: On the Psychological Activities of Reading* (New Haven: Yale University Press, 1993), 156. Hereafter cited in the text.

15. Gerrig's account draws on earlier work by Herbert H. Clark and Thomas B. Carlson, who establish the terms *overhearer* and *participant* in "Hearers and Speech Acts," *Language* 58 (1982): 332–73.

16. John Keats, *The Letters of John Keats, 1814–1821*, ed. Hyder Edward Rollins, 2 vols. (Cambridge: Harvard University Press, 1958), 2: 204

17. This essay is sometimes attributed to Mikhail Bakhtin.

18. V. N. Volosinov, "Discourse in Life and Discourse in Art (Concerning Sociological Poetics)," *Freudianism: A Critical Sketch*, trans. I. R. Titunik, ed. I. R. Titunik and Neal H. Bruss (Bloomington: Indiana University Press, 1976), 99, 103. Hereafter cited in the text.

19. L. M. Findlay, "Culler and Byron on Apostrophe and Lyric Time," *Studies in Romanticism* 24 (1985): 338.

20. Quintilian, *Institutio Oratoria*, 2: 41.

21. Although Culler explicitly calls for a "third term"—the "audience"—in contrast to any "simple oppositional structure of the I-Thou" model, his own analyses continue to elide the desired third term, as in the following remark on Shelley's "Ode to the West Wind"—"If the wind is a spirit, it can make the speaker either an it or a thou to its I" ("Apostrophe," 141–42).

22. M. H. Abrams, *A Glossary of Literary Terms*, 4th ed. (New York: Holt, Rinehart and Winston, 1981), 161.

23. Paul De Man, "Autobiography as De-Facement," *MLN* 94 (1979): 919–30, reprinted in *The Rhetoric of Romanticism* (New York: Columbia University Press, 1984), 75–76, 80.

24. Michael Macovski, *Dialogue and Literature: Apostrophe, Auditors, and the Collapse of Romantic Literature* (Oxford: Oxford University Press, 1994), 9. Hereafter cited in the text.

25. Angela Esterhammer, *The Romantic Performative: Language and Action in British and German Romanticism* (Stanford: Stanford University Press, 2000), 19.

26. Thomas Reid, *Essays on the Intellectual Powers of Man*, ed. Baruch A. Brody (Cambridge: MIT Press, 1969), 71. Hereafter cited in the text.

27. Hugh Blair, *Lectures on Rhetoric and Belles Lettres*, ed. Harold F. Harding, 3 vols. (Carbondale: Southern Illinois University Press, 1965), 1: 326. Hereafter cited in the text.

28. In his talk "Apostrophe Revisited," Culler also speaks of a "continuum" in the experience of apostrophe ("some apostrophes interrupt more surprisingly than others"), noting that the placement of an apostrophe may heighten or diminish its effect. Heather Dubrow, in a talk given as part of the same MLA special session ("'Stand and Unfold Yourself': The Partially Overheard Lyric," special session on "The Overhearing of Lyric," New Orleans, 29 December 2001), also recruits the notion of a continuum or "spectrum" in arguing for a broader conception of poetic address, one allowing for "many possibilities between direct address and overhearing an oblivious voice." I wish to thank Jonathan Culler, Heather Dubrow, and the respondent to that session, Herbert Tucker, for graciously making versions of their talks available to me at short notice.

29. See, e.g., Alan Richardson, "The Dangers of Sympathy: Sibling Incest in English Romantic Poetry," *SEL* 25 (1985): 745–47, and Anne Mellor, *Romanticism and Gender* (New York: Routledge, 1993), 19.

30. The earlier versions can be found in Samuel Taylor Coleridge, *Coleridge's Dejection: The Earliest Manuscripts and the Earliest Printings*, ed. Stephen Maxfield Parrish (Ithaca: Cornell University Press, 1988), cited here by page.

31. Addresses to household pets, however, as in Larry Kramer's apostrophe to his dog Molly (discussed above), may retain more of the familiarity and intimacy of apostrophes to friends and near relatives.

32. Compare Culler's discussion of the "sinister reciprocity" that marks certain apostrophic poems ("Apostrophe," 153).

33. Joseph E. Grady, Todd Oakley, and Seana Coulson, "Blending and Metaphor," *Metaphor in Cognitive Linguistics: Selected Papers from the Fifth International Cognitive Linguistics Conference, Amsterdam, July 1997*, ed. Raymond W. Gibbs Jr. and Gerard J. Steen (Amsterdam: Benjamins, 1999), 119.

34. See, e.g., Scott Atran, *Cognitive Foundations of Natural History: Towards an Anthropology of Science* (Cambridge: Cambridge University Press, 1990), and Michael H.

Kelly and Frank C. Keil. "The More Things Change . . . : Metamorphoses and Conceptual Structure." *Cognitive Science* 9 (1985): 403–16.

35. On "Theory of Mind" theories, see chap. 5.

36. *The Golden Age, A Poetical Epistle from Erasmus D——n, M. D. to Thomas Beddoes, M. D.* (New York: Garland, 1978), 17.

37. Raymond W. Gibbs Jr., "Process and Product in Making Sense of Tropes," *Metaphor and Thought*, 2nd ed., ed. Andrew Ortony (Cambridge: Cambridge University Press, 1993), 252–76.

38. For several especially influential statements, see Victor Shklovsky, "Art as Technique," *Russian Formalist Criticism: Four Essays*, ed. Lee T. Lemon and Marion J. Reis (Lincoln: University of Nebraska Press, 1965), 3–24; Jan Mukarovsky, "Standard Language and Poetic Language," *A Prague School Reader on Esthetics, Literary Structure, and Style*, ed. Paul L. Garvin (Washington: Georgetown University Press, 1964), 17–30; and Roman Jakobson, "Closing Statement: Linguistics and Poetics," *Style in Language*, ed. Thomas A. Sebeok (Cambridge: MIT Press, 1960), 350–77.

39. Dubrow also discusses "cultural conditions" that may have affected the positions of addressee and overhearer in the production and reception of Renaissance lyric poetry, including the "labile positions" for speaker and audience encouraged by the regular "practice of an entire congregation singing a hymn" ("'Stand and unfold yourself'"). See also Dubrow's remarks on the "social situation" evoked by many Renaissance lyrics—including the "multiple audiences" assumed in instances of poetic address—and characteristic of an "age fascinated by rhetoric" in "Lyric Forms," *The Cambridge Companion to English Literature, 1500–1600*, ed. Arthur F. Kinney (Cambridge: Cambridge University Press, 2000), 196–97.

40. Jane Austen, *Mansfield Park*, ed. Tony Tanner (Harmondsworth: Penguin, 1966), 137; hereafter cited in the text. I take it that the first phrase ("Poor William") is an apostrophe addressed (in the second person) to William; the second phrase is a comment (in the third person) on the "apostrophe" just made.

41. Jane Austen, *Sense and Sensibility*, ed. Beth Lau (Boston: Houghton Mifflin, 2002), 43.

42. F. Elizabeth Hart, "Cognitive Linguistics: The Experiential Dynamics of Metaphor," *Mosaic* 28 (1995): 14.

CHAPTER FIVE: Reading Minds—and Bodies—in *Emma*

1. Roger C. Schank and Robert P. Abelson, *Scripts, Plans, Goals, and Understanding: An Inquiry Into Human Knowledge Structures* (Hillsdale: Erlbaum, 1977); Schank, *Tell Me a Story: Narrative and Intelligence* (1990; reprint, Evanston: Northwestern University Press, 1995); and Daniel C. Dennett, "Why Everyone Is a Novelist," *TLS* (16–22 September 1988): 1016, 1028–29; reprinted as "The Self as Center of Narrative Gravity," in *Self and Consciousness: Multiple Perspectives*, ed. F. Kessell, P. Cole, and D. Johnson (Hillsdale: Erlbaum, 1992), 275–78.

2. For an introduction to this aspect of cognitive literary studies, see David Herman, ed., *Narrative Theory and the Cognitive Sciences* (Stanford: CSLI, 2003).

3. David Lodge, *Thinks . . . : A Novel* (New York: Viking, 2001).

4. Ian McEwan, *Enduring Love: A Novel* (New York: Anchor, 1999).

5. Richard Powers, *Galatea 2.2* (New York: Farrar, Straus, Giroux, 1995).

6. David Lodge, "Consciousness and the Novel," *Consciousness and the Novel: Connected Essays* (Cambridge: Harvard University Press, 2002), 1–91. Hereafter cited in the text.

7. Lisa Zunshine, "Theory of Mind and Fictions of Embodied Transparency," *Narrative* 16.1 (January 2008): 65–92. Hereafter cited in the text as "Transparency."

8. Lisa Zunshine, *Why We Read Fiction: Theory of Mind and the Novel* (Columbus: Ohio State University Press, 2006), 5.

9. Blakey Vermeule, "God Novels," *The Work of Fiction: Cognition, Culture, and Complexity*, ed. Alan Richardson and Ellen Spolsky (Aldershot: Ashgate, 2004), 147–65.

10. Alan Palmer, *Fictional Minds* (Lincoln: University of Nebraska Press, 2004), 130–47.

11. On *Persuasion*, see Richardson, *British Romanticism and the Science of the Mind* (Cambridge: Cambridge University Press, 2001), 93–113. Wendy Jones has recently made her own argument that Austen's representation of embodied subjectivity in *Emma* can be profitably understood in relation to recent work in cognitive neuroscience, though Jones does not discuss theory of mind theories. See Wendy S. Jones, "*Emma*, Gender, and the Mind-Brain," *ELH* 75 (2008): 315–43. George Butte, in his phenomenological study *I Know That You Know That I Know: Narrating Subjects from Moll Flanders to Marnie* (Columbus: Ohio State University Press, 2004), holds that "deep intersubjectivity," a complex mode of narrative representation of intersubjective relations, first appears in the novels of Austen (ix). For a parallel argument that Butte's account needs supplementing by cognitive literary theory, see Lisa Zunshine, "Why Jane Austen Was Different, and Why We May Need Cognitive Science to See It," *Style* 41.3 (Fall 2007): 273–97.

12. Simon Baron-Cohen, *Mindblindness: An Essay on Autism and Theory of Mind* (Cambridge: MIT Press, 1995), 10. Hereafter cited in the text.

13. Colin C. Trevarthen, "Communication and Cooperation in Early Infancy: A Description of Primary Intersubjectivity," *Before Speech: The Beginning of Human Communication*, ed. Margaret Bullow (Cambridge: Cambridge University Press, 1979), 321–47.

14. For an overview, see Alison Gopnik, "Theory of Mind," *The MIT Encyclopedia of the Cognitive Sciences*, ed. Robert A. Wilson and Frank C. Keil (Cambridge: MIT Press, 1999), 838–41.

15. Robert M. Gordon, "Simulation vs. Theory-Theory," *The MIT Encyclopedia of the Cognitive Sciences*, ed. Robert A. Wilson and Frank C. Keil (Cambridge: MIT Press, 1999), 765.

16. The information in this paragraph is drawn from Gopnik, "Theory of Mind"; Steven Pinker, *How the Mind Works* (New York: Norton, 1997), 329–33; and Rebecca Saxe, "Reading Your Mind: How Our Brains Help Us Understand Other People," *Boston Review* 29.1 (2004): 39–41. See also Gopnik, Andrew N. Meltzkoff, and Patricia K. Kuhl, *The Scientist in the Crib: Minds, Brains, and How Children Learn* (New York: Morrow, 1999), 23–59.

17. Matthew Belmonte, "Does the Experimental Scientist Have a 'Theory of Mind'?" *Review of General Psychology* 12.2 (June 2008): 192–204.

18. See the "Brief History of Theory of Mind" in Helen Tager-Flusberg, Simon

Baron-Cohen, and Donald Cohen, "An Introduction to the Debate," *Understanding Other Minds: Perspectives from Autism*, ed. Baron-Cohen, Tager-Flusberg, and Cohen (Oxford: Oxford University Press, 1993), 5–6.

19. Gopnik, "Theory of Mind."

20. Gordon, "Simulation vs. Theory-Theory," 765.

21. Baron-Cohen, "Theory of Mind and Autism: A Fifteen Year Review," *Understanding Other Minds: Perspectives from Cognitive Developmental Neuroscience*, ed. Simon Baron-Cohen, Helen Tager-Flusberg, and Donald J. Cohen, 2nd ed. (Oxford: Oxford University Press, 2000), 3.

22. R. Shayna Rosenbaum, Donald T. Stuss, Brian Levine, and Endel Tulving, "Theory of Mind is Independent of Episodic Memory," *Science* 23 (November 2007): 1257.

23. Saxe 40–41.

24. Jane Austen, *Emma*, ed. Fiona Stafford (Harmondsworth: Penguin, 1996), 168. Hereafter cited in the text.

25. Butte reads this scene as an instance of what he terms "intersubjective blocking" (*I Know That You Know*, 115).

26. On this point, see Zunshine, *Why We Read Fiction*, 13–16.

27. Lisa Zunshine, "Richardson's *Clarissa* and a Theory of Mind," *The Work of Fiction: Cognition, Culture, and Complexity*, ed. Alan Richardson and Ellen Spolsky (Aldershot: Ashgate, 2004), 127–46.

28. Thomas Reid, *Essays on the Intellectual Powers of Man*, ed. Baruch A. Brody (Cambridge: MIT Press, 1969), 633. Hereafter cited in the text.

29. For a review of this work, see Richardson, *British Romanticism and the Science of the Mind*, 74–82.

30. Matthew Baillie, *Lectures and Observations on Medicine* (London: Richard Taylor, 1825), 146.

31. On Joanna Baillie, see Alan Richardson, "A Neural Theater: Joanna Baillie's *Plays on the Passions*," *Joanna Baillie, Romantic Dramatist: Critical Essays*, ed. Thomas Crochunis (New York: Routledge, 2004), 130–45.

32. Edmund Burke, *A Philosophical Enquiry into the Origin of Our Ideas of the Sublime and Beautiful and Other Pre-Revolutionary Writings*, ed. David Womersley (London: Penguin, 1998), 162. For a discussion of Burke's sublime in relation to early neuroscience, see chap. 2.

33. James Hogg, *The Private Memoirs and Confessions of a Justified Sinner*, ed. John Wain (Harmondsworth: Penguin, 1986), 132.

34. James Fordyce, *Sermons for Young Women* (Boston: Thomas Hall, 1796), 242.

35. John Gregory, *A Father's Legacy to His Daughters*, ed. Gina Luria (New York: Garland, 1974), 28.

36. Fordyce 127.

37. Jean-Jacques Rousseau, *Emile: or, On Education*, trans. Allan Bloom (New York: Basic Books, 1979), 385.

38. Butte also notes the relevance of the conduct book tradition to what he calls the "intersubjectivity of anxiety" in *Emma* (*I Know That You Know*, 109–10).

39. D. Premack and G. Woodruff, "Does the Chimpanzee Have a Theory of Mind?" *Behavioral and Brain Sciences* 1 (1978): 515–26.

CHAPTER SIX: Romantic Incest

1. Claude Lévi-Strauss, *The Elementary Structures of Kinship*, trans. from the French by James Harle Bell, John Richard von Sturmer, and Rodney Needham, eds. (Boston: Beacon Press, 1969), 24.

2. Donald E. Brown, *Human Universals* (New York: McGraw-Hill, 1991), 118–29.

3. Steven Pinker, *How the Mind Works* (New York: Norton, 1997), 451–60.

4. Edward O. Wilson, *Consilience: The Unity of Knowledge* (New York: Knopf, 1998), 164–80.

5. Francis Beaumont and John Fletcher, *A King and No King, The Dramatic Works in the Beaumont and Fletcher Canon*, ed. Fredson Bowers, 5 vols. (Cambridge: Cambridge University Press, 1970), 3.1.192–97.

6. S. T. Coleridge, *Shorter Works and Fragments*, ed. H. J. Jackson and J. R. de J. Jackson, 2 vols. (Princeton University Press, 1995), 2: 1344.

7. James B. Twitchell, *Forbidden Partners: The Incest Taboo in Modern Culture* (New York: Columbia University Press, 1987), 78.

8. Twitchell 102; Peter L. Thorslev Jr. "Incest as Romantic Symbol," *Comparative Literature Studies* 1 (1965): 47; Alan Richardson, "The Dangers of Sympathy: Sibling Incest in English Romantic Poetry," *SEL* 25 (1985): 737–54.

9. Richardson, "The Dangers of Sympathy"; see also Eugene Stelzig, "'Though It Were the Deadliest Sin to Love as We Have Loved': The Romantic Idealization of Incest," *European Romantic Review* 5 (1995): 234–39.

10. George Gordon, Lord Byron, *Byron's Letters and Journals*, ed. Leslie A. Marchand, 12 vols. (Cambridge: Harvard University Press, 1973–82), 3: 199.

11. *The Bride of Abydos, A Turkish Tale*, I.xiii.420–25, in *Lord Byron: Selected Poems*, ed. Susan J. Wolfson and Peter J. Manning (Harmondsworth: Penguin, 1996). Hereafter cited in the text by canto, section, and line.

12. Mary Shelley, *Frankenstein*, ed. M. K. Joseph (Oxford: Oxford University Press, 1980), 35. Hereafter cited in the text.

13. *Thalaba*, IV.15 in *Poems of Robert Southey*, ed. M. H. Fitzgerald (London: Oxford University Press, 1909). Hereafter cited in the text by book and stanza.

14. *The Prelude*, 1805, IX.570–76, *The Prelude, 1799, 1805, 1850* (New York: Norton, 1979). Hereafter cited in the text by book and line.

15. *Laon and Cythna*, II.xxiv.874–75 in *The Complete Works of Percy Bysshe Shelley*, ed. Neville Rogers, 2 vols. (Oxford: Clarendon, 1972–). Hereafter cited in the text by canto, stanza, and line.

16. *Manfred: A Dramatic Poem*, II.2.105–10 in Byron, *Selected Poems*. Hereafter cited in the text by act, scene, and line.

17. David Hartley, *Observations on Man*, 2 vols. (1791; reprint, Poole: Woodstock, 1998), 1: 82.

18. Sir Walter Scott, *Waverley*, ed. Andrew Hook (Harmondsworth: Penguin, 1972), 474–75. The relevance of *Waverley* to Romantic incest is discussed by John Donovan in "Incest in *Laon and Cythna*: Nature, Custom, and Desire," *Keats-Shelley Review* 2 (1987): 86–87.

19. Mary Shelley, "The Brother and Sister: An Italian Story," *Collected Tales and Stories: With Original Engravings*, ed. Charles E. Robinson (Baltimore: Johns Hopkins University Press, 1976), 183, 170.

20. Twitchell 125–26. The quoted phrase is from Shelley's preface to *Laon and Cythna*, in *Complete Works*, 106.

21. *Rosalind and Helen: A Modern Eclogue*, lines 156–66, in *Shelley: Poetical Works*, 2nd ed., ed. Thomas Hutchinson, rev. G. M. Matthews (London: Oxford University Press, 1970).

22. Joanna E. Rapf, "The Byronic Heroine: Incest and the Creative Process," *SEL* 21 (1981): 644–45; Richardson, "The Dangers of Sympathy," 744.

23. Sigmund Freud, *Totem and Taboo*, trans. James Strachey (New York: Norton, 1950), 1–17.

24. Edward Westermarck, *The History of Human Marriage*, 5th ed., 3 vols. (London: McMillan, 1925), 2: 192. Hereafter cited in the text.

25. Brown, *Human Universals*, 120.

26. Arthur P. Wolf, *Sexual Attraction and Childhood Association: A Chinese Brief for Edward Westermarck* (Stanford: Stanford University Press, 1995).

27. The *bint 'amm* and kibbutzim cases are reviewed by Wolf, 423–38. See also Pierre van den Berghe, "Human Inbreeding Avoidance: Culture as Nature," *Behavioral and Brain Sciences* 6 (1983): 91–102, and Nancy W. Thornhill, "An Evolutionary Analysis of the Rules Regulating Human Inbreeding and Marriage," *Behavioral and Brain Sciences* 14 (1991): 247–61.

28. Mark T. Erickson, "Rethinking Oedipus: An Evolutionary Perspective of Incest Avoidance," *American Journal of Psychiatry* 150 (1993): 411–16. Erickson's conclusions are supported by Wolf 439–75.

29. Speculation on the incestuous character of William and Dorothy's relation began with F. W. Bateson, *Wordsworth: A Re-Interpretation* (London: Longmans, 1954) and has been revived by Kenneth R. Johnston in *The Hidden Wordsworth: Poet, Lover, Rebel, Spy* (New York: Norton, 1998), esp. 643–52.

30. *Byron's Letters and Journals*, 3: 73. The limitations of a biographical approach to the Romantic incest theme are obvious. One would have to assume that a whole series of authors harbored such desires, and, moreover, one would still have to account for the cultural situation that encouraged these writers to give such remembered, repressed, or sublimated desire a particular form of literary expression. For a revealing example of the reductiveness of a purely biographical approach, see D. L. MacDonald, who is forced to devote much of his essay "Childhood Abuse as Romantic Reality: The Case of Byron," *Literature and Psychology* 40 (1994): 24–47, to pathologizing behavior in Byron that, according to the Westermarck theory, would not be considered psychologically abnormal (however socially iconoclastic).

31. For a survey of work in evolutionary literary theory, see Joseph Carroll, "Adaptationist Literary Study: An Emerging Research Program," *Style* 36 (2002): 596–617. I have criticized the evolutionary literary theory program more broadly in Richardson, "Studies in Literature and Cognition," 12–13.

32. Joseph Carroll, *Evolution and Literary Theory* (Columbia: University of Missouri Press, 1995), 44–45.

33. Critics who adapt "possible worlds" theories to literary studies often stress this point. Lubomír Dolezel, for example, states that fictional worlds feature "properties, structures, and modes of existence" that are, "in principle, independent of the properties, structures, and existential modes of actuality" (*Heterocosmica: Fiction and Possible Worlds* [Baltimore: Johns Hopkins University Press, 1998], 23).

34. Ellen Spolsky argues for the "fitness" value of the narrative imagination on the grounds of the adaptive advantages of cognitive flexibility in "Why and How to Take the Fruit and Leave the Chaff," *SubStance* 30.1 and 2 (2001): 177–98.

35. Carroll, *Evolution*, 43.

36. Stephen Jay Gould, "Darwinian Fundamentalism," *New York Review of Books*, 12 June 1997, 34–37, and "Evolution: The Pleasures of Pluralism," *New York Review of Books*, 26 June 1997, 47–52.

37. Richard Dawkins, *The Selfish Gene*, 2nd ed. (Oxford: Oxford University Press, 1989), 57.

38. Daniel C. Dennett, *Darwin's Dangerous Idea: Evolution and the Meanings of Life* (New York: Simon and Schuster, 1995), 470–71, italics in original.

39. Richard Dawkins, "Opportunity Costs of Inbreeding," *Behavioral and Brain Sciences* 1 (1983): 105–6.

40. In addition to the studies by Thorslev, Rapf, Richardson, Twitchell, Donovan, and Stelzig, see Loren Glass, "Blood and Affection: The Poetics of Incest in *Manfred* and *Parisina*," *Studies in Romanticism* 34 (1995): 211–26.

41. Jeremy Bentham, *The Theory of Legislation*, ed. C. K. Ogden (London: Routledge and Kegan Paul, 1931), 220.

42. Alfred Owen Aldridge, "The Meaning of Incest from Hutcheson to Gibbon," *Ethics* 61 (1951): 309–13.

43. Charles de Secondat Montesquieu, *Lettres persanes*, ed. Paul Vernière (Paris: Garnier, 1975), 137–48 (*lettre 67*).

44. On the relations between these texts, see Alan Richardson, "Astarté: Byron's *Manfred* and Montesquieu's *Lettres Persanes*," *Keats-Shelley Journal* 40 (1991): 19–22.

45. Richardson, *British Romanticism and the Science of the Mind*, 151–80.

46. See Canto II of Darwin's *The Temple of Nature* (1802), *The Poetical Works of Erasmus Darwin, M.D., F.R.S.*, 3 vols. (London: J. Johnson, 1806), and William Lawrence, *Lectures on Physiology, Zoology, and the Natural History of Man, Delivered to the Royal College of Surgeons* (London: Benbow, 1822), 397–98.

47. Samuel Taylor Coleridge, *The Notebooks of Samuel Taylor Coleridge*, ed. Kathleen Coburn, 4 vols. (London: Routledge and Kegan Paul, 1957–), 1: 1637.

48. William Paley, *The Principles of Moral and Political Philosophy*, rev. ed., 2 vols. in 1 (New York: Collins and Hannay, 1831), 154–55.

49. *Osorio*, I.98–99, in *The Complete Poetical and Dramatic Works of Samuel Taylor Coleridge*, ed. J. D. Campbell (London: Macmillan, 1934).

50. Patrick Colm Hogan, "Literary Universals," *Poetics Today* 18 (1997): 223–49. See also Hogan's book-length study of the subject, *The Mind and Its Stories: Narrative Universals and Human Emotion* (Cambridge: Cambridge University Press, 2003).

51. I have tried to illustrate such caution in chapters 5 and 7 of this book, both of which do deal with thematic issues.

CHAPTER SEVEN: Language Strange

1. See the first and last chapters of Alan Richardson, *British Romanticism and the Science of the Mind* (Cambridge: Cambridge University Press, 2001), 1–38, and 151–80.

2. On the relation between feminist critique and gynocritics, see Elaine Showalter,

"Towards a Feminist Poetics," *Women Writing and Writing about Women*, ed. Mary Jacobus (London: Croom Helm, 1979), 22–41.

3. On "six-poet Romanticism," see Clifford Siskin, *The Historicity of Romantic Discourse* (New York: Oxford University Press, 1988), 8–29.

4. See the landmark collection *The Endurance of Frankenstein: Essays on Mary Shelley's Novel*, ed. George Levine and U. C. Knoepflmacher (Berkeley and Los Angeles: University of California Press, 1979).

5. Meena Alexander, *Women and Romanticism: Mary Wollstonecraft, Dorothy Wordsworth, and Mary Shelley* (London: MacMillan, 1989), 1. Hereafter cited in the text.

6. Margaret Homans, *Women Writers and Poetic Identity: Dorothy Wordsworth, Emily Brontë, and Emily Dickinson* (Princeton: Princeton University Press, 1980), 215; Susan Levin, *Dorothy Wordsworth and Romanticism* (New Brunswick: Rutgers University Press, 1987), 163. Hereafter cited in the text.

7. Stuart Curran, "Romantic Poetry: The I Altered," *Romanticism and Feminism*, ed. Anne Mellor (Bloomington: Indiana University Press, 1988), 195; Anne Mellor, *Romanticism and Gender* (New York: Routledge, 1993), 4–11.

8. Margaret Homans, "Representation, Reproduction, and Woman's Place in Language," *Bearing the Word: Language and Female Experience in Nineteenth-Century Women's Writing* (Chicago: University of Chicago Press, 1986), 3. Hereafter cited in the text.

9. Sonia Hofkosh, "The Writer's Ravishment: Women and the Romantic Author— The Example of Byron," in Mellor, ed., *Romanticism and Feminism*, 93–114.

10. Julia Kristeva, *Desire in Language: A Semiotic Approach to Literature and Art*, ed. Leon Roudiez, trans. Thomas Gora, Alice Jardine, and Leon Roudiez (New York: Columbia University Press, 1980), 133, 136.

11. Ellen Dissanayake, *Art and Intimacy: How the Arts Began* (Seattle: University of Washington Press, 2000). Hereafter cited in the text.

12. Kristeva defines the *semiotic* as a "*heterogeneousness*, detected in the first echolalias of infants as rhythms and intonations anterior to the first phonemes, morphemes, and sentences" (133).

13. Although my emphasis here is on spoken language, there is also, as Dissanayake points out, a sign-language equivalent of this repetitive, exaggerated speech to infants (*Art and Intimacy* 228, n. 9).

14. Dissanayake uses the term *baby talk* in *Art and Intimacy* and *babytalk* (one word) in her later, related essays. As she (writing with David Miall) explains in an essay explicitly devoted to infant directed speech and poetics, *babytalk* refers to "dyadic, jointly constructed engagements between a mother (or adult, or parent) and an infant (under the age of 5 or 6 months) in which vocal, visual, and kinesic behaviors (or signals) are exchanged" ("The Poetics of Babytalk," *Human Nature* 14.4 [2003]: 357).

15. Daniel Stern, *The First Relationship: Infant and Mother* (Cambridge: Harvard University Press, 1977), 15.

16. Dissanayake, "Aesthetic Incunabula," *Philosophy and Literature* 25 (2001): 336.

17. Ibid., 337.

18. Species-specific, innate, universal biases do not necessarily reflect "hardwired" responses shaped by adaptation. Rather, in this case, at least some of the universal features of infant-directed speech may reflect the psychophysiology of infants' unfolding

perceptual capacities. (In other words, they may come with the basic human body plan and the common human developmental template.) As Stern writes, the "social presence of an infant elicits variations in adult behavior that are best suited to the infant's innate perceptual biases; for example, infants prefer sounds of a higher pitch, such as are achieved in 'baby talk.'" (Infants have a higher range of hearing than do adults.) See the discussion in Daniel Stern, *The Interpersonal World of the Infant: A View from Psychoanalysis and Developmental Psychology* (New York: Basic Books, 1985), 72–74.

19. Alison Gopnik, Andrew N. Meltzkoff, and Patricia K. Kuhl, *The Scientist in the Crib: Minds, Brains, and How Children Learn* (New York: Morrow, 1999) 129.

20. Stern, *First Relationship*, 15.

21. Miall and Dissanayake, 342–43.

22. Ibid., 338.

23. Cynthia Fisher and Hisayo Tokura, "Prosody in Speech to Infants: Direct and Indirect Acoustic Cues to Linguistic Structure," *Signal to Syntax: Bootstrapping from Speech to Grammar in Early Acquisition*, ed. James L. Morgan and Katherine Demuth (Mahwah, NJ: Erlbaum, 1996), 343–63; Anne Fernald, "Intonation and Communicative Intent in Mothers' Speech to Infants: Is the Melody the Message?" *Child Development* 60: (1989): 1495–1510, and "The Perceptual and Affective Salience of Mothers' Speech to Infants," *The Origins and Growth of Communication*, ed. Lynne Feagans, Catherine Garvey, and Roberta Golinkoff (Norwood, NJ: Ablex, 1984), 5–29; Gopnik, Meltzkoff, and Kuhl, *Scientist*, 130. Note that researchers do not necessarily agree on *how* IDS facilitates language acquisition. Fisher and Tokura, for example, argue that IDS helps children understand the basics of syntactic structure, a notion criticized by Fernald (Fernald and Gerald McRoberts, "Prosodic Bootstrapping: A Critical Analysis of the Argument and the Evidence," in Morgan and Demuth, eds., *Signal to Syntax*, 365–88). Fernald instead argues that IDS gives the developing child a template for understanding speech as meaningful, "enabling the young infants from an early age to experience meaning in the sound of human speech" ("Perceptual," 26) and helps the child eventually to discriminate and produce word-meaning pairings, by providing the "first regular sound-meaning correspondences appreciated by the pre-verbal infant" ("Intonation," 1509).

24. Denis Burnham, Christine Kitamura, and Uté Vollmer-Conna, "What's New, Pussycat? Talking to Babies and Animals," *Science* 296 (24 May 2002): 1435.

25. Later in *Desire in Language*, Kristeva writes that the "*entry into syntax constitutes a first victory over the mother*, a still uncertain distancing of the mother" (289) and that "*naming . . . is a replacement* for what the speaker perceives as an archaic mother—a more or less victorious confrontation, never finished with her" (291). See the discussions of Kristeva and language in Kaja Silverman, *The Acoustic Mirror: The Female Voice in Psychoanalysis and Cinema* (Bloomington: Indiana University Press, 1988), 101–6, and Barbara Charlesworth Gelpi, *Shelley's Goddess: Maternity, Language, Subjectivity* (New York: Oxford University Press, 1992), 11–13 and 21–22.

26. Silverman 105.

27. Gelpi 33.

28. Burnham, Kitamura, and Vollmer-Conna 1435. The affective character of IDS suggests obvious links between the child's early communications with primary caretakers and its development of a "Theory of Mind" (discussed in chap. 5 in this book). For

the relation of IDS and Theory of Mind, see Anne Fernald, "Human Maternal Vocalizations to Infants as Biologically Relevant Signals: An Evolutionary Paradigm," *The Adapted Mind: Evolutionary Psychology and the Generation of Culture*, ed. Jerome H. Barkow, Leda Cosmides, and John Tooby (New York: Oxford University Press, 1992), 391–428, esp. 423.

29. Burnham, Kitamura, and Vollmer-Conna 1435.

30. Citations from Keats (book or part and line numbers given for longer poems only) follow *The Poems of John Keats*, ed. Jack Stillinger (Cambridge: Harvard University Press, 1978).

31. Walter Savage Landor, "The Hamadryad," *The Poetical Works of Walter Savage Landor*, ed. Stephen Wheeler, 3 vols. (Oxford: Clarendon Press, 1937) 2: 151–58. Cited by line number.

32. Citations of "Christabel" (by part and line) follow the text in Samuel Taylor Coleridge, *The Complete Poems*, ed. William Keach (London: Penguin, 1997).

33. Sir Walter Scott, "Glenfinlas; or, Lord Ronald's Coronach," *Minstrelsy of the Scottish Border*, ed. T. F. Henderson, 4 vols. (Edinburgh: Oliver and Boyd, 1932), 4: 138–57. Citations of the poem (by page number) follow this edition.

34. See Keach's editorial note to "Christabel" in Coleridge, *Complete Poems*, 506.

35. Gelpi 27.

36. For a good early example, see Charles J. Rzepka, "Christabel's 'Wandering Mother' and the Discourse of the Self: A Lacanian Reading of Repressed Narration," *Romanticism Past and Present* 10.2 (1986): 17–43.

37. Margery Durham, "The Mother Tongue: Christabel and the Language of Love," *The (M)Other Tongue: Essays in Feminist Psychoanalytic Interpretation*, ed. Shirley Nelson Garner, Claire Kahane, and Madelon Sprengnether (Ithaca: Cornell University Press, 1985), 175.

38. Thomas Love Peacock, *Rhododaphne: or, The Thessalian Spell*, *The Works of Thomas Love Peacock*, ed. H. F. B. Brett-Smith and C. E. Jones, 10 vols. (New York: AMS Press, 1967) 7: 22. Citations (by page) follow this edition.

39. Percy Bysshe Shelley, *Shelley's Prose; or, The Trumpet of a Prophecy*, ed. David Lee Clark (Albuquerque: University of New Mexico Press, 1954), 311.

40. Peacock, *Works*, 8: 3–25.

41. Plato, "Symposium," trans. Michael Joyce, *The Collected Dialogues of Plato, Including the Letters*, ed. Edith Hamilton and Huntington Cairns (Princeton: Princeton University Press, 1963), 534–35, 538–39.

42. Shelley, "A Discourse on the Manners of the Ancient Greeks Relative to the Subject of Love," *Shelley's Prose*, 217–23.

43. Karen Horney, *Feminine Psychology*, ed. Harold Kelman (New York: Norton, 1967), 133–46.

44. On the relation between the emotive aspect of IDS, the "poetic" function of language, and the "poetic" (or prosodic) element of poetry, see Miall and Dissanayake 353–55.

45. Wordsworth's famous passage on infancy and early cognitive development can be found in the "Two-Part *Prelude*" of 1799, 2: 268–310, the 1805 *Prelude*, 2: 237–81, and the 1850 *Prelude*, 2: 232–65, all in *The Prelude 1799, 1805, 1850*, ed. Jonathan Wordsworth, M. H. Abrams, and Stephen Gill (New York: Norton, 1979).

46. Wordsworth, "Two-Part *Prelude*," 2: 313.

47. Citations from *Sardanapalus* (cited by act, scene, and line) follow George Gordon, Lord Byron, *Selected Poems*, ed. Susan J. Wolfson and Peter Manning (London: Penguin, 1996).

48. Ann Yearsley, "To Mira, On the Care of Her Infant," *Women Romantic Poets 1785–1832: An Anthology*, new ed, ed. Jennifer Breen (London: Everyman, 1994), 96–102, cited by line.

49. Quotations from Wordsworth's poems exclusive of *The Prelude* (cited by line in the case of longer poems) follow *William Wordsworth: The Poems*, ed. John O. Hayden, 2 vols. (Harmondsworth: Penguin, 1977).

50. Jean-Jacques Rousseau, *Emile: or, On Education*, trans. Allan Bloom (New York: Basic Books, 1979), 46.

51. Gelpi 35–82.

52. James Fordyce, *Sermons for Young Women* (Boston: Thomas Hall, 1796), 23.

53. Thomas Gisborne, *An Enquiry into the Duties of the Female Sex*, ed. Gina Luria (New York: Garland, 1974), 12–13.

54. Henry Homes, Lord Kames, *Loose Hints Upon Education, Chiefly Concerning the Culture of the Heart*, 2nd ed. (Edinburgh: John Bell [et al.], 1782), 6, 10.

55. Hannah More, *Strictures on the Modern System of Education. With a View of the Principles and Conduct Prevalent among Women of Rank and Fortune*, 2 vols., 6th ed. (London: Cadell and Davies, 1799), 1: 59; Mary Wollstonecraft, *A Vindication of the Rights of Woman, with Strictures on Political and Moral Subjects*, ed. Carol Poston (New York: Norton, 1975), 151.

56. More 1: 59.

57. Fordyce 93.

58. Julie Kipp, *Romanticism, Maternity, and the Body Politic* (Cambridge: Cambridge University Press, 2003).

59. Johann Gottfried Herder, "Essay on the Origin of Language," *On the Origin of Language: Two Essays*, trans. John H. Moran and Alexander Gode (Chicago: University of Chicago Press, 1966), 88. Hereafter cited in the text.

60. Jean-Jacques Rousseau, "Essay on the Origin of Languages," *On the Origin of Language: Two Essays*, 9. Hereafter cited in the text.

61. See chap. 5 and Richardson, *British Romanticism*, 74–82.

62. William Smellie, *The Philosophy of Natural History*, 2 vols. (Edinburgh: Charles Elliot, Bell and Bradford [et al.], 1790–99). Hereafter cited in the text.

63. Wordsworth, *The Prose Works of William Wordsworth*, ed. W J. B. Owen and Jane Worthington Smyser, 3 vols. (Oxford: Clarendon Press, 1974), 1: 160.

64. Ibid., 1: 144.

65. Hofkosh, "Writer's Ravishment"; Marlon Ross, *The Contours of Masculine Desire: Romanticism and the Rise of Women's Poetry* (New York: Oxford University Press, 1989).

66. Richardson, "Romanticism and the Colonization of the Feminine," in Mellor, ed., *Romanticism and Feminism*, 13–25; Diane Long Hoeveler, *Romantic Androgyny: The Women Within* (University Park: Penn State University Press, 1990). Hereafter cited in the text.

67. Susan Luther, "A Stranger Minstrel: Coleridge's Mrs. Robinson," *Studies in*

Romanticism 33 (Fall 1994): 391–409; Daniel Robinson, "From 'Mingled Measure' to 'Ecstatic Measures': Mary Robinson's Poetic Reading of 'Kubla Khan,'" *Wordsworth Circle* 26.1 (January 1995): 4–7; Lisa Vargo, "The Claims of 'Real Life and Manners': Coleridge and Mary Robinson," *Wordsworth Circle* 26.3 (July 1995): 134–37.

    68. Quotations from "To the Poet Coleridge" follow Mary Robinson, *Selected Poems*, ed. Judith Pascoe (Peterborough, Ontario: Broadview Press, 2000).

Works Cited

Abelson, Robert P. "Artificial Intelligence and Literary Appreciation: How Big Is the Gap?" *Literary Discourse: Aspects of Cognitive and Social Psychological Approaches.* Ed. László Halász. Berlin: de Gruyter, 1987. 38–48.

Abrams, M. H. *A Glossary of Literary Terms.* 4th ed. New York: Holt, Rinehart, and Winston, 1981.

———. *Natural Supernaturalism: Tradition and Revolution in Romantic Literature.* New York: Norton, 1971.

Ackerman, Diane. *A Natural History of the Senses.* New York: Random House, 1990.

Aldridge, Alfred Owen. "The Meaning of Incest from Hutcheson to Gibbon." *Ethics* 61 (1951): 309–13.

Alexander, Meena. *Women and Romanticism: Mary Wollstonecraft, Dorothy Wordsworth, and Mary Shelley.* London: MacMillan, 1989.

Ashfield, Andrew, and Peter de Bolla. *The Sublime: A Reader in British Eighteenth-Century Aesthetic Theory.* Cambridge: Cambridge University Press, 1996.

Atran, Scott. *Cognitive Foundations of Natural History: Towards an Anthropology of Science.* Cambridge: Cambridge University Press, 1990.

Austen, Jane. *Emma.* Ed. Fiona Stafford. Harmondsworth: Penguin, 1996.

———. *Mansfield Park.* Ed. Tony Tanner. Harmondsworth: Penguin, 1966.

———. *Sense and Sensibility.* Ed. Beth Lau. Boston: Houghton Mifflin, 2002.

Austin, James H. *Zen-Brain Reflections: Reviewing Recent Developments in Meditation and States of Consciousness.* Cambridge: MIT Press, 2006.

Baillie, Matthew. *Lectures and Observations on Medicine.* London: Richard Taylor, 1825.

Balkin, J. M. *Cultural Software: A Theory of Ideology.* New Haven: Yale University Press, 1998.

Barlow, Horace. "Adaptation by Hyperpolarization." *Science* 276 (9 May 1997): 913–14.

Baron-Cohen, Simon. *Mindblindness: An Essay on Autism and Theory of Mind.* Cambridge: MIT Press, 1995.

———. "Theory of Mind and Autism: A Fifteen Year Review." *Understanding Other Minds: Perspectives from Developmental Cognitive Neuroscience.* Ed. Baron-Cohen, Helen Tager-Flusberg, and Donald J. Cohen. 2nd ed. Oxford: Oxford University Press, 2000. 3–20.

Bateson, F. W. *Wordsworth: A Re-Interpretation.* London: Longmans, 1954.

Beaumont, Francis, and John Fletcher. *The Dramatic Works in the Beaumont and Fletcher Canon.* Ed. Fredson Bowers. 5 vols. Cambridge: Cambridge University Press, 1970.

Bell, Charles. *Idea of a New Anatomy of the Brain: A Fascicle of the Privately Printed Edition of 1811*. London: Dawsons, 1966.

Belmonte, Matthew. "Does the Experimental Scientist Have a 'Theory of Mind'?" *Review of General Psychology* 12.2 (June 2008): 192–204.

Bentham, Jeremy. *The Theory of Legislation*. Ed. C. K. Ogden. London: Routledge and Kegan Paul, 1931.

Blair, Hugh. *Lectures on Rhetoric and Belles Lettres*. Ed. Harold F. Harding. 3 vols. Carbondale: Southern Illinois University Press, 1965.

Blake, William. *The Complete Poetry and Prose of William Blake*. Rev. ed. Ed. David V. Erdman. Garden City: Anchor, 1982.

Bordwell, David, and Noel Carroll, eds. *Post-Theory: Reconstructing Film Studies*. Madison: University of Wisconsin Press, 1996.

Boyd, Brian. "Jane, Meet Charles: Literature, Evolution, and Human Nature." *Philosophy and Literature* 22 (1998): 1–30.

Brooks, Peter. "Aesthetics and Ideology: What Happened to Poetics?" *Critical Inquiry* 20.3 (1994): 509–23.

Brown, Donald E. *Human Universals*. New York: McGraw-Hill, 1991.

Bucci, Wilma. *Psychoanalysis and Cognitive Science: A Multiple Code Theory*. New York: Guilford, 1997.

Burke, Edmund. *A Philosophical Enquiry into the Origin of Our Ideas of the Sublime and Beautiful and Other Pre-Revolutionary Writings*. Ed. David Womersley. London: Penguin, 1998.

Burnham, Denis, Christine Kitamura, and Uté Vollmer-Conna. "What's New, Pussycat? Talking to Babies and Animals." *Science* 296 (24 May 2002): 1435.

Burwick, Frederick. "Romanticism as Cognitive Process." *Prism(s): Essays in Romanticism* 15 (2007): 7–32.

Butte, George. *I Know That You Know That I Know: Narrating Subjects from Moll Flanders to Marnie*. Columbus: Ohio State University Press, 2004.

Byrd, Don. *The Poetics of the Common Knowledge*. Albany: State University of New York Press, 1994.

Byron, George Gordon, Lord. *Byron's Letters and Journals*. Ed. Leslie A. Marchand. 12 vols. Cambridge: Harvard University Press, 1973–82.

———. *Selected Poems*. Ed. Susan J. Wolfson and Peter Manning. London: Penguin, 1996.

Cabanis, Pierre-Jean-Georges. *On the Relations Between the Physical and Moral Aspects of Man*. Trans. Margaret Duggan Saidi. Ed. George Mora. 2 vols. Baltimore: Johns Hopkins University Press, 1981.

Carroll, Joseph. "Adaptationist Literary Study: An Emerging Research Program." *Style* 36 (2002): 596–617.

———. *Evolution and Literary Theory*. Columbia: University of Missouri Press, 1995.

Chase, Cynthia. "'Viewless Wings': Intertextual Interpretation of Keats's 'Ode to a Nightingale.'" *Lyric Poetry: Beyond New Criticism*. Ed. Chaviva Hosek and Patricia Parker. Ithaca: Cornell University Press, 1985. 208–25.

Churchland, Paul M. *The Engine of Reason, the Seat of the Soul: A Philosophical Journey into the Brain*. Cambridge: MIT Press, 1995.

Clark, Herbert H., and Thomas B. Carlson. "Hearers and Speech Acts." *Language* 58 (1982): 332–73.

Coleridge, Samuel Taylor. *Biographia Literaria or Biographical Sketches of My Literary Life and Opinions.* Ed. James Engell and W. J. Bate. 2 vols. Princeton: Princeton University Press, 1983.

———. *Coleridge's Dejection: The Earliest Manuscripts and the Earliest Printings.* Ed. Stephen Maxfield Parrish. Ithaca: Cornell University Press, 1988.

———. *The Complete Poems.* Ed. William Keach. London: Penguin, 1997.

———. *The Complete Poetical and Dramatic Works.* Ed. J. D. Campbell. London: MacMillan, 1934.

———. *The Notebooks of Samuel Taylor Coleridge.* Ed. Kathleen Coburn. 4 vols. London: Routledge and Kegan Paul, 1957–.

———. *Shorter Works and Fragments.* Ed. H. J. Jackson and J. R. de J. Jackson. 2 vols. Princeton: Princeton University Press, 1995.

Crane, Mary Thomas. "'Fair is Foul': *Macbeth* and Binary Logic." *The Work of Fiction: Cognition, Culture, and Complexity.* Ed. Alan Richardson and Ellen Spolsky. Aldershot: Ashgate, 2004.

———. *Shakespeare's Brain: Reading with Cognitive Theory.* Princeton: Princeton University Press, 2001.

Crane, Mary Thomas, and Alan Richardson. "Literary Studies and Cognitive Science: Toward a New Interdisciplinarity." *Mosaic* 32 (1999): 123–40.

Crick, Francis. *The Astonishing Hypothesis: The Scientific Search for the Soul.* New York: Simon and Schuster, 1995.

Cronin, Richard. "Shelleyan Incest and the Romantic Legacy." *Keats-Shelley Journal* 45 (1996): 61–76.

Culler, Jonathan. "Apostrophe." *The Pursuit of Signs: Semiotics, Literature, Deconstruction.* Ithaca: Cornell University Press, 1981. 135–54.

———. "Apostrophe Revisited." Special session on "The Overhearing of Lyric." Modern Language Association Convention. New Orleans. 29 December 2001.

———. *Structuralist Poetics: Structuralism, Linguistics, and the Study of Literature.* Ithaca: Cornell University Press, 1975.

Curran, Stuart. "Romantic Poetry: The I Altered." In Mellor, ed., *Romanticism and Feminism*, 186–207.

Darwin, Erasmus. *The Poetical Works of Erasmus Darwin, M.D., F.R.S.* 3 vols. London: J. Johnson, 1806.

Dawkins, Richard. "Opportunity Costs of Inbreeding." *Behavioral and Brain Sciences* 1 (1983): 105–6.

———. *The Selfish Gene.* 2nd ed. Oxford: Oxford University Press, 1989.

De Man, Paul. "Autobiography as De-Facement." *MLN* 94 (1979): 919–30. Rpt. in *The Rhetoric of Romanticism.* New York: Columbia University Press, 1984. 67–92.

———. "The Epistemology of Metaphor." *Critical Inquiry* 5 (1978): 13–30. Rpt. in *On Metaphor.* Ed. Sheldon Sacks. Chicago: University of Chicago Press, 1979. 11–28.

———. "Lyrical Voice in Contemporary Theory: Riffaterre and Jauss." *Lyric Poetry: Beyond New Criticism.* Ed. Chaviva Hosek and Patricia Parker. Ithaca: Cornell University Press, 1985. 55–72.

———. "Semiology and Rhetoric." *Allegories of Reading: Figural Language in Rousseau, Nietzsche, Rilke, and Proust.* New Haven: Yale University Press, 1979. 3–19.

Dennett, Daniel C. *Consciousness Explained.* Boston: Little, Brown, 1991.

————. *Darwin's Dangerous Idea: Evolution and the Meanings of Life*. New York: Simon and Schuster, 1995.

————. "Why Everyone Is a Novelist." *TLS*, 16–22 September 1988, 1016, 1028–29. Rpt. as "The Self as Center of Narrative Gravity." *Self and Consciousness: Multiple Perspectives*. Ed. F. Kessell, P. Cole, and D. Johnson Hillsdale: Erlbaum, 1992. 275–78.

Derrida, Jacques. "White Mythology: Metaphor in the Text of Philosophy." *Margins of Philosophy*. Trans. Alan Bass. Chicago: University of Chicago Press, 1982. 207–71.

Dissanayake, Ellen. "Aesthetic Incunabula." *Philosophy and Literature* 25 (2001): 335–46.

————. *Art and Intimacy: How the Arts Began*. Seattle: University of Washington Press, 2000.

Dolezel, Lubomír. *Heterocosmica: Fiction and Possible Worlds*. Baltimore: Johns Hopkins University Press, 1998.

Donovan, John. "Incest in *Laon and Cythna*: Nature, Custom, and Desire." *Keats-Shelley Review* 2 (1987): 49–90.

Dubrow, Heather. "Lyric Forms." *The Cambridge Companion to English Literature, 1500–1600*. Ed. Arthur F. Kinney. Cambridge: Cambridge University Press, 2000. 178–99.

————. "'Stand and unfold yourself': The Partially Overheard Lyric." Special session on "The Overhearing of Lyric." MLA Convention. New Orleans. 29 December 2001.

Duchan, Judith F., Gail A. Bruder, and Lynne E. Hewitt. *Deixis in Narrative: A Cognitive Science Perspective*. Hillsdale, NJ: Lawrence Erlbaum, 1995.

Durham, Margery. "The Mother Tongue: Christabel and the Language of Love." *The (M)Other Tongue: Essays in Feminist Psychoanalytic Interpretation*. Ed. Shirley Nelson Garner, Claire Kahane, and Madelon Sprengnether. Ithaca: Cornell University Press, 1985. 169–93.

Edelman, Gerald M. *Bright Air, Brilliant Fire: On the Matter of the Mind*. New York: Basic Books, 1992.

Eichenbaum, Boris. "The Theory of the 'Formal Method.'" *Russian Formalist Criticism: Four Essays*. Ed. Lee T. Lemon and Marion J. Reis. Lincoln: University of Nebraska Press, 1965. 99–139.

Ekman, Paul. Afterword to Charles Darwin, *The Expression of the Emotions in Man and Animals*. 3rd ed. Ed. Paul Ekman. New York: Oxford University Press, 1998. 363–93.

Erickson, Mark T. "Rethinking Oedipus: An Evolutionary Perspective of Incest Avoidance." *American Journal of Psychiatry* 150 (1993): 411–16.

Esrock, Ellen J. *The Reader's Eye: Visual Imagining as Reader Response*. Baltimore: Johns Hopkins University Press, 1994.

Esterhammer, Angela. *The Romantic Performative: Language and Action in British and German Romanticism*. Stanford: Stanford University Press, 2000.

Farah, Martha J. "The Neural Bases of Mental Imagery." *The New Cognitive Neurosciences*. Ed. Michael S. Gazziniga. 2nd ed. Cambridge: MIT Press, 2000. 965–74.

Ferguson, Frances. *Solitude and the Sublime: The Romantic Aesthetics of Individuation*. New York: Routledge, 1992.

Fernald, Anne. "Human Maternal Vocalizations to Infants as Biologically Relevant Signals: An Evolutionary Paradigm." *The Adapted Mind: Evolutionary Psychology and the Generation of Culture*. Ed. Jerome H. Barkow, Leda Cosmides, and John Tooby. New York: Oxford University Press, 1992. 391–428.

————. "Intonation and Communicative Intent in Mothers' Speech to Infants: Is the Melody the Message?" *Child Development* 60: (1989): 1495–1510.

————. "The Perceptual and Affective Salience of Mothers' Speech to Infants." *The Origins and Growth of Communication.* Ed. Lynne Feagans, Catherine Garvey, and Roberta Golinkoff. Norwood, NJ: Ablex, 1984. 5–29.

Fernald, Anne, and Gerald McRoberts. "Prosodic Bootstrapping: A Critical Analysis of the Argument and the Evidence." *Signal to Syntax: Bootstrapping from Speech to Grammar in Early Acquisition.* Ed. James L. Morgan and Katherine Demuth. Mahwah, NJ: Erlbaum, 1996. 365–88.

Findlay, L. M. "Culler and Byron on Apostrophe and Lyric Time." *Studies in Romanticism* 24 (1985): 335–53.

Fisher, Cynthia, and Hisayo Tokura. "Prosody in Speech to Infants: Direct and Indirect Acoustic Cues to Linguistic Structure." *Signal to Syntax: Bootstrapping from Speech to Grammar in Early Acquisition.* Ed. James L. Morgan and Katherine Demuth. Mahwah, NJ: Erlbaum, 1996. 343–63.

Fodor, Jerry A. *The Modularity of Mind: An Essay on Faculty Psychology.* Cambridge: MIT Press, 1983.

Fordyce, James. *Sermons for Young Women.* Boston: Thomas Hall, 1796.

Foucault, Michel. *Discipline and Punish: The Birth of the Prison.* Trans. Alan Sheridan. New York: Vintage, 1995.

Freeland, Cynthia A. "The Sublime in Cinema." *Passionate Views: Film, Cognition, and Emotion.* Ed. Carl Plantinga and Greg M. Smith. Baltimore: Johns Hopkins University Press, 1999. 65–83.

Freud, Sigmund. *Totem and Taboo.* Trans. James Strachey. New York: Norton, 1950.

Fried, Debra. *The Norton Anthology of Poetry, Third Edition: Course Guide for the Complete and Shorter Editions.* New York: Norton, 1986.

Gall, François Joseph. *On the Functions of the Brain and of Each of Its Parts: With Observations on the Possibility of Determining the Instincts, Propensities, and Talents, or the Moral and Intellectual Dispositions of Men and Animals by the Configuration of the Brain and Head.* Trans. Winslow Lewis. 6 vols. Boston: Marsh, Capen, and Lyon, 1835.

Galperin, William H. *The Return of the Visible in British Romanticism.* Baltimore: Johns Hopkins University Press, 1993.

Gardner, Howard. *The Mind's New Science: A History of the Cognitive Revolution.* New York: Basic Books, 1985.

Gazzaniga, Michael S., ed. *The Cognitive Neurosciences 3.* Cambridge: MIT Press, 2004.

————, ed. *The New Cognitive Neurosciences.* 2nd ed. Cambridge: MIT Press, 2000.

Gelpi, Barbara Charlesworth. *Shelley's Goddess: Maternity, Language, Subjectivity.* New York: Oxford University Press, 1992.

Gerrig, Richard J. *Experiencing Narrative Worlds: On the Psychological Activities of Reading.* New Haven: Yale University Press, 1993.

Gibbs, Raymond W., Jr. *The Poetics of Mind: Figurative Thought, Language, and Understanding.* Cambridge: Cambridge University Press, 1994.

————. "Process and Product in Making Sense of Tropes." *Metaphor and Thought.* 2nd ed. Ed. Andrew Ortony. Cambridge: Cambridge University Press, 1993. 252–76.

Gisborne, Thomas. *An Enquiry into the Duties of the Female Sex.* Ed. Gina Luria. New York: Garland, 1974.

Glass, Loren. "Blood and Affection: The Poetics of Incest in *Manfred* and *Parisina*." *Studies in Romanticism* 34 (1995): 211–26.

The Golden Age, A Poetical Epistle from Erasmus D——n, M. D. to Thomas Beddoes, M. D. 1794. Reprint, New York: Garland, 1978.

Gombrich, E. H. *Art and Illusion: A Study in the Psychology of Pictorial Representation.* 2nd ed., rev. Princeton: Bollingen, 1969.

Gopnik, Alison. "Theory of Mind." In Wilson and Keil, eds., *The MIT Encyclopedia of the Cognitive Sciences*, 838–41.

Gopnik, Alison, Andrew N. Meltzkoff, and Patricia K. Kuhl. *The Scientist in the Crib: Minds, Brains, and How Children Learn.* New York: Morrow, 1999.

Gordon, Robert M. "Simulation vs. Theory-Theory." In Wilson and Keil, *The MIT Encyclopedia of the Cognitive Sciences*, 765–66.

Gould, Stephen Jay. "Darwinian Fundamentalism." *New York Review of Books* 12 June 1997, 34–37.

———. "Evolution: The Pleasures of Pluralism." *New York Review of Books* 26 June 1997, 47–52.

Grady, Joseph E., Todd Oakley, and Seana Coulson. "Blending and Metaphor." *Metaphor in Cognitive Linguistics: Selected Papers from the Fifth International Cognitive Linguistics Conference, Amsterdam, July 1997.* Ed. Raymond W. Gibbs Jr. and Gerard J. Steen. Amsterdam: Benjamins, 1999. 101–24.

Greenblatt, Stephen. *Shakespearean Negotiations: The Circulation of Social Energy in Renaissance England.* Berkeley and Los Angeles: University of California Press, 1988.

Gregory, John. *A Father's Legacy to His Daughters.* Ed. Gina Luria. New York: Garland, 1974.

Haraway, Donna J. "Situated Knowledges: The Science Question in Feminism and the Privilege of Partial Perspective." *Simians, Cyborgs, and Women: The Reinvention of Nature.* New York: Routledge, 1991. 183–203.

Hart, F. Elizabeth. "Cognitive Linguistics: The Experiential Dynamics of Metaphor." *Mosaic* 28 (1995): 1–23.

———. "The Epistemology of Cognitive Literary Studies." *Philosophy and Literature* 25.2 (2001): 314–34.

Hartley, David. *Observations on Man.* 2 vols. 1791. Reprint, Poole: Woodstock, 1998.

Hayles, N. Katherine. "Constrained Constructivism: Locating Scientific Inquiry in the Theater of Representation." *Realism and Representation: Essays on the Problem of Realism in Relation to Science, Literature, and Culture.* Ed. George Levine. Madison: University of Wisconsin Press, 1993. 27–43.

Hazlitt, William. *Lectures on the English Poets and The Spirit of the Age.* Ed. Catherine MacDonald Maclean. London: Dent, 1967.

Herder, Johann Gottfried. "Essay on the Origin of Language." *On the Origin of Language: Two Essays.* Trans. John H. Moran and Alexander Gode. Chicago: University of Chicago Press, 1966. 85–166.

Herman, David, ed. *Narrative Theory and the Cognitive Sciences.* Stanford: CSLI, 2003.

———. *Story Logic: Problems and Possibilities of Narrative.* Lincoln: University of Nebraska Press, 2002.

Hitt, Christopher. "Toward an Ecological Sublime." *New Literary History* 30.3 (1999): 603–23.

Hobbes, Thomas. *Leviathan: Or the Matter, Forme and Power of a Commonwealth Ecclesiasticall and Civil*. Ed. Michael Oakeshott. New York: Collier, 1962.

Hoeveler, Diane Long. *Romantic Androgyny: The Women Within*. University Park: Penn State University Press, 1990.

Hoffman, Donald D. *Visual Intelligence: How We Create What We See*. New York: Norton, 1998.

Hofkosh, Sonia. "The Writer's Ravishment: Women and the Romantic Author—The Example of Byron." In Mellor, ed., *Romanticism and Feminism*, 93–114.

Hogan, Patrick Colm. *Cognitive Science, Literature, and the Arts: A Guide for Humanists*. New York: Routledge, 2003.

———. "Literary Universals." *Poetics Today* 18 (1997): 223–49.

———. *The Mind and Its Stories: Narrative Universals and Human Emotion*. Cambridge: Cambridge University Press, 2003.

Hogg, James. *The Private Memoirs and Confessions of a Justified Sinner*. Ed. John Wain. Harmondsworth: Penguin, 1986.

Holmqvist, Kenneth, and Jaroslaw Pluciennik. "A Short Guide to the Theory of the Sublime." *Style* 36.4 (2002): 718–41.

Homans, Margaret. "Representation, Reproduction, and Woman's Place in Language." *Bearing the Word: Language and Female Experience in Nineteenth-Century Women's Writing*. Chicago: University of Chicago Press, 1986. 1–39.

———. *Women Writers and Poetic Identity: Dorothy Wordsworth, Emily Brontë, and Emily Dickinson*. Princeton: Princeton University Press, 1980.

Horney, Karen. *Feminine Psychology*. Ed. Harold Kelman. New York: Norton, 1967.

Hume, David. *Hume's Moral and Political Philosophy*. Ed. Henry D. Aiken. New York: Hafner Press, 1948.

Hutcheon, Linda, and Michael Hutcheon. "A Convenience of Marriage: Collaboration and Interdisciplinarity." *PMLA* 116.5 (2001): 1364–76.

Jacobus, Mary. "Apostrophe and Lyric Voice in The Prelude." *Lyric Poetry: Beyond New Criticism*. Ed. Chaviva Hosek and Patricia Parker. Ithaca: Cornell University Press, 1985. 167–81.

Jakobson, Roman. "Closing Statement: Linguistics and Poetics." *Style in Language*. Ed. Thomas A. Sebeok. Cambridge: MIT Press, 1960. 350–77.

Johnson, Barbara. "Apostrophe, Animation, and Abortion." *A World of Difference*. Baltimore: Johns Hopkins University Press, 1987. 184–99.

Johnson, Samuel. *Lives of the English Poets*. Ed. Arthur Waugh. 2 vols. London: Oxford, 1952.

Johnston, Kenneth R. *The Hidden Wordsworth: Poet, Lover, Rebel, Spy*. New York: Norton, 1998.

Jones, Wendy S. "*Emma*, Gender, and the Mind-Brain." *ELH* 75 (2008): 315–43.

Jütte, Robert. *A History of the Senses: From Antiquity to Cyberspace*. Trans. James Lynn. Cambridge: Polity Press, 2005.

Kames, Henry Home, Lord. *Loose Hints Upon Education, Chiefly Concerning the Culture of the Heart*. 2nd ed. Edinburgh: John Bell [et al.], 1782.

Kant, Immanuel. *Critique of Judgment*. Trans. Werner S. Pluhar. Indianapolis: Hackett, 1987.

Keach, William. *Shelley's Style*. New York: Methuen, 1984.

Keats, John. *The Letters of John Keats, 1814–1821.* Ed. Hyder Edward Rollins. 2 vols. Cambridge: Harvard University Press, 1958.

———. *The Poems of John Keats.* Ed. Jack Stillinger. Cambridge: Harvard University Press, 1978.

Keen, Suzanne. *Empathy and the Novel.* Oxford: Oxford University Press, 2007.

Kelly, Michael H., and Frank C. Keil. "The More Things Change . . . : Metamorphoses and Conceptual Structure." *Cognitive Science* 9 (1985): 403–16.

Kermode, Frank. *Romantic Image.* New York: Vintage, 1957.

Kipp, Julie. *Romanticism, Maternity, and the Body Politic.* Cambridge: Cambridge University Press, 2003.

Kneale, J. Douglas. "Romantic Aversions: Apostrophe Reconsidered." *Rhetorical Traditions and British Romantic Literature.* Ed. Don Bialostosky and Lawrence D. Needham. Bloomington: Indiana University Press, 1995.

Kosslyn, Stephen M. *Image and Brain: The Resolution of the Imagery Debate.* Cambridge: MIT Press, 1994.

Kosslyn, Stephen M., and Olivier Koenig. *Wet Mind: The New Cognitive Neuroscience.* New York: Free Press, 1992.

Kosslyn, Stephen M., and William L. Thompson. "Shared Mechanisms in Visual Imagery and Visual Perception: Insights from Cognitive Neuroscience." In Gazzaniga, ed., *The New Cognitive Neurosciences*, 975–85.

Kristeva, Julia. *Desire in Language: A Semiotic Approach to Literature and Art.* Ed. Leon S. Roudiez. Trans. Thomas Gora, Alice Jardine, and Leon Roudiez. New York: Columbia University Press, 1980.

Kuhl, Patricia K. "Language, Mind, and Brain: Experience Alters Perception." In Gazzaniga, ed., *The New Cognitive Neurosciences*, 99–105.

Lakoff, George. *Women, Fire, and Dangerous Things: What Categories Reveal about the Mind.* Chicago: University of Chicago Press, 1987.

Lakoff, George, and Mark Johnson. *Metaphors We Live By.* Chicago: University of Chicago Press, 1980.

———. *Philosophy in the Flesh: The Embodied Mind and Its Challenge to Western Thought.* New York: Basic Books, 1999.

Landor, Walter Savage. "The Hamadryad." *The Poetical Works of Walter Savage Landor.* Ed. Stephen Wheeler. 3 vols. Oxford: Clarendon Press, 1937. 2: 151–58.

Lawrence, William. *Lectures on Physiology, Zoology, and the Natural History of Man, Delivered to the Royal College of Surgeons.* London: Benbow, 1822.

Leighton, Angela. *Shelley and the Sublime: An Interpretation of the Major Poems.* Cambridge: Cambridge University Press, 1984.

Lerdahl, Fred, and Ray Jackendoff. *A Generative Theory of Tonal Music.* Cambridge; MIT Press, 1983.

Levin, Susan M. *Dorothy Wordsworth and Romanticism.* New Brunswick: Rutgers University Press, 1987.

Levine, George, and U. C. Knoepflmacher. *The Endurance of Frankenstein: Essays on Mary Shelley's Novel.* Berkeley and Los Angeles: University of California Press, 1979.

Lévi-Strauss, Claude. *The Elementary Structures of Kinship.* Trans. from the French by James Harle Bell, John Richard von Sturmer, and Rodney Needham, eds. Boston: Beacon Press, 1969.

Livingstone, Margaret. *Vision and Art: The Biology of Seeing.* New York: Abrams, 2002.

Locke, John. *An Essay Concerning Human Understanding.* Ed. Peter H. Nidditch. Oxford: Clarendon Press, 1975.

Lodge, David. "Consciousness and the Novel." *Consciousness and the Novel: Connected Essays.* Cambridge: Harvard University Press, 2002. 1–91.

———. *Thinks . . . : A Novel.* New York: Viking, 2001.

Luther, Susan. "A Stranger Minstrel: Coleridge's Mrs. Robinson." *Studies in Romanticism* 33 (Fall 1994): 391–409.

MacDonald, D. L. "Childhood Abuse as Romantic Reality: The Case of Byron." *Literature and Psychology* 40 (1994): 24–47.

———. "Incest, Narcissism and Demonality in Byron's *Manfred.*" *Mosaic* 25 (1992): 25–38.

Macovski, Michael. *Dialogue and Literature: Apostrophe, Auditors, and the Collapse of Romantic Literature.* Oxford: Oxford University Press, 1994.

McEwan, Ian. *Enduring Love: A Novel.* New York: Anchor, 1999.

McGuire, Kathryn B. "The Incest Taboo in *Wuthering Heights*: A Modern Appraisal." *American Imago* 45 (1988): 217–24.

Mellor, Anne K., ed. *Romanticism and Feminism.* Bloomington: Indiana University Press, 1988.

———. *Romanticism and Gender.* New York: Routledge, 1993.

Miall, David S. *Literary Reading: Empirical and Theoretical Studies.* New York: Peter Lang, 2006.

Miall, David S., and Ellen Dissanayake. "The Poetics of Babytalk." *Human Nature* 14.4 (2003): 337–64.

Mitchell, W. J. T. "Visible Language: Blake's Wond'rous Art of Writing." *Romanticism and Contemporary Criticism.* Ed. Morris Eaves and Michael Fischer. Ithaca: Cornell University Press, 1986. 46–86.

Monk, Samuel Holt. *The Sublime: A Study of Critical Theories in XVIII-Century England.* 1935. Ann Arbor: University of Michigan Press, 1960.

Montesquieu, Charles Secondat de. *Lettres persanes.* Ed. Paul Vernière. Paris: Garnier, 1975.

More, Hannah. *Strictures on the Modern System of Education. With a View of the Principles and Conduct Prevalent among Women of Rank and Fortune.* 2 vols. 6th ed. London: Cadell and Davies, 1799.

Mouffe, Chantal. "Hegemony and New Political Subjects: Toward a New Conception of Democracy." *Marxism and the Interpretation of Culture.* Ed. Cary Nelson and Lawrence Grossberg. Urbana: University of Illinois Press, 1988. 89–102.

Mukarovsky, Jan. "Standard Language and Poetic Language." *A Prague School Reader on Esthetics, Literary Structure, and Style.* Ed. Paul L. Garvin. Washington: Georgetown University Press, 1964. 17–30.

Ortony, Andrew, ed. *Metaphor and Thought.* 2nd ed. Cambridge: Cambridge University Press, 1993.

Oyama, Susan. *Evolution's Eye: A Systems View of the Biology-Culture Divide.* Durham: Duke University Press, 2000.

Paivio, Allan. *Mind and Its Evolution: A Dual Coding Theoretical Approach.* Mahwah, NJ: Erlbaum, 2007.

———. "The Mind's Eye in Arts and Science." *Poetics* 12 (1983): 1–18.

Paley, William. *The Principles of Moral and Political Philosophy*. Rev. ed. 2 vols. in 1. New York: Collins and Hannay, 1831.

Palmer, Alan. *Fictional Minds*. Lincoln: University of Nebraska Press, 2004.

Peacock, Thomas Love. *The Works of Thomas Love Peacock*. Ed. H. F. B. Brett-Smith and C. E. Jones. 10 vols. 1924–34. Reprint, New York: AMS Press, 1967.

Perkins, David. *Is Literary History Possible?* Baltimore: Johns Hopkins University Press, 1992.

———, ed. *English Romantic Writers*. 2nd ed. Fort Worth: Harcourt Brace, 1995.

Pinker, Steven. *How the Mind Works*. New York: Norton, 1997.

Plato. *The Collected Dialogues of Plato, Including the Letters*. Ed. Edith Hamilton and Huntington Cairns. Princeton: Princeton University Press, 1963.

Pottle, Frederick A. "The Eye and the Object in the Poetry of Wordsworth." *Romanticism and Consciousness: Essays in Criticism*. Ed. Harold Bloom. New York: Norton, 1970. 273–87.

Powers, Richard. *The Echo Maker*. New York: Picador, 2006.

———. *Galatea 2.2*. New York: Farrar, Straus, Giroux, 1995.

Premack, D., and G. Woodruff. "Does the Chimpanzee Have a Theory of Mind?" *Behavioral and Brain Sciences* 1 (1978): 515–26.

Quintilian. *Institutio Oratoria*. Trans. H. E. Butler. 4 vols. Cambridge: Harvard University Press, 1921.

Ramachandran, V. S., and Sandra Blakeslee. *Phantoms in the Brain: Probing the Mysteries of the Human Mind*. New York: William Morrow, 1998.

Rapf, Joanna E. "The Byronic Heroine: Incest and the Creative Process." *SEL* 21 (1981): 637–45.

Reid, Thomas. *Essays on the Intellectual Powers of Man*. Ed. Baruch A. Brody. Cambridge: MIT Press, 1969.

Richardson, Alan. "Astarté: Byron's *Manfred* and Montesquieu's *Lettres Persanes*." *Keats-Shelley Journal* 40 (1991): 19–22.

———. *British Romanticism and the Science of the Mind*. Cambridge: Cambridge University Press, 2001.

———. "Cognitive Science and the Future of Literary Studies." *Philosophy and Literature* 23 (1999): 157–73.

———. "The Dangers of Sympathy: Sibling Incest in English Romantic Poetry." *SEL* 25 (1985): 737–54.

———. *Literature, Education, and Romanticism: Reading as Social Practice*. Cambridge: Cambridge University Press, 1994.

———. "A Neural Theater: Joanna Baillie's *Plays on the Passions*." *Joanna Baillie, Romantic Dramatist: Critical Essays*. Ed. Thomas Crochunis. New York: Routledge, 2004. 130–45.

———. "Romanticism and the Colonization of the Feminine." In Mellor, ed., *Romanticism and Feminism*, 13–25.

———. "Studies in Literature and Cognition: A Field Map." *The Work of Fiction: Cognition, Culture, and Complexity*. Ed. Alan Richardson and Ellen Spolsky. Aldershot: Ashgate, 2004. 1–29.

Robinson, Daniel. "From 'Mingled Measure' to 'Ecstatic Measures': Mary Robinson's Poetic Reading of 'Kubla Khan.'" *Wordsworth Circle* 26.1 (January 1995): 4–7.

Robinson, Mary. *Mary Robinson: Selected Poems.* Ed. Judith Pascoe. Peterborough, Ontario: Broadview Press, 2000.

Rosenbaum, R. Shayna, Donald T. Stuss, Brian Levine, and Endel Tulving. "Theory of Mind is Independent of Episodic Memory." *Science* 23 (November 2007): 1257.

Ross, Marlon B. *The Contours of Masculine Desire: Romanticism and the Rise of Women's Poetry.* New York: Oxford University Press, 1989.

Rousseau, Jean-Jacques. *Emile: or, On Education.* Trans. Allan Bloom. New York: Basic Books, 1979.

———. "Essay on the Origin of Languages." *On the Origin of Language: Two Essays.* Trans. John H. Moran and Alexander Gode. Chicago: University of Chicago Press, 1966. 1–74.

Ruston, Sharon. *Shelley and Vitality.* Houndmills: Palgrave Macmillan, 2005.

Ryan, Vanessa L. "The Physiological Sublime: Burke's Critique of Reason." *Journal of the History of Ideas* 62.1 (April 2001): 265–79.

Rzepka, Charles J. "Christabel's 'Wandering Mother' and the Discourse of the Self: A Lacanian Reading of Repressed Narration." *Romanticism Past and Present* 10.2 (1986): 17–43.

Saxe, Rebecca. "Reading Your Mind: How Our Brains Help Us Understand Other People." *Boston Review* 29.1 (2004): 39–41.

Scarry, Elaine. *Dreaming by the Book.* New York: Farrar, Strauss, and Giroux, 1999.

Schank, Roger C. *Tell Me a Story: Narrative and Intelligence.* 1990. Reprint, Evanston: Northwestern University Press, 1995.

Schank, Roger C., and Robert P. Abelson. *Scripts, Plans, Goals, and Understanding: An Inquiry into Human Knowledge Structures.* Hillsdale: Erlbaum, 1977.

Scott, Sir Walter. *Minstrelsy of the Scottish Border.* Ed. T. F. Henderson. 4 vols. Edinburgh: Oliver and Boyd, 1932.

———. *Waverley.* Ed. Andrew Hook. Harmondsworth: Penguin, 1972.

Searle, John R. *The Rediscovery of the Mind.* Cambridge: MIT Press, 1992.

Semino, Elena, and Jonathan Culpeper, eds. *Cognitive Stylistics: Language and Cognition in Text Analysis.* Amsterdam: J. Benjamins, 2002.

Shelley, Mary. "The Brother and Sister: An Italian Story." *Collected Tales and Stories: With Original Engravings.* Ed. Charles E. Robinson. Baltimore: Johns Hopkins University Press, 1976. 166–89.

———. *Frankenstein.* Ed. M. K. Joseph. Oxford: Oxford University Press, 1980.

Shelley, Percy Bysshe. *The Complete Works of Percy Bysshe Shelley.* Ed. Neville Rogers. 2 vols. Oxford: Clarendon, 1972–.

———. *Shelley: Poetical Works.* 2nd ed. Ed. Thomas Hutchinson and G. M. Matthews. London: Oxford University Press, 1970.

———. *Shelley's Poetry and Prose.* Ed. Donald H. Reiman and Sharon Powers. New York: Norton, 1977.

———. *Shelley's Prose, or, The Trumpet of a Prophecy.* Ed. David Lee Clark. Albuquerque: University of New Mexico Press, 1954.

Shen, Yesayahu. "Cognitive Aspects of Metaphor." *Poetics Today* 13 (1992): 567–74.

Shklovsky, Victor. "Art as Technique." *Russian Formalist Criticism: Four Essays.* Ed. Lee T. Lemon and Marion J. Reis. Lincoln: University of Nebraska Press, 1965. 3–24.

Showalter, Elaine. "Towards a Feminist Poetics." *Women Writing and Writing about Women.* Ed. Mary Jacobus. London: Croom Helm, 1979. 22–41.

Silverman, Kaja. *The Acoustic Mirror: The Female Voice in Psychoanalysis and Cinema.* Bloomington: Indiana University Press, 1988.

Sircello, Guy. "How Is a Theory of the Sublime Possible?" *Journal of Aesthetics and Art Criticism* 51.4 (1993): 541–50.

Siskin, Clifford. *The Historicity of Romantic Discourse.* New York: Oxford University Press, 1988.

Smail, Daniel Lord. *On Deep History and the Brain.* Berkeley and Los Angeles: University of California Press, 2007.

Smellie, William. *The Philosophy of Natural History.* 2 vols. Edinburgh: Charles Elliot, Bell and Bradford [et al.], 1790–99.

Smith, Johanna M. "'My Only Sister Now': Incest in *Mansfield Park.*" *Studies in the Novel* 19 (1987): 1–15.

Snyder, Gary. "Entering the Fiftieth Millennium." *The Gary Snyder Reader: Prose, Poetry, and Translations, 1952–1998.* New York: Counterpoint, 1999. 390–94.

Southey, Robert. *Poems of Robert Southey.* Ed. M. H. Fitzgerald. London: Oxford University Press, 1909.

Spolsky, Ellen. "Cognitive Literary Historicism: A Response to Adler and Gross." *Poetics Today* 24.2 (2003): 161–83.

———. "Darwin and Derrida: Cognitive Literary Theory as a Species of Post-Structuralism." *Poetics Today* 23.1 (2002): 43–62.

———. *Gaps in Nature: Literary Interpretation and the Modular Mind.* Albany: State University of New York Press, 1993.

———. *Satisfying Skepticism: Embodied Knowledge in the Early Modern World.* Aldershot: Ashgate, 2001.

———. "Why and How to Take the Fruit and Leave the Chaff." *SubStance* 30.1 and 2 (2001): 177–98.

———. *Word vs. Image: Cognitive Hunger in Shakespeare's England.* Basingstoke: Palgrave Macmillan, 2007.

Starr, Gabrielle G. "Multi-Sensory Imagery." *Introduction to Cognitive Cultural Studies.* Ed. Lisa Zunshine. Baltimore: Johns Hopkins University Press, forthcoming.

Stelzig, Eugene. "'Though It Were the Deadliest Sin to Love as We Have Loved': The Romantic Idealization of Incest." *European Romantic Review* 5 (1995): 230–51.

Stern, Daniel. *The First Relationship: Infant and Mother.* Cambridge: Harvard University Press, 1977.

———. *The Interpersonal World of the Infant: A View from Psychoanalysis and Developmental Psychology.* New York: Basic Books, 1985.

Stockwell, Peter. *Cognitive Poetics: An Introduction.* London: Routledge, 2002.

Sutton, John. *Philosophy and Memory Traces: Descartes to Connectionism.* Cambridge: Cambridge University Press, 1998.

Tager-Flusberg, Helen, Simon Baron-Cohen, and Donald Cohen. "An Introduction to the Debate." *Understanding Other Minds: Perspectives from Autism.* Ed. Simon Baron-Cohen, Helen Tager-Flusberg, and Donald Cohen. Oxford: Oxford University Press, 1993. 3–9.

Temperley, David. *The Cognition of Basic Musical Structures.* Cambridge: MIT Press, 2004.

Thornhill, Nancy W. "An Evolutionary Analysis of the Rules Regulating Human Inbreeding and Marriage." *Behavioral and Brain Sciences* 14 (1991): 247–61.

Thorslev, Peter L., Jr. "Incest as Romantic Symbol." *Comparative Literature Studies* 1 (1965): 41–58.

Trevarthen, Colin. C. "Communication and Cooperation in Early Infancy: A Description of Primary Intersubjectivity." *Before Speech: The Beginning of Human Communication.* Ed. Margaret Bullow. Cambridge: Cambridge University Press, 1979. 321–47.

Tsur, Reuven. *Toward a Theory of Cognitive Poetics.* Amsterdam: North-Holland, 1992.

———. *What Makes Sound Patterns Expressive: The Poetic Mode of Speech Perception.* Durham: Duke University Press, 1992.

Turner, Mark. "The Cognitive Study of Art, Language, and Literature." *Poetics Today* 23.1 (2002): 9–20.

———. *Death Is the Mother of Beauty: Mind, Metaphors, and Criticism.* Chicago: University of Chicago Press, 1987.

———. *The Literary Mind.* New York: Oxford University Press, 1996.

———. *Reading Minds: The Study of English in the Age of Cognitive Science.* Princeton: Princeton University Press, 1991.

Twitchell, James B. *Forbidden Partners: The Incest Taboo in Modern Culture.* New York: Columbia University Press, 1987.

Van den Berghe, Pierre. "Human Inbreeding Avoidance: Culture as Nature." *Behavioral and Brain Sciences* 6 (1983): 91–102.

Varela, Francisco J., Evan Thompson, and Eleanor Rosch. *The Embodied Mind: Cognitive Science and Human Experience.* Cambridge: MIT Press, 1991.

Vargo, Lisa. "The Claims of 'Real Life and Manners': Coleridge and Mary Robinson." *Wordsworth Circle* 26.3 (July 1995): 134–37.

Vermeule, Blakey. "God Novels." *The Work of Fiction: Cognition, Culture, and Complexity.* Ed. Alan Richardson and Ellen Spolsky. Aldershot: Ashgate, 2004. 147–65.

Vinge, Louise. *The Five Senses: Studies in a Literary Tradition.* Lund: CWK Gleerup, 1975.

Volosinov, V. N. "Discourse in Life and Discourse in Art (Concerning Sociological Poetics)." *Freudianism: A Critical Sketch.* Trans. I. R. Titunik. Ed. Titunik and Neal H. Bruss. Bloomington: Indiana University Press, 1976. 93–116.

Weiskel, Thomas. *The Romantic Sublime: Studies in the Structure and Psychology of Transcendence.* Baltimore; Johns Hopkins University Press, 1986.

Westermarck, Edward. *The History of Human Marriage.* 5th ed. 3 vols. London: McMillan, 1925.

Wilson, Edward O. *Consilience: The Unity of Knowledge.* New York: Knopf, 1998.

Wilson, Robert A., and Frank C. Keil. *The MIT Encyclopedia of the Cognitive Sciences.* Cambridge: MIT Press, 1999.

Wilson, Timothy D. *Strangers to Ourselves: Discovering the Adaptive Unconscious.* Cambridge: Belknap Press, 2002.

Winner, Ellen, and Howard Gardner. "The Comprehension of Metaphor in Brain-Damaged Patients." *Brain* 100 (1977): 717–29.

Wittreich, Joseph Anthony, Jr., ed. *The Romantics on Milton: Formal Essays and Critical Asides.* Cleveland: Case Western Reserve University Press, 1970.

Wolf, Arthur P. *Sexual Attraction and Childhood Association: A Chinese Brief for Edward Westermarck.* Stanford: Stanford University Press, 1995.

Wollstonecraft, Mary. *Mary and The Wrongs of Women*. Ed. Gary Kelly. Oxford: Oxford University Press, 1980.

———. *A Vindication of the Rights of Woman, with Strictures on Political and Moral Subjects*. Ed. Carol Poston. New York: Norton, 1975.

Wordsworth, William. *The Prelude 1799, 1805, 1850*. Ed. Jonathan Wordsworth, M. H. Abrams, and Stephen Gill. New York: Norton, 1979.

———. *The Prose Works of William Wordsworth*. Ed. W J. B. Owen and Jane Worthington Smyser. 3 vols. Oxford: Clarendon Press, 1974.

———. *Selected Prose*. Ed. John O. Hayden. Harmondsworth: Penguin, 1988.

———. *William Wordsworth: The Poems*. Ed. John O. Hayden. 2 vols. Harmondsworth: Penguin, 1977.

Yeager, Patricia. "Toward a Female Sublime." *Gender and Theory: Dialogues on Feminist Criticism*. Ed. Linda Kauffman. London: Basil Blackwell, 1989.

Yearsley, Ann. *A Poem on the Inhumanity of the Slave-Trade*. London: Robinson, 1788.

———. "To Mira, On the Care of Her Infant." *Women Romantic Poets 1785–1832: An Anthology*. New ed. Ed. Jennifer Breen. London: Everyman, 1994. 96–102.

Zeki, Semir. *Inner Vision: An Exploration of Art and the Brain*. Oxford: Oxford University Press, 1999.

Zunshine, Lisa. Introduction to *Introduction to Cognitive Cultural Studies*. Ed. Lisa Zunshine. Baltimore: Johns Hopkins University Press, forthcoming.

———. "Rhetoric, Cognition, and Ideology in A. L. Barbauld's *Hymns in Prose for Children* (1781)." *Poetics Today* 23.1 (2002): 9–20.

———. "Richardson's *Clarissa* and a Theory of Mind." *The Work of Fiction: Cognition, Culture, and Complexity*. Ed. Alan Richardson and Ellen Spolsky. Aldershot: Ashgate, 2004. 127–46.

———. "Theory of Mind and Fictions of Embodied Transparency." *Narrative* 16.1 (January 2008): 65–92.

———. "Why Jane Austen Was Different, and Why We May Need Cognitive Science to See It." *Style* 41.3 (Fall 2007): 273–97.

———. *Why We Read Fiction: Theory of Mind and the Novel*. Columbus: Ohio State University Press, 2006.

Index